HYDROBOTANICAL METHODS

Richard D. Wood, Ph.D.
Professor of Botany
University of Rhode Island

University Park Press
Baltimore · London · Tokyo

UNIVERSITY PARK PRESS
International Publishers in Science and Medicine
Chamber of Commerce Building
Baltimore, Maryland 21202

Typeset by The Composing Room of Michigan, Inc.
Printed in the United States of America by Bay Printing, Inc.

Library of Congress Cataloging in Publication Data
Wood, Richard Dawson, 1918-
Hydrobotanical methods.

Bibliography: p.
Includes index.
1. Aquatic plants–Laboratory manuals. 2. Aquatic ecology–Laboratory manuals. I. Title. [DNLM: 1. Marine biology. 2. Plankton. QH91.57.A1 W878h]
QK930.W66 1975 581.5'263'028 75-25840
ISBN 0-8391-0830-3

Hydrobotanical Methods

Contents

Preface

In recent years, there has been a burgeoning of interest in ecological problems. Trained environmentalists are thus becoming increasingly in demand. But environmentalists are often generalists, while at the same time traditional academic departments of colleges and universities may continue to produce specialists. This manual is one attempt to bridge the gap—to assist the professor in a traditional department in preparing students, through these realistic exercises, for today's job market in environmentally oriented work, and in improving the understanding of environmental reality by persons who will not ultimately make this their life work.

The purposes of this guide are to provide a series of field and laboratory projects for training university students in aquatic ecology, with emphasis on the autophyte, and to offer detailed instructions for a set of methods useful in aquatic investigation. The exercises progress from taxonomic aspects, with which most students are familiar, to more sophisticated methodology of quantitative and physiological ecology. Each project is an actual task that a professional aquatic biologist may be expected to handle. In essence, the guide provides on-the-job training. The sequence best fits the fall term, taking advantage of the fine autumn days for field work and reserving the strictly laboratory projects for the colder, unsettled days of late autumn and winter.

For individual tests, one workable and accepted technique is provided. Each was selected from available methods for its accuracy, feasibility, and adaptability to a variety of field conditions, with both salt- and fresh-water habitats. The student can apply these techniques directly on the job, modifying them as needed to fit special conditions; and he should retain them as basic reliable methods against which he can test other seemingly desirable procedures. For the graduate student, the use of this program of procedures, pretested and perfected, can free him from the task of developing methods and enable him to devote more of his energies to resolving biological aspects of his thesis.

Whereas the major thrust of this work is to provide training for aquatic plant ecologists, in reality the coverage is very much the same as that for aquatic animal ecologists. The primary difference is the nature of the biota under consideration, but even here the sampling and collecting methods are often similar. Therefore, where practical, the term ("fauna") is added in the text where directions suggest a study of the flora. This may assist the instructor in shifting the emphasis of the projects to fit the particular demands of his situation.

The book is designed for biologists, and in an effort to promote ease in comparison of data from widely varying areas (both marine and fresh-water: academic and practical), units are expressed as far as possible in ppm, or its equivalent mg/liter. Formulas are provided to simplify conversions. For certain cases where other units are advantageous, the use of special units is of course justified, and the manner of conversion is presented.

To help develop ease and skill in writing reports, the text is arranged to approximate the format common in scientific journals, especially as in *Limnology and Oceanography*. In addition, the style, abbreviations, and symbols for the most part follow those recommended by the American Institute of Biological Sciences (*CBE Style Manual*).

A feature employed to help the nonmathematically oriented student is the manner of presenting formulas, in which they are expanded so as to show all factors and to make the logic for each step apparent. Adapting factors to fit modifications in experimental conditions is also facilitated by this mode of handling.

Two projects, those on indirect sampling and on general hydrobotany, can be run separately or together in one major project. For this reason, these have been numbered 5 and 5a, respectively.

It is anticipated that from time to time new projects may be added as an appendix. Suggestions from readers for projects they would like to have added would be appreciated.

To the Student

The tools of aquatic plant ecology are drawn from widely divergent sciences or technologies including agronomy, civil engineering, geology, hydrology, limnology, oceanography, quantitative analysis, statistics, systematics, etc. One cannot be an expert in all these areas, but he can develop a working knowledge of useful aspects of the various fields.

The advanced student with experience in several of the associated specialities will find that the projects are straightforward applications of his knowledge. The course may help him orient his information for submarine studies. The novice, however, may find each project a challenge and may have to make a special effort to learn to run the procedures and to appreciate how the findings contribute to ecological understanding.

Of particular importance, the student will have an opportunity to become efficient at summarizing his findings, and is expected to report on each project. This report should be organized without delay just as soon as the data are available. As a minimum (Figure 1), such a report would include a statement

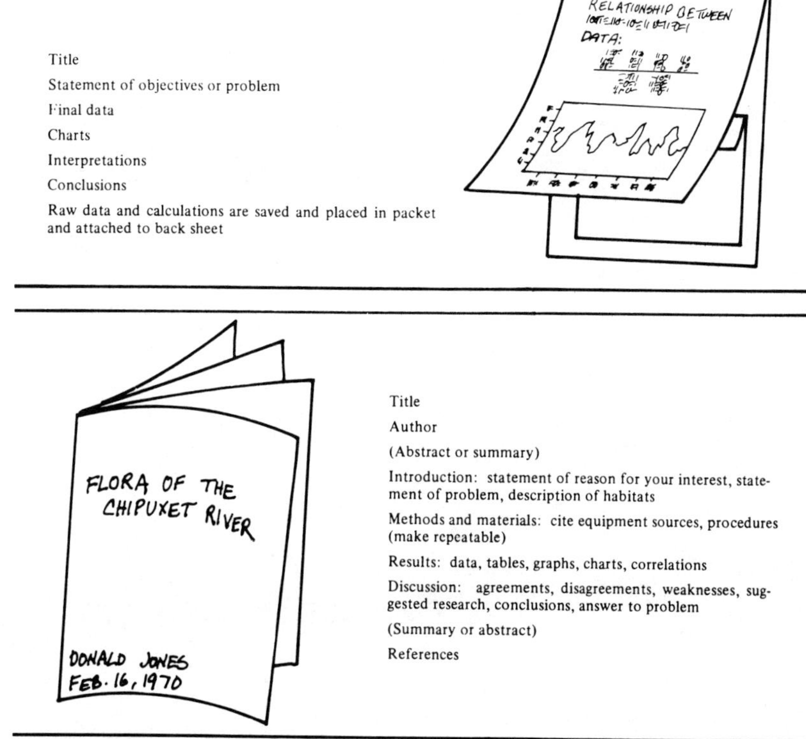

Title
Statement of objectives or problem
Final data
Charts
Interpretations
Conclusions
Raw data and calculations are saved and placed in packet and attached to back sheet
RELATIONSHIP BETWEEN
DATA:
FLORA OF THE CHIPUXET RIVER
DONALD JONES
FEB. 16, 1970
Title
Author
(Abstract or summary)
Introduction: statement of reason for your interest, statement of problem, description of habitats
Methods and materials: cite equipment sources, procedures (make repeatable)
Results: data, tables, graphs, charts, correlations
Discussion: agreements, disagreements, weaknesses, suggested research, conclusions, answer to problem
(Summary or abstract)
References

Figures 1 (*top*) and 2 (*bottom*). Two types of written reports are the minimal report (Figure 1) and the optimal report (Figure 2). The former, common in business, gives just the barest presentation of facts and conclusions needed for decision making. The latter is the manuscript for an article in professional journals, and although succint it is organized and thoroughly documented. The contents of the two types are shown with each figure.

of what is being done, a table of final data together with pertinent statements and graphs, interpretations, and conclusions. Raw data and calculations are critical and must be saved, and they may be attached to the back sheet of the report or filed with the project. On the other hand, one should also become adept at preparing optimal reports (Figure 2) which are the efficient, space-saving format used in articles published in scientific journals (e.g., *Limnology and Oceanography*). Early difficulty in deciding what information belongs in the introduction, results, and discussion vanishes as one practices this style. Keep in mind that the results comprise the data, the facts, and not opinions. Similarly, the discussion is the place to discuss, not to introduce, your information. Any new data cited must appear in the results. Once again, the raw data must be saved, either filed with the project records or appended to the report.

PROJECT 1 Reconnaissance

OBJECTIVE

To examine area with special regard to conditions contributing to aquatic habitats (e.g., trip from mountain, along river, to sea).

METHOD

Cover area noting topographic features, water drainage patterns, impoundments, rock outcrops and ledges, soil types, centers of human habitation and activity (industry, agriculture, marinas and harbors, dumps), and evidence of effects on aquatic life.

DATA

Summarize findings concisely including both maps and statements of the following:

A. General topography.
B. Drainage pattern.
C. Impoundments.
D. Influence of underlying or outcropping rocks.
E. Human activity.
F. Vegetation.
G. Aquatic habitats.

Photographs or pictures, such as from newspapers, are helpful.

REFERENCES

Coast & Geodetic Survey. Hydrographic charts. (Available from local agents).

Coker, R. E. 1954. Streams, Lakes, Ponds. Univ. North Carolina Press, Chapel Hill. 327 p.

Fenneman, N. M. 1938. Physiography of Eastern United States. McGraw-Hill, New York. 714 p.

Hunt, C. B. 1967. Physiography of the United States. W. H. Freeman & Co., San Francisco. 479 p.

Johnson, D. W. 1919. Shore Processes and Shoreline Development. John Wiley & Sons, New York. 584 p. (Reprinted 1965).

Lobeck, A. K. 1956. Things Maps Don't Tell Us. Macmillan, New York. 159 p.

Reid, G. K. 1967. Pond Life. Golden Press, New York. 160 p. (See pp. 4–9, 24, 25).

Strahler, A. N. 1965. Introduction to Physical Geography. John Wiley & Sons, New York. 455 p.

U.S. Coast & Geodetic Survey (now Coast & Geodetic Survey). Hydrographic charts. (Available from local agents).

U.S. Geological Survey. Topographic charts. (Available from local agents).

Zim, H. S., and L. Ingle. 1955. Seashores. Simon & Schuster, New York. 160 p. (See pp. 8–13).

NOTES

Reconnaissance[1]

A first step in any type of field project, as in any type of research at all, is to get acquainted with the area and its problems. This might involve merely checking on

[1] Note to instructor: As an example of reconnaissance and as an introduction to this course, I have managed a 6-hr bus trip

where to install slides, or it could be preparatory to a large-scale study of a drainage region.

Topographic Features These can well be examined from car or on foot, especially in conjunction with a topographic map. Also helpful are maps of rock outcropping and a prior study of the geological reports of the area. Note that each topographic structure has resulted from geological processes (or that of man) such as deposition by a glacier, erosion of old mountain tops by ice and water, valley cut by a river, terrace caused by uplift of land, and rejuvenation by stream cutting (see especially Lobeck, 1956, for examples). Man may level hills here and build others there (as for a viaduct in flat country). However, even flat regions have a history, such as a floodplain of a river or the peneplain of a mountain region. Much can be understood by learning of the strata of rock beneath the surface, and these can often be observed in road cuts, stream-valley walls, and quarries; or information can be obtained from the records for home well drillings.

Drainage Patterns The flow of surface water in hilly areas can be traced by following the rivers and tributaries upstream to their sources. The entire area from which rainwater drains down these tributaries into a central stream is the watershed. Micromodels of such watersheds can be observed commonly in gently sloping piles of sand or gravel; but at the other extreme, drainage systems can be vast, as in the case of the Amazon River. Even one's own small study area may be difficult to envision, and hiring a small plane to make a reconnaissance could be well worth the investment. In studying the drainage patterns with a topographic map, note that the contour lines form a V at each stream, the point of the V indicating upstream. This helps trace the direction of flow. Also, note that the altitude of the lake and pond water surface is usually printed on each impoundment, and this also helps establish direction of drainage.

The area of a watershed can be calculated from the scale given in the legend of the map, or it can be measured with a polar planimeter. If the map is too big, portions of it can be measured at a time.

The pattern of the drainage system often gives a clue to the geological history of the area, such as radial pattern around volcanic cones and dendroid pattern in tilted planes.

Impoundments Water accumulates in any basin, forming an impoundment. Each body of water must be blocked from draining by some more or less impermeable structure such as a dam, rock outcrop across a valley, or wall of glacial debris. Locate this feature. Impoundments usually have one or more inlets and an outlet, but others may lack one or the other. Water entering impoundments below the waterline are said to be spring fed, information which is common knowledge to fishermen in the area.

The position of impoundments in a drainage system is important to note, and once again the geological information on the nature and condition of underground rock strata is important, together with information on which strata are permeable and which do not carry water. Here the records of hydrologists on both the surface and subterranean flow can be useful. Recall that, wherever a permeable stratum of rock projects into a valley or into a lake or breaks off in an area of soil, water will flow. If the water reaches the surface, the evidence is a spring. Water carried down along these aquifers can develop high pressure, which can cause it to come out forcibly in an artesian spring or well. If water barely oozes out of the rock, a moist area or seep is recorded.

Underlying and Outcropping Rocks The type and structure of the underlying rocks affect topography, drainage, and impound-

---

covering a river from the source in a mountain brook habitat, following down along the river, on to the estuary and the open sea. The nature of such an introductory trip depends, of course, upon the geology of the region.

ment. Tilting, bending, folding, and faulting all can have effects on the water system of an area. Study surface rocks, outcrops in valleys and quarries; record dip and strike; and synthesize your findings into a picture of the underground conditions. See geological survey reports for help and hard-to-find information.

Centers of Human Habituation and Activity These can be plotted on your working map. It is important to note where these occur in a watershed, where along a stream, and whether upstream or downstream from an impoundment. Compare condition of aquatic life above and below such areas of activity to get information on the effects of the habitation. Compare a clean and a polluted pond, and clean and polluted parts of a river, to obtain some standard for evaluating the degree of effect of civilization.

Written Report of Reconnaissance Organize your findings in a logical outline, describe structures and conditions succinctly, and indicate clearly when you are stating opinions rather than citing facts.

To help in writing reports, an organized set of word groups is presented below. Note that the word groups are entered under broad terms. This thesaurus-type of listing can help recall terms that you will need in describing or citing certain structures.

Topical List of Some Terms Useful in Reporting Reconnaissance

General Topics Topography, relief, drainage, impoundments, coastal features, bedrock and outcrops, soils, sediments, climates, human influences and pollution, plant and vegetation types, succession.

Terms

Atoll: see coral reef.

Beaches: shore, coastline, coast; –cliff, berm, backshore, beach scarp, foreshore, high-water line, strand line, low-tide terrace, low-water (shore) line, offshore trough, bar.

Bedrock: igneous, metamorphic, sedimentary; –lava, glass, obsidian, basalt, tuffa, breccia; –boulder and gravel → conglomerate → gneiss and schist; sand → sandstone → quartzite → schist; silt and clay → shale → slate and schist; lime → limestone and marl → marble and schist; coarse igneous → gneiss; fine igneous → schist; –mechanical, conglomerate, sandstone, clay, shale; organic, calcareous, limestone, marl, carbonaceous; precipitated, limestone, gypsum, rock salt, iron ore; metamorphic, marble, quartzite; –ledge, fault, anticline and syncline folds, strike, dip, cliff, erratics.

Climates: continental, maritime, polar; –rain-forest, savannah, tundra, permafrost, monsoon, mountain, steppe, desert; –tropical types: equatorial, summer rain, monsoon, high plateau, hot desert; –warm temperate lands, types: warm eastern margins, mediterranean, interior lowland, plateau; –cool temperate lands, types: eastern margins, interior lowland, western margin, mountain; –cold lands, types: tundra, cold desert.

Coastal ponds and bays: sound, bight, bay, cove, lagoon, pond.

Coral reef: fringing, barrier, atoll; –seaward slope, windward reef, buttresses, algal ridge, encrusting reef flat, coral heads, inlet, islands (motu), passes; –lagoon floor, lagoon reef, lagoon slope, knolls, microatoll, reef margin, reef flat.

Deltas: arcuate, bayhead, bird-foot, cuspidate, estuarine; –delta-flood plain, alluvial fan, levee, distributary.

Dissection: youthful, mature, old age.

Drainage: dendritic, trellis, anastomosing (braided), radial; –inlet (influent), outlet (effluent), tributary.

Escarpments: volcanic (crater wall, lava flow), eroding (river, wind, glacier, water), fault.

Flow: laminar (ordered), turbulent (disordered); –current, convection, eddy; –inflow, outflow; –waterfall, submerged waterfall.

Human influences: habitation, dam, industry, marina, harbor, pollution outfall;

–agriculture, animal stock, dump, recreation, conservation, pollution.

Impoundments: occan, sea, saline lakes, playa, vlai, lake, pond, pool, farm pond (dam), reservoir, borrow pit.

Islands: oceanic, continental; –high, low; –barrier, fringing, atoll, motu; –vegetation island (in desert), organic; –faulting, ocean volume change, volcanic action, organic, isolated by glacier or wave action, deposits.

Lakes: oligotrophic, eutrophic, dystrophic; –open, closed, seepage, solution; –rift valley, moraine dammed, caldera, crater, raft, beaver, brush pile, plant growth, artificial, oxbow, ribbon, paternoster, kettle, tarn, playa, lagoon, bog, morainal, glacial, saline; –circular, subcircular, lunate, triangular; –types: amictic, cold monomictic (polar), subpolar, dimictic (temperate), 1st, 2nd, 3rd order; warm monomictic (subtropical), oligomictic, polymictic, holomictic, meromictic.

Landscape: see topography.

Mangrove: red, white, black; –swamps.

Moraines: terminal, lateral, interlobate, recessional, ground, end, outwash plain, drumlin, esker, kame.

Mountains: volcanic, horst, folded, faulted, overthrust, tilted, residual, crust block, laccolith, batholith; –dome, roche moutonnée, foothill, piedmont, monadnock, horst, horn, arête, col, comb ridge, fault scarp, escarpment (scarp), fold, cuesta; –boulders, relict, irratic.

Outcrops: cliff, ledge, road cut, escarpment, scarp, fold, fault, cuesta; –boulder, relict, irratic; –dip, strike.

Plains: peneplain, plateau, alluvial, deltaic, glacial drift, outwash, terrace, butte, lake bed, flood plain, loess plain, lava flow, mesa, sand plain (desert), rock field (felsenfel).

Plant types: woody, herbaceous; –annual, perennial, biennial; –monocot, dicot; –laminar, foliar, graminoid; –cryptogam, angiosperm, gymnosperm, coniferous, thallophyte, bryoid, algal (see vegetation).

Pollution: effluents: industrial, petrochemical, domestic, sewage (raw), farm fertilizer, thermal, radiation, winter salt, detergent (biodegradable, nonbiodegradable), pesticides, herbicides, algicides; –oligosaprobic, polysaprobic (septic), alpha and beta mesosaprobic; –zones: recent pollution, active decomposition, strong pollution, mild pollution, clean water.

Rock outcrops: see outcrops.

Rocky coasts: headland, rocky head, outcrop, neck, beach, reef, atoll; –sea cliff, nip, arch, notch, stack, cave, crevice, wave-cut terrace, abrasion platform, shore-faced terrace, wave-cut rock bench, wave-cut platform; –sinking shoreline, shoreline of submergence; –drowned valley (see beaches).

Sandy coasts: beach, bar, spit, recurved spit, baymouth bar, hook, tombolo, cuspidate bar, bayhead beach, barrier island, lagoon, tidal inlet, offshore bar, haff, nehrung; –longshore currents and drifting, backwash and swash, waves, storm waves, wave refraction, tidal currents and deposit (see also beaches, rocky coasts, shorelines).

Sediments: sand, fine sand, mud, silt, clay; –dy, gyttja, sapropel, peat; –rock, boulder, cobble, pebbles, shingle, gravel, sand, mud, clay, ooze (see C&GS Chart no. 1); –inorganic, organic, reducing; –marine oozes: calcareous (globigerina, pteropod, coccolith), siliceous (diatom, radiolarian); –terrigenous, pelagic, autochthonous, allochthonous.

Shorelines: of submergence, emergence, sinking, rising; –concordant, discordant, neutral; –drowned valley, drowned river; –stable, estuarine; –longitudinal, transverse, ria coast, fjord coast, volcanic coast; –submergence, shorelines of: mountainous coasts, submerged coastal plain, fjord, glacial deposit; –emergence, shorelines of: coastal plain, steeply sloping (faulted), neutral, alluvial fan, delta, volcanic, coral reef.

Soils: forest, grassland, desert; –podzol, laterosol, chernozem, sierozem, red and yellow, dark brown, prairie, caliche; –forest: podzols, brown earth, red and yellow;

–grassland: black earth, brown steppe; –white, brown, dark brown, black, red, yellow.

Streams: torrential, mountain brook, river, creek, seep: –young, mature, old age; –intermittent, permanent, interrupted; –equilibrium, graded, base level; –courses: upper, middle, lower; –spring, source, headwater, mouth, estuary; –flow: shooting, laminar, riffle; –modifications: canal, ditch, lock, dam; –structures: meander, oxbow, fall, plunge basin, pothole, levee, yazoo stream, entrenched meander, alluvial terrace, alluvial fan, delta; –meander structure: cutaway or undercut slope (bluff), depositing or slipoff slope, point-bar deposit; –mouths: ria, fjord, deltaic; –anticedent, consequent, subsequent, superimposed; –springs, caves, caverns, sink holes, honeycombed, efflorescence (surface salt); –bottom type: rock, boulder, cobble, gravel, sand, mud, silt, clay; –filling: river bar, alluvial fan and apron, flood plain, delta, delta-flood plain (see also deltas).

Substrates: see sediments.

Succession: habitat, microclimate, vegetation; –oligotrophic, eutrophic, marsh, swamp, forest; –oligotrophic, mat covering, acidification, bog, closed bog, swamp, forest; –estuary, tidal marsh, marsh, forest; –eutrophication, shoaling, vegetating, oxygen depletion, anaerobic decomposition; –stream, lake, flood plain, meadow, forest.

Tidal marsh: tidal flat, tidal marsh; –open and closed; –erosion cliff, terrace, salt pan, levee, strand line, shrub border, upper border, upper slope, lower slope, channel, seaward margin.

Tides: storm, equinoctial, high and low, neap and spring, maximum and minimum, tropic and equatorial, diurnal and semidiurnal, mixed; –LLLW, LLW, HLW, MLW, MSL, LHW, HHW, MHW, HHW, HHHW; –MHWS(pring), MHWN(eap).

Topography: types: flat, undulating, knob and kettle, karst, incised, dissected, foothill or piedmont, mountainous, glaciated, cliff-cuesta, hog-back, badland; –action: weathering, erosion, corrasion, exfoliation, solution, deflation, aggradation, degradation, extrusion, intrusion, folding, faulting, sinking, rising, volcanic, glacial, precipitation, mechanical, chemical, rejuvenation, sandblasting, wave-cutting (see also dissection).

Valleys: rill, trench, gully, V-shaped, arroyo, canyon, box canyon, gorge, glaciated, U-shaped, hanging, rejuvenated, incised, cirque, amphitheater, graben, rift.

Vegetation: marsh, swamp, tidal marsh, bog, forest; –intertidal zone: black, brown, green, red, kelp; –littoral, supralittoral, eulittoral, midlittoral, sublittoral, infralittoral (littoral, sublittoral, and infralittoral fringes); –algal mat; –psammon, benthon, epibenthon, ephemeral, plankton, periphyton (aufwuchs), neuston, epiphytic, epizoic, submerged, submerged attached, floating, floating attached, emergent, amphibious, terrestrial.

Waves: oscillation, translation; –cycloidal traveling (progressive), standing; –waves: storm, hurricane, earthquake, tsunamis; –nodal points, antinode; –seich, internal seich; –period, height, length; –fetch (duration); –breakers, surf, chop, ground swell; –long, short; –wind streaks.

PROJECT 2 Flora

OBJECTIVE

To prepare a qualitative report, a voucher-supported floristic list of plants of a selected area (e.g., stream plant life).

METHOD

1. Collecting by hand or rake, gather optimum specimens (with flowers, seeds, and roots if feasible); carry in pail, plastic bags, vasculum, or wet paper; mark each with tag having field number, etc.
2. On return to laboratory, mount part of the material, dry, and prepare for permanent collection; the other part keep fresh and identify as soon as possible. Save bit for fluid preservation if desirable (especially microscopic forms).
3. Identify, using any suitable method and references. A reference herbarium is most useful; and regional floras, lists, and punch-card sets are helpful.
4. Prepare final specimens, labeled completely, for reference herbarium.
5. Prepare list of species, with authors. Arrange in rational order (e.g., alphabetical or systematic).

DATA

A. Voucher specimens.
B. Floristic list: organize alphabetically or systematically (i.e., family, genus, etc.). For example:

1. *Callitriche heterophylla* Pursh. Water chickweed
2. *Ceratophyllum demersum* L. Hornwort or Coontail
3. *Peltandra virginica* (L.) Schott & Endl. Arrow Arum

REFERENCES

Conard, H. S. 1959. Mosses. *In* W. T. Edmondson (ed.), Fresh-water Biology, pp. 1161–1169. 2nd Ed. John Wiley & Sons, New York. 1248 p.

Fassett, N. C. 1940. A Manual of Aquatic Plants. 1st Ed. McGraw-Hill, New York. 382 p. (Also, 2nd Ed., 1957, Univ. Wisconsin Press, Madison. 405 p.)

Fernald, M. L. 1950. Gray's Manual of Botany. 8th Ed. American Book Co., New York. 1632 p.

Fosberg, F. R., and M. H. Sachet. 1965. Manual for tropical herbaria. Regnum Vegetabile 39: 1–132.

Muenscher, W. C. 1944. Aquatic plants of the United States. Comstock Publ. Assoc., Ithaca, N.Y. 374 p. Reprinted, Cornell Univ. Press, Ithaca, N.Y.

Muenscher, W. C. 1959. Vascular plants. *In* W. T. Edmondson (ed.), Fresh-water Biology, pp. 1171–1193. 2nd Ed. John Wiley & Sons, New York. 1248 p.

Prescott, G. W. 1962. Algae of the western Great Lakes area. Rev. ed. W. C. Brown, Dubuque, Iowa. 977 p. (Orig. 1951. Cranbrook, Bloomfield Hills, Mich. 946 p.)

Prescott, G. W. 1969. How to Know the

Aquatic Plants. W. C. Brown, Dubuque, Iowa. 171 p.

Prescott, G. W. 1970. How to Know the Fresh-water Algae. 2nd Ed. W. C. Brown, Dubuque, Iowa. 348 p.

Rollins, R. C. 1955. The Archer method for mounting herbarium specimens. Rhodora 57(682): 294–299.

deRoon, A. C. 1958. International directory of specialists in plant taxonomy. Regnum Vegetabile 13: 1–266.

Smith, G. M. 1950. The Fresh-water Algae of the United States. 2nd Ed. McGraw-Hill, New York. 719 p.

Stearn, W. T. 1966. Botanical Latin. Hafner, New York. 566 p.

Wood, R. D. 1967. Charophytes of North America. Publ. by author. (Available from Bookstore, Univ. Rhode Island, Kingston, R.I. 02881). 72 p.

NOTES

Collecting

Gather complete specimens, in flower and fruit if possible. If too large, take representative parts. Rinse off mud in field. Collect and place in pail, vasculum, plastic bags, or jars. With each, place tag (strip of herbarium paper, ca. 2 × 8 cm) with code number, and possibly also location and field identification.

Process as soon as possible or hold in refrigerator. Specimens keep adequately in freezer. Marine algae decompose overnight at room temperatures, and many microscopic algae disappear rapidly. Angiosperms last several days in refrigerator, but wilt rapidly if dry.

For further details for handling collections, see Fosberg and Sachet (1965).

Sorting

Strong forms of aquatics are treated as for ordinary flowering plants. Sort soft forms in sink or large pan with water. Selected parts may need to be transferred to clean sink or pan for mounting.

Labeling

Before wetting mounting paper, add complete data in soft pencil, lightly written, directly to sheet in lower righthand corner (in area which will be covered by label). Final label (Figure 1), hand written with India ink, or typed, is pasted in corner with library or tin paste. Do not use rubber cement. Note that the author's name or abbreviation is always included in the scientific name on labels. These can be verified in books such as

```
No. 62-7-18-2

        Ceratophyllum demersum L.

Common in ca. 14 cm of clear, flow-
ing water, on sandy mud bottom, fast
flowing stream, Jones Brook, 1.3
miles upstream from Cannonfodder
Crossing, Blakes Co., Yukon, Canada

Coll.:  James Jennings    July 18, 1962

Det.:  H. Barnard          Dec. 6, 1963
```

Figure 1. Herbarium label.

the floras by Fassett (1940), Fernald (1950), Muenscher (1944), etc. Fluid specimens should have label (pencil, India ink, or typed—not ballpoint pen) on herbarium paper, which is slipped around inside wall of jar.

Drying and Mounting

1. Sufficiently sturdy specimens can be handled as are ordinary flowering plant collections; i.e., lay between fold of newspaper, mark data on newspaper margin and on label included, and dry in plant press (weaker or filamentous plants, bryophytes, and algae require special handling). Attach to herbarium paper with tin glue, linen strips, or attach with straplike drops of mounting resin[1] (not suitable in tropics) over spots on the stem or portions of the leaf, etc. Do not use Scotch tape or similar adhesive plastic tapes.

2. Small filamentous algae: preserve some in fluid; mount some on herbarium paper (usually 1/8 or 1/4 sheet) and allow to air dry. Mount directly or place in packet.

3. Larger algae and flimsy angiosperms: float out in pan of water, slide herbarium paper (with data entered) under specimen, and gradually lift paper up under specimen. Drain by hanging over edge of (nonwaxed) table edge until water gloss on paper is gone. Place in fold of newspaper, cover algal side with wax paper, and dry in plant press as done for flowering plants.

4. Mosses: place in fold of newspaper; dry without heat and under gentle pressure (not over 2 lb). Place in labeled packets. Paste on herbarium sheet, or keep in shoe boxes.

5. Brittle or calcareous algae: air dry, and mount in packet or in small box. Paste packet or box on herbarium sheet.

6. Slimy masses of blue-green algae: smear over herbarium sheet, then air dry at room temperature.

Specimens to be pressed are separated by corrugates, stacked in plant press, bound up as tightly as possible with straps or nylon Venetian blind cord, and dried on edge at ca. 90°F (32°C).

Duplicates

Generally make a minimum of three mounts: one for yourself, one to send away for identification, and one to file in a permanent herbarium. For advanced work, make more duplicates for wider distribution and exchange, especially of good material.

Collection Numbers

These are variously concocted. The author prefers a chronological system (see Figure 1) composed of, first, the year, month, and date, and then the number of the collection of the day—e.g., 62-7-18-2 indicates a collection of 1962, July, 18th, 2nd sampling. Hyphens are needed to prevent duplication of collection numbers, such as for January 23 (1-23) and December 3 (12-3), which without hyphens could be an indistinguishable 123.

Identifying

Use keys, monographs, pictures in books, reference herbaria, local lists, or any other assistance available (see Figure 2). Once identification is made, enter complete scientific name, with author, on label. It is often helpful to record the reference used in deciding a name.

Changes in Identification If identification is changed later, make an annotation (Figure 3) label with the new name (dated), and attach above the previous label. Do not revise the label.

---

[1] *Mounting resin:* Mix 880 ml of toluene and 220 ml of methanol. Then completely dissolve mixture in 75 g of Dow Resin 276 V-Z. Finally, while stirring, gradually work in 1,750 ml (560–650 g) of Ethocel (standard 10 cps) until partly dissolved. Let stand to clear overnight. If bubbles form, add a little more solvent and stir them out. (Ref.: Rollins, 1955: 294).

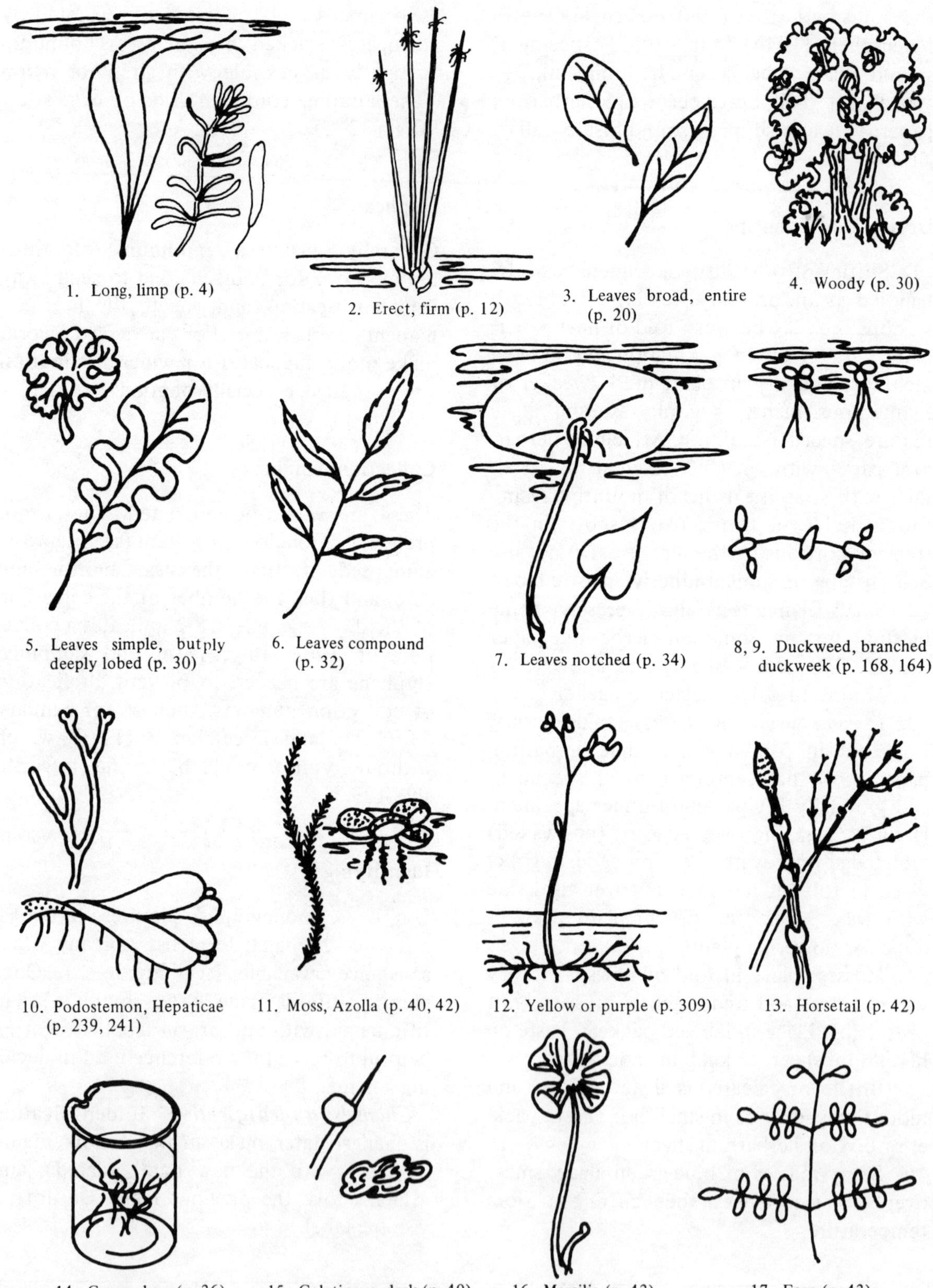

Figure 2. Pictorial guide to Fassett's "General Key," p. 3 of his *Manual of Aquatic Plants.*

No. 62-7-18-2

Myriophyllum spicatum L.

Annotated: H. Barnard, Dec. 18, 1963

Figure 3. Annotation label.

Help in Identification Refer to local taxonomists, scientists in herbaria of universities, regional museums, United States National Herbarium; or seek names of specialists in de Roon (1958) for help.

Uncertainties in Identification If uncertain, place question mark (?) before the name or epithet of which you are uncertain. For unknown species, use "sp." For example:
Callitriche ?heterophylla
?Sphagnum macrophyllum
Vaucheria sp.

Note that the "sp." is not italicized.

Preserving

Use 4% formalin (4 parts of fresh commercial "formaldehyde" + 96 parts water; neutralize to litmus with borax if water or solution is acid). For marine specimens, 5% in seawater is used. For freshwater algae, FAA or 6-3-1 (see Prescott, 1962: ix) are also popular preservatives.

Pronouncing Scientific Names

See accent marks on names in Fernald (1950) or Fassett (1940) in which (′) means to accent syllable but make vowel short, and (`) means to accent and make vowel long. For example:
Callítriche = cal-IT-trick-ee
Ceratophýllum = sir-at-oh-PHIL-um
Potamogèton = POTE-am-oh-JEE-ton

For rules on pronunciation, see Stearn (1966).

Curating

Place final sheets, with specimens face up, in genus or species covers with the opening on the right. File covers according to system used in the herbarium, and with name written on outer lower right corner. For an ecological reference herbarium, it is convenient to prepare two sets, one a general collection alphabetically arranged and one arranged by station or habitat. Place specimens in herbarium box or steel herbarium case. See Fosberg and Sachet (1965) for details.

Fumigating

Certain plants, especially angiosperms and pteridophytes, are subject to insect damage. Marine algae are rarely bothered, neither are bryophytes nor charophytes. For angiosperms, to deter insects keep paradichlorobenzene crystals in open containers in the herbarium case. If specimens become infested, remove specimens and heat in hot-air oven to 110°F for several hours (Fosberg and Sachet, 1965: 66). Thoroughly clean or fumigate shelves or boxes before restoring specimens.

In very humid regions, to prevent fungal growth, store collection in drying closet with one light bulb near floor, or in dry upstairs, or heated room (l.c., p. 68).

PROJECT 3 Vegetation Analysis by Line Transect

OBJECTIVE

To prepare a quantitative report of the vegetation of an area by the line transect (line intercept) method (e.g., shoreline of moderately eutrophic pond).

METHOD

1. Establish base points at regular intervals along the shore, marking with surveying pins.
2. Follow parallel compass bearings out into the water and, starting from the high water berm, or present water's edge, lay meter stick progressively in a line along bottom. Measure depth with second meter stick. Record *each plant* (depth and position on meter stick) which touches or lies within 1 cm of the stick. Record by name or, if not known, use descriptive code word (see Figure 1).
3. Take voucher specimen (from outside the transect) of each species met, assigning name or code name together with collection number.
4. Where plants occur in dense masses, count number of stems per unit length and indicate the distance along which the mass occurs (enter under "Remarks").
5. Work can be continued beyond wading depth by use of mask and snorkel or by SCUBA. Observing vegetation from boat through viewing box is also helpful.
6. On return to the laboratory, identify specimens and prepare dried or fluid voucher specimens.
7. Process the field data, and organize it for presentation in a diagram (bisect), life form diagrams of each association, and a gradient chart (depth; species).

DATA

A. Field data (save original, e.g., store in packet).
B. Pictorial bisect of transect made to scale.
C. Life form diagram of each major association.
D. Species-depth gradient table.
E. Tabulate other data that may be obtained, such as soil (sediment) mechanical analysis, pH, dissolved oxygen, temperature.

REFERENCES

Dansereau, P. 1959. Vascular aquatic plant communities of southern Quebec. A preliminary analysis. Trans. N.E. Wildl. Conf. (Montreal) 1: 27–54.

Distance					
Reading on meter stick (cm)	Distance from shore (m)	Depth (cm)	Species	Voucher no.	Remarks
33	64.33	22	Elodea	1	Sand
37	64.37	23	Twisted leaf ///	2	Sand
50	64.50	25	" " //		"
82	64.82	25	" " ~~////~~		"
92	64.92	32	Scirpus sp //	3	Mud
76	64.96	38	"		Sand
99	64.99	39	Needles ///	4	Muck
99.5	64.995	39	" //		~~Sand~~
100	65.	39	Twisted leaf // →		Mud → Sand

Figure 1. A sample of field data for pond shore transect arranged in table form. Tabulation gives number of shoots. Note errors and corrections made.

Golubic, S. 1968. Die Verteilung der Algenvegetation in der Umgebung von Rovinj (Istrien) unter dem Einfluss häuslicher und industrieller Abwässer. Zeitsch. Wasser Abwasser Forsch. (München) 1968(3): 87–95.

Hubbs, C. L., and C. Hubbs. 1953. An improved graphical analysis and comparison of series of samples. Syst. Zool. 2(2): 49–57.

Neushul, M. 1967. Studies of subtidal marine vegetation in western Washington. Ecology 48(1): 83–94.

Oosting, H. J. 1948. The study of plant communities. W. H. Freeman, San Francisco. 389 p.

Spence, D. H. N. 1964. The macrophyte vegetation of fresh-water lochs, swamps and associated fens. *In* J. H. Burnett (ed.), The Vegetation of Scotland, pp. 306–425. Oliver & Boyd, Edinburgh. 613 p.

Tansley, A. G. 1939. The British Islands and Their Vegetation. Cambridge Univ. Press, Cambridge. 930 p.

NOTES

Field Notes

See Figure 1.

Bisect (or Profile Diagram)

Using black ink, prepare diagram so as to give viewer a clear idea of what you found. Select scale to fit 8½ × 11 inch page; and choose vertical exaggeration (usually 2×) so as to make plants and slope of bottom look realistic. Assign approximate value to each plant symbol used. Make plants resemble the field appearance. See bisect (Figure 2).

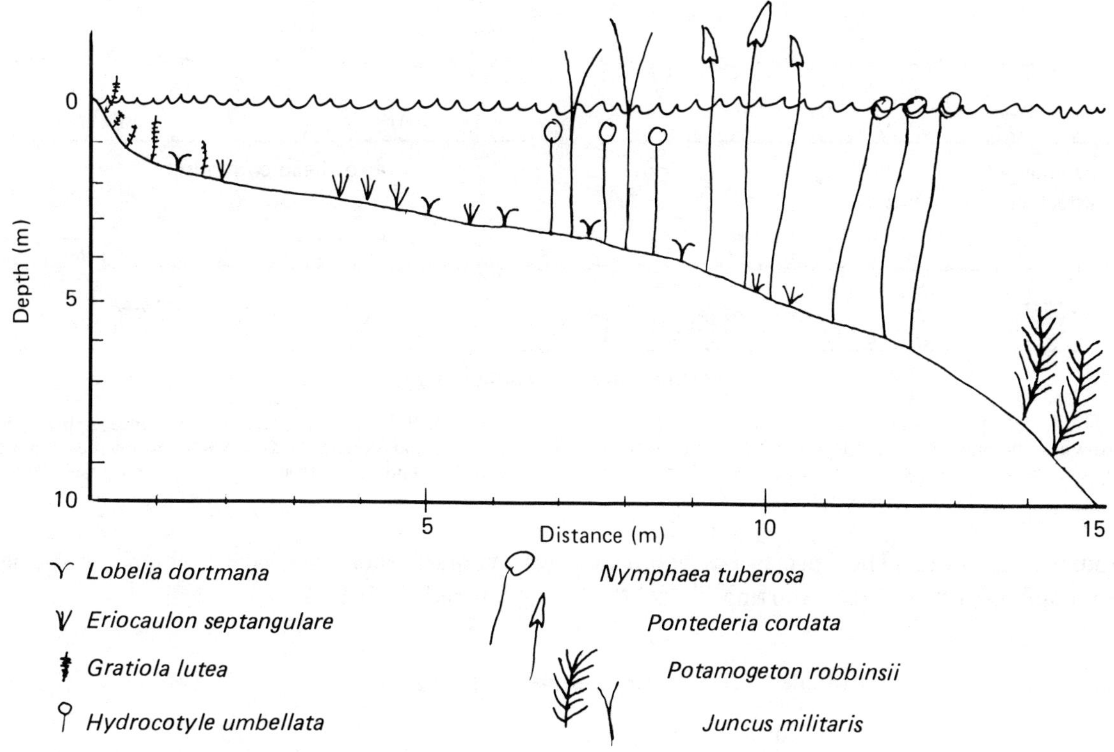

Figure 2. Bisect of littoral vegetation of Snars Pond, Snars, R.I. From point 10.8 ft west of town dock, on bearing mag 275 (WNW). Vertical exaggeration 2.5×.

Life Form Association Diagram

Using Dansereau's symbols (Figure 3), make vegetation diagram for each different community you observe (Figure 4).

Gradient Table

A gradient table is for analyzing the relationship of occurrence to some factor. These data will be at intervals of 10 cm along a

Structure	Leaf Form
erect woody plants	needle or spine
climbing or decumbent	graminoid (leaf of grass)
epiphytes	medium or small
herbs	broad
bryoid (mosses	compound
	thalloid (liverwort or prothallus)

Function			
deciduous	semideciduous	evergreen	evergreen-succulent

Figure 3. Life form symbols. (After Dansereau, 1959.)

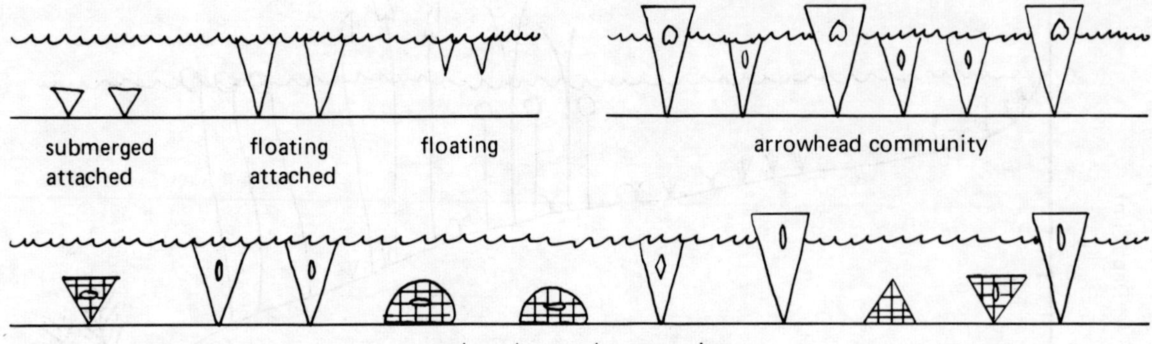

Figure 4. Life form diagrams for community or association structure. Upper left: Shoreline zones of pond. Upper right: Arrowhead community or association (*Sagittarietum rigidae*) with *Sagittaria* and *Juncus.* Lower: Northern bur reed community or association (*Sparganietum boreale*) with *Sparganium, Isoëtes,* and *Fontinalis.* For association naming, see project 8.

gradient of depth. The species are listed in sequence of occurrence, starting from the left. Mark each interval in which the species occurred (Table 1).

Table 1. Sample depth-species gradient table[a]

(Gradient at intervals of *10 cm*) / Interval along a gradient of *depth*	*Gratiola lutea*	*Juncus militaris*	*Elatine minor*	*Numphaea odorata*	*Pontederia cordata*	*Potamogeton gramineus*	*Vallisneria americana*
0	X	X	–	–	X	–	–
10	X	X	X	–	–	–	–
20	–	X	X	–	–	–	–
30	–	X	–	–	–	–	–
40	–	–	–	X	X	–	–
50	–	–	–	X	X	–	–
60	–	–	–	X	–	X	–
70	–	–	–	–	–	X	X

[a]For more quantitative detail of occurrence, use phytosociological classes (project 8), number of shoots per m^2, or Hubbs-Hubbs (1953) diagrams.

PROJECT 4 Vegetation Analysis by Quadrat

OBJECTIVE

To prepare a quantitative report of vegetation and biomass of an area of a stream by the quadrat method; and to determine velocity, discharge, substrate type, and certain useful parameters.

METHOD

Field Work

1. Establish base points along the water's edge.
2. Lay out transect directly across the stream.
3. Measure depth at regular intervals across stream, as basis for calculating cross section area.
4. At regular intervals along transect, lay out quadrat; quadrats are generally 1 m^2, but size depends upon type and density of vegetation (see species-area curve, project 8), and smaller quadrats (e.g., 4 dm^2 [= 0.04 m^2]) are useful in small vegetation.
5. Examine flora (fauna) of quadrat, and report all species (use code words for unknowns).
6. Obtain vouchers from outside the quadrat.
7. Count number of shoots of each species in quadrat.
8. Harvest all material in quadrat by cutting at soil level, excluding all plant parts not within volume directly above the quadrat.
9. Measure volume: a) shake and mop off excess water, such as by twisting in towel; b) insert part or all of sample into large graduate partly filled with water; c) record increase in volume caused by plant material; and d) obtain total volume for m^2.
10. Measure wet weight: a) shake and remove excess water (as in step 9); b) place part or all of sample in scoop-equipped (with suitable counterweight) balance; and c) obtain total wet weight for m^2. (Save sample for laboratory analysis by tying up in newspaper or putting in plastic bag.)
11. Obtain ca. a 100-ml sample of sediment for laboratory analysis.
12. Measure water velocity; a) by Dutchman's log by timing a floating twig or chip over a measured distance (e.g., 100 ft), or b) with current meter, in which case check flow rates in channel, amid vegetation, and along shore.
13. It is desirable to measure certain chemical-physical factors including pH, temperature, dissolved oxygen (see project 5).

Laboratory Work

1. Measure dry weight: a) dry sample at 105° C in forced-air oven to constant weight (overnight is usually adequate) by placing

part or all in open baskets; or, in absence of oven, air dry on loosely stacked newspaper; b) cool; and c) weigh with scoop-equipped pan balance to 0.1 g.

2. Measure ash weight by analyzing a representative sample from well mixed dried and ground-up quadrat material: a) predry and weigh combustion crucible to 0.001 g; b) using dried sample (step 1), grind entire material from a quadrat with plant grinder; c) mix grindings thoroughly; d) take small, representative sample (ca. 0.25–1 g), enough to half fill a small combustion crucible; e) weigh grindings and crucible to 0.001 g to determine dry weight; f) cover crucible, and ash at 550°C for 6 hrs (*note:* if lime-encrusted plants are included, first remove lime by soaking sample in dil. acetic acid and redrying); g) open crucible, and cool in disiccator; h) reweigh to 0.001 g; and i) calculate % ash weight of sample, and then the ash material in g/m^2.

3. Run mechanical analysis of sediment: a) spread sediment on newspaper in enamel pan, removing vegetable matter; b) mix and work out lumps gently to a flowing state; c) weigh out suitable sample (usually 100 g, but 10 g may suffice); d) sift through set of stacked standard soil sieves arranged from largest to smallest pore size from top down; e) shake sieves laterally for ca. 1 min (or preferably use Rotap); f) help particles through sieves gently with rubber messenger; g) weigh soil that is caught on each sieve; and h) calculate % of each class size (for finer grain sizes, clays, and silts, run Bouyoucos hydrometer method, involving prior peroxide digestion of organic matter).

4. Estimate productivity (clipped quadrat) by assuming no grazing and a known growing season; calculate mg dry wt/m^2 per day and mg wet wt/m^2 per day, and mg C/m^2 per day to produce the biomass.

DATA

A. Flora (fauna): species list, together with supporting vouchers.

B. Vegetation: quantitative quadrat, giving species number (species diversity), number of shoots (density), and number of shoots of each species/m^2.

C. Biomass (or standing crop): of autophytes, reported by volume (ml/m^2), and wet weight, dry weight, ash weight, and weight of organic matter in g/m^2.

D. Sediment: report as % of sample of each soil size range, and as % of total sample finer than each successive sieve size (i.e., per cent finer). Plot the two curves on graph with particle size (mm) on abscissa and % on ordinate (Figure 1).

E. Velocity: in cm/sec (and ft/sec) at dif-

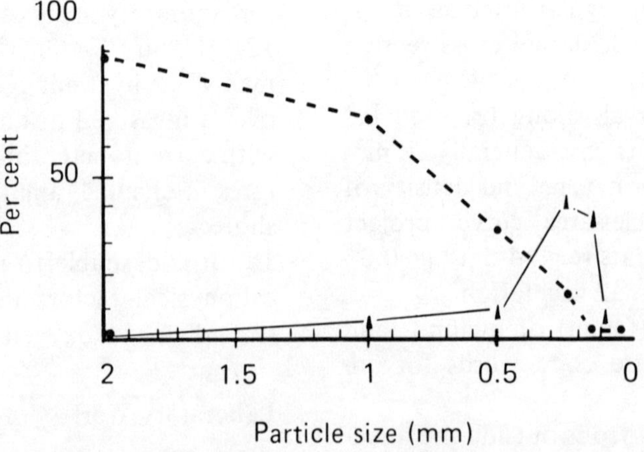

Figure 1. Mechanical analysis of sediment taken at depth of 10 ft. Solid line = % per size class. Broken line = % finer.

ferent portions of the stream (and from depth data, graph cross section diagram on paper, measure area with planimeter, calculate area; and with cross sectional area and velocity, calculate discharge).

F. Discharge: from cross section area and velocity, calculate and report discharge in ft^3/sec (cfs), m^3/sec, liter/min, gal/min (*note:* 1 ft^3 = 7.481 U.S. gallons, and 1 ft^3/sec = 450 gal/min).

G. Breadth: summarize breadth data: mean breadth and range of breadth for segment of stream investigated.

H. Depth: summarize depth data: mean depth and range of channel depth and range.

I. Chemical-physical data: tabulate values, and possibly summarize as mean values and range of variation.

J. Productivity (from clipped quadrat): report as mg dry wt/m^2 per day or mg wet wt/m^2 per day.

REFERENCES

Baldwin, M., C. E. Kellogg, and J. Thorp. 1938. Soil classification. *In* Yearbook of Agriculture, pp. 979–1001. U.S. Dept. Agric., Washington, D.C.

Goldman, C. R. (ed.). 1965. Primary Productivity in Aquatic Environments. Mem. Ist. Ital. Idrobiol. Suppl. 18. Univ. California Press, Berkeley. 464 p.

Hartman, R. T. (pers. comm).

McLean, R. C., and W. R. Ivimey Cook. 1946. Practical Field Ecology. George Allen & Unwin, London. 216 p.

Phillips, E. A. 1959. Methods of Vegetation Study. Holt-Dryden, Henry Holt & Co., New York. 107 p.

Reid, G. K. 1961. (See "References" in project 5).

Smith, R. L. 1966. Ecology and Field Biology. Harper and Row, New York. 686 p.

Strahler, A. N. 1965. (See "References" in project 1).

Tansley, A. G. 1939. (See "References" in project 3).

Welch, P. S. 1948. Limnological Methods. Blakiston Co., Philadelphia. 381 p. (now by McGraw-Hill Book Co., N.Y.).

Westlake, D. F. 1965. Some basic data for the investigation of the productivity of aquatic macrophytes. *In* C. R. Goldman (1965), pp. 231–248, see above.

Wood, R. D., and P. E. Hargraves. 1969. Comparative benthic plant ecology by SCUBA-monitored quadrats. Hydrobiologia 33: 561–586.

NOTES

Quadrat Count

Quadrats For aquatic work, a convenient quadrat consists of rope laced through the eyes of four surveying pins. The length of rope determines the area enclosed (e.g., 4-m rope gives 1 m^2). Romex can be bent to form a convenient quadrat (Wood and Hargraves, 1969: 567). Size and number of quadrats needed for significance is determined by species-area curves. Plot number of species against area in m^2, and use area above plateau of curve (Smith, 1966: 611, 612).

Diversity Number of species per m^2; (see "Method," step 5).

Density Number of shoots (of each species, or total) per m^2; (see "Method," step 7).

Harvest* (clip) *Quadrat (See "Method," step 8).

Biomass

Compare with available standing crop data (e.g., Hartman, pers. comm.).

Wet Weight (See "Method," step 10).

Dry Weight (See "Method," step 1).

Ash Weight (See "Method," step 2).

Ash-free Dry Weight ("organic carbon") Often called (e.g., Westlake, 1965) organic carbon and abbreviated "C," this is more nearly a measure of organic matter:

dry wt/m^2 – ash wt/m^2 = ash-free dry wt/m^2

Carbon The inorganic carbon, C/m^2, in organisms predominantly carbohydrate in composition, would be approximately 12/30 of the ash-free dry weight (i.e., C/m^2 = 0.4 [ash-free wt/m^2], expressed in g).

Volume (Displacement Volume) (See "Method," step 9).

Stream parameters

Length Total length of stream, or length of segment under study.

Breadth Width at either actual water level or flood level. Mean breadth is average width over segment under study.

Depth Either actual depth or depth at flood level. Mean depth, $\bar{d} = A/w$, where A = area of cross section and w = width.

Area Either the surface area of water of segment under study, or area of a cross section of the stream. For the latter, plot cross section of stream from depth measurements, obtain area with polar planimeter (or graph paper), and calculate cross section in ft^2 or m^2.

Velocity (See "Method," step 12). The Dutchman's log, or surface float method (Welch, 1948: 151), is subject to many errors caused by wind, current variations, etc. Weighting down float reduces wind errors. Mean velocity is estimated at 0.8 times the float velocity. With a current meter, average velocity can be measured by taking readings at intervals across stream and at intervals of depth. With the Gurley current meter, the number of clicks/min divided by 60 = ft/sec velocity.

Discharge (Volume of Flow) Product of average velocity and cross sectional area of stream. When using the Dutchman's log, it can be calculated from Embody's formula, as given by Welch (1948: 153):

$$r = \frac{wdal}{t} \quad \text{or} \quad r = \frac{Aal}{t}$$

where r = discharge in ft^3/sec; w = width of channel in ft (average); d = average depth (ft); a = a constant depending on smoothness of bottom (0.8 if rough, 0.9 if smooth) and depth (1.33 if less than 2 ft, 1.05 if more than 10 ft, and interpolate if between 2 and 10 ft); l = length of channel measured (ft); t = time (average of three tests) to cover the length (sec); and A = cross section area (replaces W and d when area is measured directly) (*note:* 1 ft^3/sec = 450 gal/min; 1 ft^3 = 7.481 U.S. gal).

Mean Channel Slope Channel slope is the ratio of the vertical drop of the channel along a segment of a stream to the horizontal distance along the segment (S = height/length); mean channel slope is the average of all the slopes measured along a segment (Strahler, 1965: 493).

Shoal Area of bottom being markedly shoal (shallow) divided by area of bottom, × 100, gives % shoal.

Volume The product of mean depth, mean breadth, and length, all in ft, gives volume of that segment of river (in ft^3).

Sediment

Mechanical Analysis (See "Method," step 3; Figure 1). Note also that uniform shaking of screnes (sieves) for 3–4 min is indicated, but more uniform results are obtained with standard Rotap shaking machine. Methods are well established, and counsel of soils expert is recommended.

Per Cent Finer (See "Data," item D).

Classification For soil texture grades, see Table 1. For soils triangle to classify soils on

Table 1. Soil texture grades used by the U.S. Department of Agriculture (after Strahler, 1965: 168)

Name of grade	Diameter (inches)	Diameter (mm)
Coarse gravel	Above 0.08	Above 2
Fine gravel	0.04 – 0.08	1 – 2
Coarse sand	0.02 – 0.04	0.5 – 1
Medium sand	0.01 – 0.02	0.25 – 0.5
Fine sand	0.004 – 0.01	0.1 – 0.25
Very fine sand	0.002 – 0.004	0.05 – 0.1
Silt	0.00008 – 0.002	0.002 – 0.05
Clay	Below 0.00008	Below 0.002

Table 2. Relationship between stream velocity and sediment type and nature of habitat (Tansley's 1939 data as arranged by Reid, 1961: 139)

Velocity in ft (m)/sec	Sediment	Habitat
4+ (1.21)	Rock	Torrential
3 – 4 (0.91 – 1.21)	Heavy shingle	Torrential
2 – 3 (0.60 – 0.91)	Light shingle	Nonsilted
1 – 2 (0.30 – 0.60)	Gravel	Partly silted
8 in. – 1 (0.2 – 0.3)	Sand	Partly silted
5 in. – 8 in. (0.12 – 0.2)	Silt	Silted
0 – 5 in. (→ 0.12)	Mud	Pondlike

the per cent of clay, silt, and sand, see Strahler (1965: 168).

Sediment-Velocity Relationship See Tansley's data (listed by Reid, 1961: 139) on sediment type and its relationship to water velocity (see Table 2).

Substrate For terms to describe the bottom material, see listings under "Sediments," in "Notes" section, project 1.

Polar Planimeter Lay out large paper on smooth surface so that angle does not approach 180° (sectioning map may be necessary); rotate wheel to zero in the meter. Operate clockwise. To check in advance, draw square inch and check accuracy of planimeter. (Ref.: Welch, 1948:79.)

PROJECT 5 Vegetation Analysis in Deep Water by Indirect Sampling

OBJECTIVE

To investigate deep-water benthic vegetation (fauna) and environmental factors beyond the limit of direct sampling; and to sample and study phytoplankton.

METHOD

1. Benthon

Establish two stations, one on each shore. Run transect across water from one to the other by either of two methods, boat team or SCUBA team. Investigate depth, substrate, vegetation, and certain chemical and physical factors.

Boat Team Using a broadbeam skiff (rowboat) pulled by oars and equipped with lead line and grapnel, follow transect across basin, taking dredgings at regular intervals for benthic vegetation, locating station by bearings, compass bearings, or sextant, and taking a sediment sample by Ekman dredge and a plankton tow between stations. Process samples in laboratory.

SCUBA Team The same transect is followed by divers using SCUBA (self-contained underwater breathing apparatus), by compass or by swimming along a previously laid out plastic rope or weighted line. Record per cent cover, depth, changes in vegetation and substrate. Obtain samples, and make other observations of interest.

2. Plankton

Base station boat team (vertical gradient team): Anchor upwind, drift downwind, and secure line when over station; take measurements (temperature, light intensity), Secchi disk reading, and samples of water for analysis and for plankton at 1-m intervals from surface to bottom. Samples are largely processed in the laboratory, and may include water color, pH, alkalinity, carbon dioxide, conductivity, dissolved oxygen and its saturation, redox, and total filterable residue. Sec "Notes" for details.

DATA

A. Flora (fauna): make two species lists, one of benthon and another of plankton.
B. Vegetation: tabulate data on species by per cent composition or density.

C. Physical-chemical factors:tabulate data.
D. Voucher specimens of macrophytes: herbarium specimens.
E. Vouchers of microphytes: preserve sample together with slides, sketches, drawings, or photomicrographs of individual species of plankton.
F. Graphs showing vertical gradients of physical–chemical factors, especially of light, temperature, and dissolved oxygen.

REFERENCES

APHA. 1965. Standard Methods for the Examination of Water and Wastewater, Including Bottom Sediments and Sludges. 12th Ed. American Public Health Association, 1790 Broadway, New York. 769 p. (Reissued periodically).

Chapman, C. F. 1968. Piloting, Seamanship and Small Boat Handling. (1968–1969 Ed.) Motor Boating, New York. 664 p. (New editions issued frequently).

Chemical Rubber Publ. Co. (current year). Handbook of Chemistry and Physics. Chemical Rubber Publ. Co., Cleveland.

CNCA (Conference for National Cooperation in Aquatics). 1959. The science of skin and scuba diving. Association Press, New York. 306 p. (Reissued periodically).

Dansereau, P. 1959. (See "References" in project 3).

Hargraves, P. E., and R. D. Wood. 1967. Periphyton algae in selected aquatic habitats. Int. J. Oceanol. Limnol. 1(2): 55–67.

Hodgman, C. D. (ed.) 1943. Handbook of Chemistry and Physics. Chemical Rubber Publ. Co., Cleveland. 2553 p. (Issued annually).

Mackereth, F. J. H. 1963. Some Methods of Water Analysis for Limnologists. Freshwater Biological Association, Ambleside, Westmorland, England. 70 p.

Reid, G. K. 1961. Ecology of Inland Waters and Estuaries. Reinhold, New York. 375 p.

Saila, S. B., and D. Horton. 1957. Fisheries investigations and management in Rhode Island lakes and ponds. Publ. 3, Fisheries, Rhode Island Dept. Agric. and Conserv., Div. Fish and Game, Providence. 134 p.

Strickland, J. D. H., and T. R. Parsons. 1965. A Manual of Sea Water Analysis. Queen's Printer, Ottawa. 203 p.

Strickland, J. D. H., and T. R. Parsons. 1968. A Practical Handbook of Seawater Analysis. Bull. No. 167. Fisheries Res. Board of Canada. Queen's Printer, Ottawa. 311 p.

Sverdrup, H. U., M. W. Johnson, and R. H. Fleming. 1942. The Oceans, their Physics, Chemistry, and General Biology. Prentice-Hall, Englewood Cliffs, N.J. 1087 p.

Ward, H. B., and G. C. Whipple. 1918. Freshwater Biology. John Wiley & Sons, New York. 1111 p. (Out of print; for 2nd Ed., see Edmondson, "References" in project 7).

Welch, P. S. 1948. (See "References" in project 4).

Wood, R. D. 1963. Adapting SCUBA to aquatic plant ecology. Ecology 44: 416–419.

Wood, R. D., and P. E. Hargraves. 1969. (See "References" in project 4).

NOTES

Field Operations

Boat Team Transect Using topographic map or hydrographic chart, select a station on each shore and two permanent bearing objects visible from the work area. Starting from one station, pull a fixed number of oar strokes (e.g., 2 or 4). Stop, lower grapnel to bottom, jerk line up and down to test nature of bottom, and record depth from line's graduations. Fix location by bearings or taking compass reading on the two fixed objects. Haul grapnel a uniform short distance, then raise to surface. Retrieve vegetation, recording density on a 0.1–5 scale (5 = very dense), and save sample in plastic bag, or wrap in newspaper, labeled clearly. Lower

Ekman dredge to bottom and send down messenger to release, raise, and remove ca. 100 ml of sediment into plastic bag or bottle, labeled clearly. Repeat samplings at regular intervals (or number of oar strokes) along transect. Between stops, take plankton tow with net, saving half as is and preserving half with enough formalin (to make 4% [5% in seawater]). Process plant and plankton samples (see below) in laboratory.

SCUBA Team Transect Team of two or three divers: don wet suits and gear, enter water, dive sufficiently deep to drive out air from suit, surface, and adjust weight belt to neutral buoyancy (or slightly heavy). Take compass, depth gauge, armored thermometer, light meter, roughened lucite slate and pencil (or submarine tape recorder), plastic bags and jars and samplers (Kemmerer sampler[1] or W-Z diver's sampler[1]) in bug bag[2] (tie items to body with strings). Begin from one station with one diver maintaining compass course, the second making observations. A third may be of help by remaining at the surface to supply needs or give assistance. Record depth at which changes in vegetation or conditions occur; note species of plants, substrate, rocks, etc.; and take light and temperature readings. Take light readings with back to light direction, and find maximum reading when passing meter back and forth 1 ft above open hand. Note vegetation types, per cent cover, dominant species, depth limits. Take voucher specimens of each species, recording collection by name or code word, and depth. Take sediment by forcing plastic tube into substrate and stoppering ends or scooping up into jar. Take water sample by opening sampler, pushing tube sharply through water to area to be sampled, then plugging ends. Trap periphyton by sliding sampler over algal mass and stoppering ends. (*Note:* Position of samples can be estimated later by plotting course on hydrographic chart and fixing location by depth record, or similarly correlating with transect data from boat team.) On return, wash diving gear carefully and air dry. Prepare voucher specimens. Tabulate data. Process samples that are taken of sediment, water, plankton, periphyton, etc.

Vertical Gradients Team Using steady, well equipped boat as base station, anchor upwind or upcurrent, and pay out anchor line sufficient to bring boat over study area (usually deep hole). At 1-m intervals, take measurements of light and temperature, recording depth by graduated line from one end of the boat. Take water samples with 1,000-ml Kemmerer water sampler at 1-m intervals from surface down, filling 250-ml gs bottles, one for dissolved oxygen (overflowing 1–2 times its volume), a second for alkalinity and other analyses, a third for plankton, and use rest of water for immediate measurement of pH, redox, CO_2, and water color. Process the dissolved oxygen sample through the sulfuric acid stage immediately. Preserve (see "Notes") half of each phytoplankton collection, and keep the rest shaded and cool until microscope examination at the very first opportunity. If time permits, lower Secchi disk until it just disappears, raise it until it appears, and take depth reading at the midpoints between the two readings (see "Procedures" in project 5a).

For details on use of Ekman dredge, compass bearings, electronic thermometer, Secchi disk, and submarine photometer, see these items as treated in "Notes" of project 5a.

Laboratory Procedures

For details on *phytoplankton analysis, dissolved oxygen* concentration (Winkler), *conductivity,* or *pH,* see these items under "Procedures" of project 5a.

Processing of Benthic Vegetation Sort out each grapnel haul in a separate pan, and determine the number of different kinds of

[1] See "Procedures" of project 5a.

[2] Skin diver's nylon net lobster bag.

plants. Identify all that can be classified; and, if there is a large enough sample to make it somewhat meaningful, calculate the per cent composition. Vouchers should be prepared for permanent record.

Preservation of Phytoplankton Obtain plankton sample, or tow, and add sufficient commercial formalin to make up to 4% (5% in seawater) of that solution. If resulting preservative is acidic, dissolve in sufficient borax to make neutral litmus. If diatoms are present, and are to be studied later by a phycologist, the preservative should be changed the following day. Centrifuge plankton down, then cautiously pipet out as much fluid as practical. Replace with 70% ethanol, and redisperse the plankton. Store in screw-capped bottles, label carefully (see "Labeling" under "Notes" of project 1), and store in dark case or closet.

Slides of Phytoplankton These can be fairly easily made with karo solution or with glycerine jelly. For the former, make up fresh 30% karo solution in water. Put drop of preserved plankton on slide, and mix in a drop of 30% karo. Cover with coverslip, label, and allow to dry several weeks during which time a drop of increasingly stronger karo solution (e.g., 50%, 80%) should be added to the edge of the coverslip to compensate for evaporation. For glycerine jelly technique, see books on microtechnique.

Drawing of Phytoplankton Using a drawing prism or camera lucida and balancing light through microscope and that falling on drawing paper by using two lamps, sketch outline of the plankton cell. With aid of micrometer slide, or micrometer ocular scale, the magnification of the drawing can be determined. Once the outline is made, fill in details. Label carefully and indicate magnification. If final results are desired, trace onto a quality paper using tracing box, and ink with India ink.

Processing and Preservation of Periphyton Samples obtained in the W-Z diver's sampler can be gently floated out in an enamel pan and examined with a swingarm stereoscopic microscope. For more detailed analysis, the material can be preserved and processed as for plankton in 4% neutral formalin, then mixed vigorously to separate the cells preparatory to counting. See procedures under "Plankton" in the "Procedures" section of project 5a. In this step, 1 ml of thoroughly mixed sample is delivered into a Sedgwick-Rafter counting chamber, and the slide is examined at 100X with a laboratory microscope. The number of different kinds, the flora (fauna), and per cent composition can be reported. It is also possible to obtain density and biomass per unit area of host if desired. (Ref. Hargraves and Wood, 1967, and Wood and Hargraves, 1969.)

PROJECT 5a General Hydrobotanical Investigation

OBJECTIVE

To investigate and report on the vegetation (fauna), hydrography, and chemical-physical factors in a given basin.

METHOD

Teams, each assigned special parts of the job and trained in the special techniques for that phase of work, make an overall field study of a basin. The total job includes extensive work, both in the field and in the laboratory. A third important aspect is the planning.

Field Work

1. Reconnaissance: to examine surrounding area and drainage system involved.
2. Surveying: to obtain outline map and shoreline information.
3. Fathometry: to obtain transects, and ultimately contours, of depths of the basin.
4. Transects of benthos: to fix location and range of benthic species and vegetation, both attached and periphytic forms.
5. Transect of sediment samples: to locate sediment types.
6. Shoreline vegetation: to determine species and vegetation of shoreline and littoral regions.
7. Vertical sampling of water: to measure chemical-physical factors, and to obtain data on phytoplankton.
8. Horizontal sampling of water: to determine current- or wind-related variations in physical-chemical factors and phytoplankton.

Planning

1. Schedule and procedures
2. Supplies
3. Distribution of supplies
4. Division of labor

Laboratory Work

1. Analyzing samples for chemical-physical factors
2. Identifying biota
3. Counting plankton
4. Preparing vouchers (herbarium, fluid, photographs, drawings)
5. Tabulating data
6. Calculating results
7. Interpreting results (including preparation of final data in tables, charts, graphs, maps), and statements of conclusion and relevant implications

DATA

Tabulate raw and final data for each aspect of the work, and prepare illustrations (transects, bisects, maps, or charts) as needed.

Flora and Vegetation (Fauna)

A. Benthic macrophytes (macrophytobenthon).
B. Benthic algae (microphytobenthon).
C. Plankton (phytoplankton).
D. Periphytic algae (phytoperiphyton).
E. Epibenthic algae (phytoepibenthon).

Basin and Morphometry

A. Region
 1. Geology
 2. Drainage
 3. Map
B. Surface outline chart of basin
C. Hydrographic chart (contours at suitable depth intervals [2.5 ft is practical if 5-ft charts are provided])
D. Parameters, such as length, mean breadth, volume, mean slope, circumference, shoreline development

Chemical-Physical Factors

A. Vertical (and horizontal?) gradients
 1. Light intensity (% transmitted); spectrum
 2. Dissolved oxygen, and % saturation
 3. Alkalinity
 4. Carbon dioxide
 5. pH
 6. Temperature
 7. Solutes
B. Fixed values
 1. Secchi disk
C. Sediment types and distribution

REFERENCES

APHA. 1965. (See "References" in project 5).

Armstrong, F. A. J. 1951. (See "Silicates").

Atkins, W. R. G. 1923. (See "Phosphates").

Chapman, C. F. 1968. (See "References" in project 5).

Dansereau, P. 1959. (See "References" in project 3).

Deevey, E. S. 1940. Limnological studies in Connecticut. V. A contribution to regional limnology. Amer. J. Sci. 238: 717–741.

Denigès, G. 1920. (See "Phosphates").

Eastman Kodak Co. 1970, 1974. (See "Photomicrography").

IBP. 1969. Methods for chemical analysis of fresh waters. International Biological Programme. Blackwell Scientific, Oxford. 166 p. (Text by H. L. Golterman).

Mackereth, F. J. H. 1963. (See "References" in project 5).

Mullin, J. B., and J. P. Riley. 1955. (See "Nitrates").

Patrick, R. 1949. A proposed biological measure of stream conditions, based on a survey of the Conestoga Basin, Lancaster County, Pennsylvania. Proc. Nat. Acad. Sci. 101: 277–341.

Pratt, D. M. (pers. comm.). (See "Nitrates," "Phosphates," "Silicates").

Reid, G. K. 1967. (See "References" in project 1).

Ruttner, F. 1963. Fundamentals of Limnology. 3rd Ed. Univ. Toronto Press, Toronto. 295 p. (Translated by D. G. Frey and F. E. J. Fry).

Saila, S. B., and D. Horton. 1957. (See "References" in project 5).

Saunders, G. W., F. B. Trama, and R. W. Bachman. 1962. Evaluation of a modified ^{14}C technique for shipboard estimates of photosynthesis in large lakes. Great Lakes Res. Div., Inst. Sci. and Technol., Univ. Mich. Publ. no. 8: 1–61. (Also JI/GTFE, 1969: 30).

Strickland, J. D. H., and T. R. Parsons. 1968. (See "References" in project 5).

Sverdrup, H. U., M. W. Johnson, and R. H. Fleming. 1942. (See "References" in project 5).

Wattenberg, H. 1937. (See "Phosphates").
Ward, H. B., and G. C. Whipple. 1918. (See "References" in project 5).
Wood, R. D. 1963. (See "References" in project 5).

NOTES

Preparations

Advanced Preparations Sample of steps required in planning field work.

1. Select station: depends on access, size for surveying, local regulations on boating or motors, attitude of property owners.
2. Select date: during growing season before abscission or dormancy, weather trends, time required for prior training of personnel.
3. Select procedures: those usually made for survey of this type.
4. Organize personnel: select team to cover each job, with concern for having an advanced worker on each team, matching interests of personnel to job.
5. Train personnel: each worker should carry out in advance the sampling and analyzing procedures he will need to use. He should have established a degree of proficiency.
6. Provide instructions: a copy of full instructions to all personnel will enable each to know where he fits. These should be provided in advance.
7. Assemble equipment: each person specializing in a given task needs to conduct trial runs to see what he needs, then make sure all items he needs are included in equipment and supplies being assembled.
8. Arrange for moving of equipment to field: a) boats and motors, b) supplies and equipment (including rinse water), c) personnel, d) instructions, e) diving gear (probably to be handled strictly by divers themselves).
9. Provide transportation: bus, private cars, trailers.
10. Place markers (rags) at regular intervals on shore around pond.
11. Arrange to have equipment removed from field, cleaned up, and returned to storage; also arrange to clean up markers in the field.

Program of Field Operation Sample of job distribution and teams for one hydrobotanical investigation.

1. SCUBA team: two or three persons, doing a benthic transect for a) vegetation, b) light intensity, c) sediment type, d) general notes, and e) vouchers. If time permits, a) calibrate light meter with submarine photometer, and b) take deep-water samples for water and epibenthic algae.
2. Boat team: four persons, doing transect by rowing, fixing stations by compass bearing (or sextant), taking samples of benthic vegetation from bottom and surface samples of water and plankton: a) sediment samples, b) depth by lead line, c) location by compass bearings, d) net plankton samples, and e) benthic vegetation grapnel samples.
3. Plankton sampling and survey: two persons, doing a) vertical distribution (by person in "gradients team"), b) horizontal distribution (by person in "boat team").
4. Surveying team: two to three persons, on shore a) making outline map, b) fixing location of all stations.
5. Fathometer team: three persons, in boat with motor, taking transects between fixed points around basin.
6. Vertical gradients team: five or more persons, aboard main boat, obtaining data from different depths, a) recording data, b) measuring light intensity by submarine photometer, c) obtaining water samples with Kemmerer water sampler (for pH, dissolved oxygen, color, redox, conductivity, alkalinity, temperature), d) taking readings in the field of temperature, pH, and if possible also redox and color, e) taking plankton samples, preserving half of each, and assisting with jobs member "d" cannot handle.
7. Littoral plant survey: two persons, recording and charting vegetation of shoreline to waist deep.

8. Littoral chemical-physical factors: two persons, testing for local conditions which cause variations in oxygen, temperature, pH, light, etc.

9. Sediment: one person (in "boat team") making samples along transect, but more help will be required for sediment analyses.

10. Deep-water macrophyte survey: one person (with "boat team") obtaining samples from grapnel hauls, and possibly a second person (with "boat team") with peep box making sight observations of shallow-water vegetation.

11. Aufwuchs or periphyton: two (or three) persons, one with "littoral plant survey team" checking on periphyton found, and sampling, for later analysis; and one with "boat team" watching for periphyton on grapnel samples. A third person (one with "SCUBA team") will watch for and sample a) aufwuchs on plants, rocks, stumps, and b) benthic microflora on sediment and in sediment.

Procedures

1. ***Alkalinity*** (Time required: ca. 10 min)

Reagents

1. *Methyl purple indicator* (or methyl orange).

2. *Phenolphthalein indicator:* in 500 ml of 95% ethanol, dissolve 5 g of phenolphthalein, and dil. to 1,000 ml with dist. water; add 0.02 N NaOH until faint pink disappears.

3. *0.02 N sulfuric acid* (see APHA, 1965: 50).

Procedure Work under bright fluorescent light.

1. Pipet 100 ml of sample into white evaporating dish.

2. Add 4 drops of phenolphthalein indicator.

3. Stir; if not pink, record phenolphthalein alkalinity as 0 and continue; but, if pink develops, titrate until pink disappears (ca. pH 8.3) and record volume.

4. Add 3 (or more) drops of methyl purple indicator.

5. Titrate cautiously until color shifts from green to pink (ca. pH 4.6) and record volume.

6. Rinse with tap water, and proceed to next sample.

Closing steps:

7. Rinse evaporating dish with tap water and air dry.

8. Rinse buret with dist. water.

Calculations Total alkalinity as mg of $CaCo_3$/liter = 10× V; where V = volume of acid titrated (ml). For calculations, amount titrated to phenolphthalein end point (phenolphthalein alkalinity) may be needed. For other factors (carbonate alkalinity and total CO_2) see IBP Handbook no. 8 (IBP, 1969: 28) or APHA (1965).

Conversions

$$\frac{\text{meq}}{\text{liter}} = \frac{\text{ppm}}{50} = \frac{1}{50} \times \frac{\text{mg}}{\text{liter}}$$ (expressed as ppm $CaCO_3$, etc.)

Ranges Inland waters: 0–500 mg of $CaCO_3$/liter or 0–10 meq of $CaCO_3$/liter (APHA, 1965: 50); marine: 0–140 mg of $CaCO_3$/liter or 0.5–2.8 meq of $CaCO_3$/liter (Strickland and Parsons, 1968: 31).

Notes See project 15 for conversions to carbonates or available carbon. See "Conductivity," procedure 8, for relationship to total filterable residue and conductance.

References APHA (1965: 48); Welch (1948: 214).

2. ***Bearings***

Methods useful to pinpoint location of boat in lake or cove are:

Bearings: orient boat in line with two shore objects (e.g., chimney, telephone pole) from one direction, and two shore objects from another direction. Also referred to as *ranges.*

Compass bearings: by hand-held compass, take readings in degrees of two fixed shore points and record as magnetic bearing (e.g., mag 270 for west); correct for compass variation and deviation (see "Note" below).

Compass and range finder: take compass reading on known point, together with distance by range finder; correct for compass errors.

Sextant: take angle measurement between known points, together with a compass bearing. (See "Sextant," procedure 48, for details.)

Two transits: with transits at known points, take simultaneous sightings and a compass bearing.

Plane table alidade: with stadia rod held aloft on boat, draw line toward boat and read distance from stadia rod.

Note See "Compass," procedure 7, for corrections of variation (of locality) and deviation (of boat).

References Not well documented, but see Chapman (1968: 351).

3. Bisect

For method, see "Notes" and Figure 2 in project 3. Sediment information can be added as done by Dansereau (1959).

4. Carbonates and total carbon

See "Notes" in project 15.

5. Carbon dioxide

Procedure The available titrimetric methods (APHA, 1965: 82) are too uncertain, and the gasometric method (Strickland and Parsons, 1968: 35) is too tedious, to recommend for field ecology. Use Mackereth's (1963: 20) graph (Figure 1) for normal lakes, which requires only pH and total alkalinity. For less average waters, use the nomographs by APHA (1965: 78) which, in addition to alkalinity and pH, also require total filterable residue and temperature. The nomograph methods give free CO_2.

Conversions

$$\text{millimole } CO_2 = \frac{\text{ppm}}{36} = \frac{\text{mg } CO_2/\text{liter}}{36}$$

Ranges Inland waters: 0–200 mg of CO_2/liter (Reid, 1961: 160) or 0–6 millimoles of CO_2; marine: near 0.

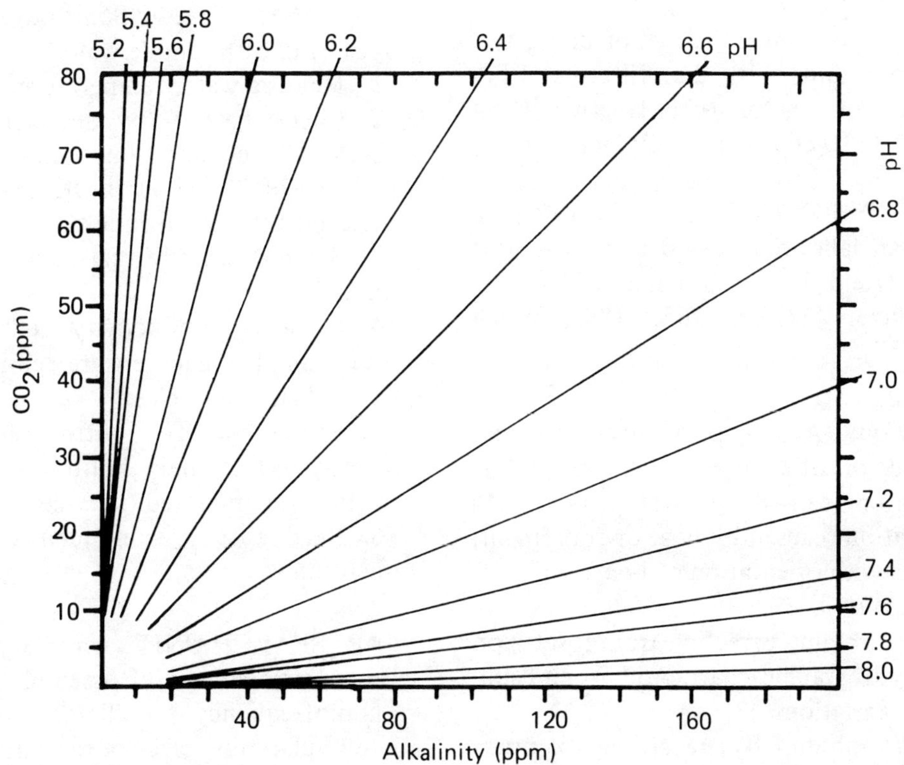

Figure 1. Dissolved free carbon dioxide concentration (ppm or mg/liter) as related to alkalinity and pH. (Data from Mackereth, 1963: 20.)

References Mackereth (1963: 20); APHA (1965: 78).

6. Color

Procedure Using the Hellige "U.S.G.S." color measuring unit with platinum-cobalt-colored filter disks:

1. Use clean, dry 20-cm standard tube, mounting filters in spring at far end; or fill with dist. water.
2. Select suitable sample tube (usually the 20-cm tube unless color is unusual), fill completely (avoiding bubbles), and plug.
3. Hold both toward light of low sky area, and compare simultaneously.
4. Accumulate (or interchange as needed), increasing total values marked on disks, until color (not density) matches.
5. Record sum of values marked on disks.

Note If color is more extreme, use shorter sample tubes (10- or 5-cm). If tubes leak, soak occasionally for several hours.

Calculation

$$C = F \times U$$

where C = platinum-cobalt color units; U = sum of color units marked on filters; and F = factor to correct for tube length (20-cm tube, F = 1; 10-cm tube, F = 2; 5-cm tube, F = 4).

Ranges 0–500 (APHA, 1965: 129); inland, clean lakes are near 0 and dark bogs near 300 (Reid, 1961: 101); marine ?.

References APHA (1965: 129); Welch (1948: 137).

7. Compass

Precautions Avoid proximity to iron, electronic, or other magnetic items. Errors are variation (caused by location on earth) and deviation (caused by boat or equipment, and varies with orientation of boat).

Corrections

Variation: obtain correction from rosette on local hydrographic chart. Add W, and subtract E, variations.

Deviation: obtain by recording compass readings while boat is rotated stepwise through a circle of known true compass bearings.

Divers must make a special effort to hold wrist compass *ahead,* away from tank, and to avoid slight reading errors which tend to accumulate and result in turning to the left.

Reference Chapman (1968: 256).

8. Conductivity

Conductivity can be measured conveniently with industrial-model bridges, or can be more accurately determined in the laboratory by research units.

•INDUSTRIAL MODEL The Beckman RB-3 SoluBridge with CEL VS2 cell (cell constant 2.00/cm) covers low solute range (50–8,000 μmhos), while a separate cell (cell constant 0.20/cm) is needed for very pure waters. The RB3-349 with CEL VH20 cell (cell constant 20.0/cm) covers marine conditions (0–40 ^{o}/oo S; 0–60,000 μmhos).

Procedure To use SoluBridge, clean cell by rinsing with sample water.

1. Measure water temperature.
2. Check battery by depressing "battery check" switch and simultaneously pressing the "on–off" button. If OK, needle deflects right, into the green zone.
3. Set temperature dial to water temperature.
4. Immerse conductivity cell completely into sample, and ensure elimination of trapped air or bubbles.
5. Press "on–off" button and simultaneously rotate main knob until needle deflection is eliminated (i.e., meter reads zero).
6. Read specific conductance directly in micromhos.

•RESEARCH UNIT An effective research unit may consist of assembled parts, the audiofrequency oscillator, conductivity cell, platinum electrodes, earphones, and Wheatstone bridge.

Reagents

1. *Stock 0.100 N KC1* (specially prepared; see APHA, 1965: 283).

2. *0.100 N KC1 working standard* (remake regularly) (into 100-ml vol. flask with 10-ml vol. pipet, add 10.0 ml 0.1 N stock KC1 (sol. 1) and dil. to 100 ml with top quality dist. water).

Procedure

To determine cell constant:

1. Bring standard and sample solutions to uniform temperature between 20 and 30°C (preferably 25°C).
2. Turn on audiofrequency oscillator, and allow to warm up for 10 min.
3. Rinse conductivity cell thoroughly with dist. water, and shake off clinging drops. (Handle electrodes carefully, do not strike, keep erect lest mercury spill out.)
4. Rinse and fill lower portion of conductivity cell with standard solution (0.01 N KC1).
5. Immerse electrode into fluid.
6. Set bridge at ca. 300 ohms.
7. Lock down BA (battery) button.
8. Tapping GA (galvanometer) button, listen to buzz, and raise and lower the resistance by means of the dials until buzz disappears or becomes minimal. (Always start with highest resistance knobs first, working stepwise to lower ones, and finally to multiplier.)
9. Record resistance. (Be sure to note multiplier value.)
10. It is well to repeat, using second sample or standard, until constant reading is obtained, to eliminate possible dilution.

> ***Note*** Extreme imbalance may occur if wires to electrodes have poor contact. Move wires up and down to correct.

To determine unknown:

11. Rinse conductivity cell thoroughly, and shake off excess water from electrodes.
12. Rinse cell and electrodes with unknown.
13. Partly fill conductivity cell with unknown.
14. Determine and record resistance (steps 4–10, above) in ohms.
15. Finally, rinse out with dist. water, and leave electrode standing in dist. water in conductivity cell.

Calculations For cell constant:

$$K_c = R_s \times C_s$$

where K_c = cell constant, R_s and C_s are the resistance (ohms) and specific conductance (μmhos) of the standard 0.01 N KC1 (C_s = 0.001413 mhos at 25°C, or 1,413 μmhos).

For specific conductance of unknown:

$$C_u = K_c/R_u \quad \text{or} \quad C_u = 1{,}413 \times R_s/R_u$$

where C_u = specific conductance of unknown, in μmhos; R_u = resistance of unknown, in ohms (for K_c, R_s, 1,413, see above).

Conversions 1 mho = 10^6 μmhos; $K_{18} \times 10^6$ = specific conductance in micromhos at 18°C, a common form used in Europe, and called reciprocal megohms; 0.001413 mhos = 1,413 μmhos; 1 millimho = μmhos/1,000.

Ranges 0.5–52,000 μmhos; fresh dist. water (0.5–2), tap water (50–500), brackish water (S = 16 ‰) (ca. 26,000), seawater (S = 34 ‰) (ca. 52,000). For one cell, the resistance of these in ohms is about 8 for seawater, 340 for 0.01 N KCl standard, 40,000–60,000 for tap water, 100,000–1,000,000 for dist. water.

References APHA (1965: 280 ff); Sverdrup, Johnson, and Fleming (1942: 72).

Notes

1. Relation of conductance to total filterable residue:

total filterable residue (mg/liter) = K × specific conductance (μmhos at 25°C)

where K = ranges normally from 0.55 to 0.7, being lower with free acid or caustic alkalinity and higher with highly saline water.

2. Note relationship of specific conductance to salinity in Figure 2, or see Mackereth (1963: 22) for inland waters. Also, see

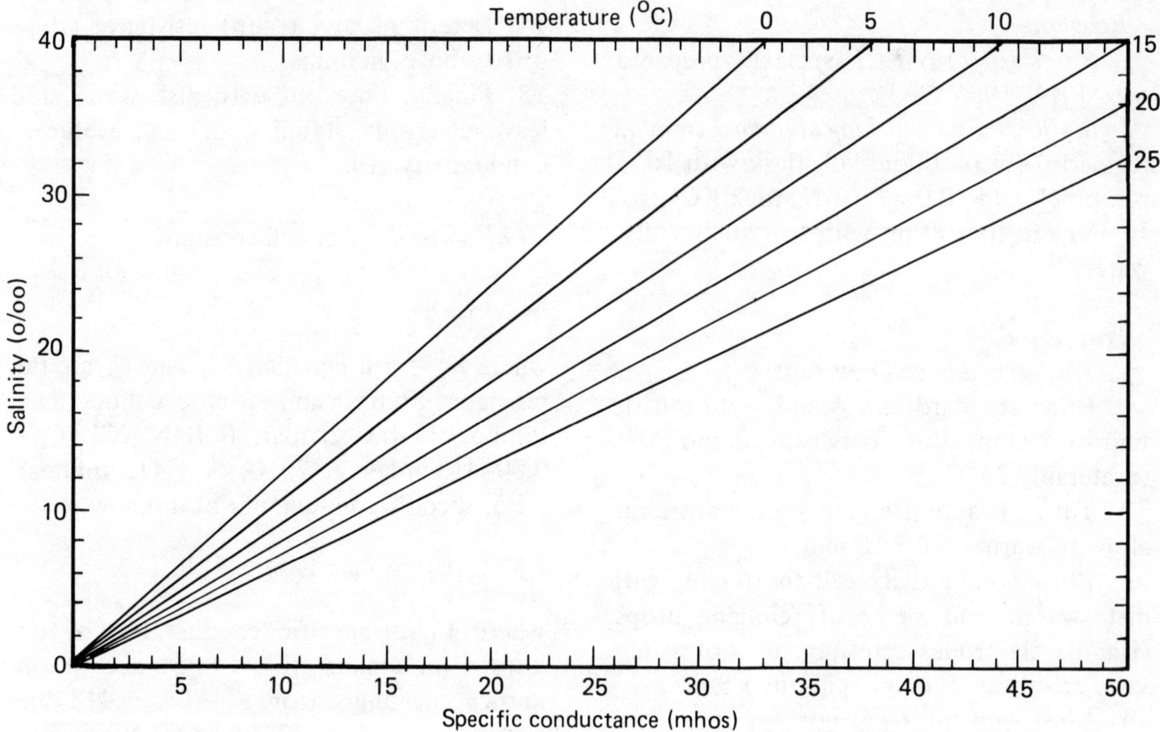

Figure 2. Salinity of seawater as related to specific conductance and temperature. (Data from Beckman Instruments, Inc., Cedar Grove Operations, Cedar Grove, N.J.)

Table 1 for relationship between specific conductance and alkalinity.

9. Depth

Methods useful for determining depth are direct (meter stick, staff) or indirect (lead line, graduated lines of sampling instruments, fathometer, diver's depth gauge).

Corrections Indirect methods often involve errors in graduations or readings and need to be checked. Ropes may swell and shrink, buckle or twist. Standardize on a good depth chain, correcting for temperature and expansion. Diver's depth gauges should be carefully chosen, and in use should be checked at the water surface when starting dive for possible error in the zero reading.

Table 1. Relationship between specific conductance and alkalinity in fresh water[a]

Alkalinity (as $CaCO_3$)		
mg/liter	meq/liter	Conductance (micromhos)
50	1	85
100	2	166
150	3	244
200	4	320
250	5	394

[a]Data by Ruttner (1963: 59).

10. Dissolved oxygen

See "Oxygen, dissolved," procedures 26 and 27.

11. Ekman dredge

Caution! Avoid catching fingers in trap while setting.

When using Ekman dredge, open each jaw one at a time, and hook chain to hole in trigger mechanism. Slide messenger up the line, and retain it as you lower dredge slowly to bottom. After allowing dredge to settle a moment, slide messenger down the the line. Hoist, and deliver sample into pan or wide container.

Reference Welch (1948: 176, Figure 50).

12. Electronic thermometer

Thermometers (e.g., those by Research Associates [Linden, N.J.] or Austin Science Associates [Austin, Tex.]) with a sensitive probe on a 50-ft wire are very convenient in field work and the readings are nearly instantaneous.

1. Lower probe (weighted with 1–2 lb of lead if necessary) to desired depth.
2. Switch on.
3. Record temperature.
4. Switch off.

Note Keep unit dry, e.g., in plastic bag (manufacturer, pers. comm.). Battery, Eveready ElN 1.5 volt, is easily replaced.

13. Epibenthic algae

See "Vegetation," procedure 59.

14. Fathometry

See project 6.

15. Gradient curve

For vertical gradients, plot factor on abscissa and depth (from surface down) on ordinate (Figure 3) with surface (depth 0) at the top.

16. Grapnel or grapple

A 4-lb grapnel anchor, or preferably a Pieters plant hook (Ward and Whipple, 1918: 68) can be used for qualitative sampling. Limitations are several (Wood, 1963: 418), but indication of density and composition are obtained.

1. Lower to bottom.
2. Drag for desired distance.
3. Hoist smoothly, not hesitating lest plant material be lost.

Reference Ward and Whipple (1918: 68).

17. Hydrogen ion concentration

Hydrogen ion concentration is usually measured as pH, the negative log of the hydrogen ion concentration. Hydrogen ion concentration and pH are not the same. The

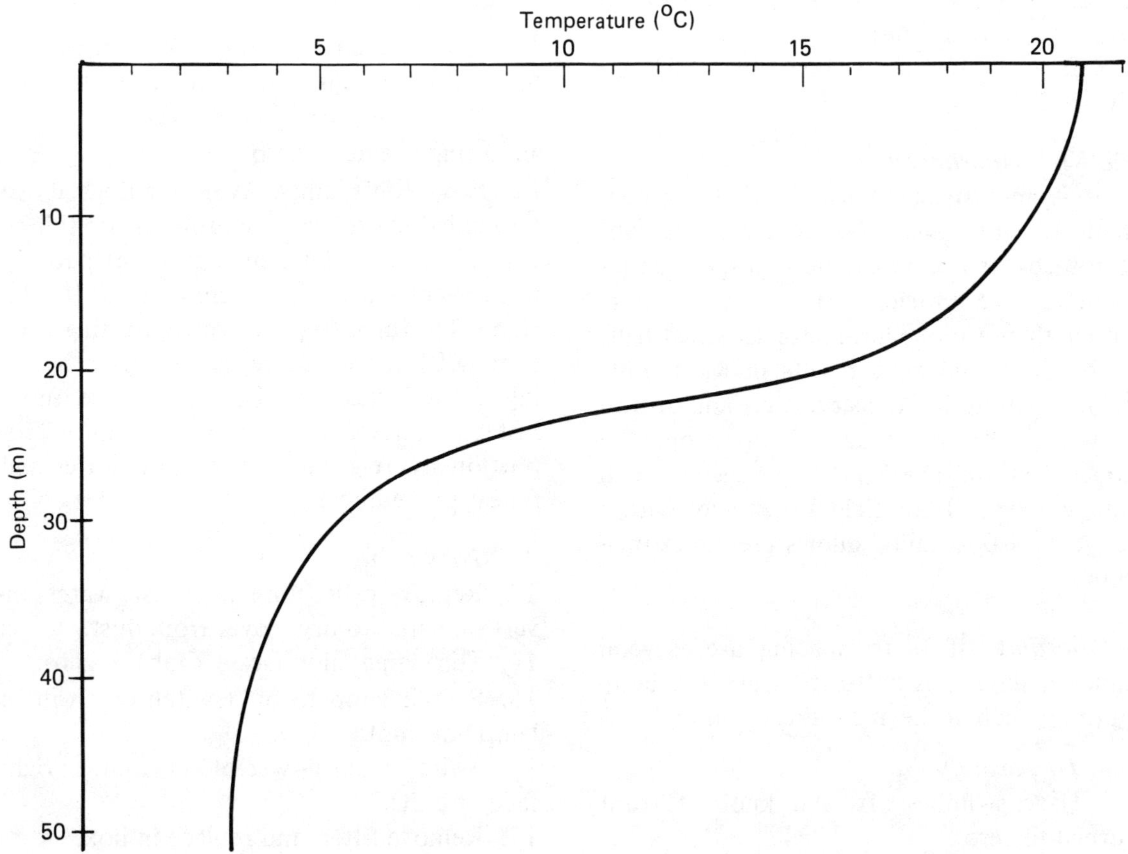

Figure 3. Typical gradient curve, in this case displaying the gradient of temperature with depth.

former can be averaged; but pH, as a log function, should not be averaged. Rather, pH can be converted to antilog, averaged, then reexpressed as pH.

A table for converting pH and hydrogen ion activity is given by Strickland and Parsons (1968: 297).

18. Kemmerer water sampler

The Kemmerer water sampler is an ideal unit for taking dissolved oxygen samples or water samples in fairly deep water. Newer, nonmetallic units, not toxic to organisms, are available, such as the new models of the Kemmerer sampler, and the Van Dorn sampler.

To open Kemmerer sampler, release end stoppers and extend to maximum; then set trigger, slip line through messenger and retain it as you lower to desired depth, release messenger, hoist sampler, insert drain hose into container, and release drain plug. For dissolved gases (e.g., O_2), allow bottle to overflow several times.

Reference Welch (1948: 199, 200, and Figure 59).

19. Klett colorimeter

This is an instrument for determining concentration of a solute by measuring the light it absorbs. It is comparable to a spectrophotometer (see project 14), but uses filters rather than a monochromator to select light to be used, and gives results in Klett units rather than optical density. Klett and optical density units are equally proportional to concentration. The Klett is a rugged, small unit convenient for field work; and, with a range of 1,000 units, allows precise estimation.

Procedure If Klett is being used several times a day, it is better to leave the lamp burning than to keep turning it on and off.

To warm up:

1. Have switches off, and knob at front turned to zero.
2. Install correct filter for the procedure.
3. With knob on top of unit (pointer-setting knob), bring needle to zero.
4. Flip up the switch on face of right side of instrument to turn on electricity in unit.
5. Check to see that filter knob (left side, toward back) is pulled out completely if rectangular cell is to be used; or pushed in if cuvets (round) are to be used.
6. Fill "blank" cell 3/4 full with dist. water, wipe dry, and clean with tissue; install in cuvet well (top right, near back); orient cell lengthwise for a 4-cm light path, and crosswise for a 2-cm path.
7. Flip on switch on front of light housing toward back to turn on lamp.
8. With knob (zero adjustment knob) just left of cuvet well, bring needle to zero. Check until constant.

To make reading:

9. Allow Klett to run a few minutes, and readjust needle to zero with top left rear knob.
10. Into test cuvet, pour unknown sample to 3/4 full, and insert in place of blank.
11. Turn main knob (scale knob) in front and bring needle to zero.
12. Read Klett units. Avoid readings above 600 units. (*Notes:* a) if solution is too thin to get effective reading, increase light path by using 4-cm rather than 2-cm path. b) If solution is too thick to get effective reading [i.e., over 800], either decrease light path by using 2-cm instead of 4-cm path, use tubes instead of rectangular cuvet, or dilute proportionally [e.g., 1:1] with dist. water and repeat procedure.)

To close up:

13. Remove cells, rinse with dist. water, invert on paper to dry, cover from dust.
14. Turn large knob (scale knob) to zero.
15. Switch lamp to off (switch on front of lamp housing).
16. Switch main power off (switch on right face of unit).
17. Remove filter, and replace in box.
18. Allow unit to cool, then recover.

Calculations Made exactly as in the case of spectrophotometer. The usual calculation is:

$$C_u = \frac{R_u \times C_s}{R_s}$$

where C_u = concentration of unknown (in unit being used); C_s = concentration of standard; R_s = reading of standard (against dist. water) in Klett units; and R_u = reading of unknown in Klett units.

Where there are complications of using a different light path length (than specified in the procedure) or of having to dilute in order to get a feasible reading, depth and dilution factors are included as follows:

$$C_u = \frac{R_u}{R_s} \times C_s \times \frac{P_o}{P_a} \times \frac{V_a}{V_o}$$

where C_u, R_u, R_s, and C_s are as above; and P_o/P_a = the light path correction, where P_a = the light path length used in the actual analysis and P_o = the light path length specified in the procedure; and V_a/V_o = the dilution (volume) correction, in which V_a = the volume used in the actual analysis and V_o = the volume specified in the procedure.

Notes *Klett units* differ considerably from those found on spectrophotometers, and 1,000 Klett units cover the same logarithmic set as do 100 per cent transmittance or the 2.0 optical density range of spectrophotometers. However, as set up in the formulas, the same results are obtained either by Klett or optical density units since the ratio (R_u/R_s) will be the same in either case.

To convert Klett units to transmittance (per cent T) or extinction (optical density), see conversion table in the back of the instruction manual for the Klett. Optical density = Klett units/500.

20. Light-depth gradient curves

See "Gradient curve," procedure 15.

21. Light meter

See also "Submarine photometer," project 14.

For underwater work, a photographic light meter is enclosed in a plastic housing. It should be so constructed as to permit low and high light readings.

While in use, keep meter in dark sack to protect it against light. Dive to desired depth, peel off sack and select effective sensitivity; and, with back to sun, take and record maximum reading on palm of hand at distance of one foot. Cover unit with sack. Convert this reading to ft-c by using a previously established calibration curve.

Calibration curve: cooperating with an operator on a boat, diver accompanies sea cell of submarine photometer, taking readings at each depth interval (e.g., 1 m) at which boatside operator is taking photometer readings. Construct curve of ft-c on abscissa and light meter units on ordinate.

22. Light quality

To obtain a measure of quality of light of the water in a basin, use three special transmission filters, approximately 400 mμ, 500 mμ, and 600 mμ, and mount each, in turn, in the ring just above the photocell of the sea unit of a submarine photometer. Obtain the per cent transmission at the surface and at 1-m depth. Record as a color code in a 1–10 basis, rounding off to the nearest 10%. For example, Saila and Horton recorded 014 for Barber Pond, R.I., meaning 0% in 400 mμ, 10% in 500 mμ, and 40% in 600 mμ range.

Range 014–498 of T at 400, 500, and 600 mμ.

References Ruttner (1963: 19); Saila and Horton (1957: 41).

23. Mechanical analysis of soil

See "Sediment" under "Notes" in project 4.

24. Net coefficient

The ratio of actual plankton obtained to that which would have been caught by a net if all the water through which the net passed had actually been filtered through the net is the net coefficient. It must be determined for each net and speed.

Select a uniformly mixed water course in which to standardize net. Using Kemmerer sampler (or closing net), take samples at 1-m intervals across the course at a uniform depth. Fix samples immediately with formalin. Take plankton tow at proposed speed over same course at same depth. Measure volume of sample and then fix sample. In the laboratory, carefully count a major species, or set of species, in a 1-ml sample (in Sedgwick-Rafter chamber) for each Kemmerer sampler, and calculate the actual population expected along the entire course. Similarly, count net sample and, after correcting for concentration of water by the net (distance towed, area of mouth), calculate expected true number of individuals of major species which occur.

$$\frac{P_t}{P_n} = K_n$$

where P_n = number of the plankter caught by net, P_t = total number of the plankter actually in path of net, and K_n = net coefficient.

To correct a net tow count for net efficiency, multiply the count by net coefficient (observed count × K_n = true count, or $P_t = K_n \times P_n$).

Reference Welch (1948: 278).

25. Nitrates

Time required: ca. 90 min first day and 40 min second day

Glassware To conserve time and glassware, and to facilitate general use of a detailed analysis, special glassware items needed in the procedure are set aside for each step. They are coded below by geometric symbols and numbered serially by use. When analysis is done, they need only to be carefully rinsed with tap, then dist., water and returned to their special clamp or peg to air dry.

Cylinders, graduated: three 50-ml ① ② ③

Pipets, graduated: two 10-ml [2] [8]

Pipets, volumetric: four 1-ml [5] [7] [10] [11]; two 2-ml [6] [9]; one 5-ml [4]; two 25-ml [1] [3]

Flasks, Erlenmeyer: several 125-ml for samples ⟨5⟩; six 125-ml for standard and for standard curve ⟨6⟩; one 126-ml for blank ⟨7⟩

Flasks, volumetric: two 50-ml ⟨1⟩⟨3⟩; three 100-ml ⟨2⟩⟨4⟩⟨8⟩; one 250-ml; one 1,000-ml ⟨9⟩

Chemicals Acetone, copper sulfate (5-hydrated), hydrazine sulfate, hydrochloric acid, one-naphthylamine hydrochloride (discard when not white), phenol (keep dry), potassium nitrate, sodium acetate (hydrated), sodium hydroxide, sulfanilic acid, sulfuric acid (for rinsing).

Reagents (store in polyethylene containers):

1. *1.0 N NaOH:* in 100-ml vol. flask with some dist. water, dissolve 4.01 g of NaOH; dil. to 100 ml with dist. water.

2. *Phenol stock solution*[1] (discard when brown): in 250-ml vol. flask with ca. 200 ml of dist. water, dissolve 9.40 g of phenol; dil. to 250 ml with dist. water.

*3. *Phenol sodium phenate buffer*[2] (make just before use and avoid contact with air): into 50-ml vol. flask ⟨1⟩ with 25-ml vol. pipet [1] *add 25 ml of phenol solution* (sol. 2) and with 10-ml grad. pipet [2] *add 8 ml of 1.0 N NaOH* (sol. 1); dil. to 50 ml with dist. water.

4. *Copper sulfate catalyst solution* (stable): in 1,000-ml vol. flask with some dist. water, dissolve 0.393 g of copper sulfate; dil. to 1,000 ml with dist. water.

5. *Hydrazine sulfate:* preweigh out 0.48-g amounts and store in vials for use in sol. 6.

*6. *Hydrazine sulfate stock solution*[2] (make fresh): in 100-ml vol. flask ⟨2⟩ with ca. 80 ml of dist. water, dissolve 0.48 g of hydrazine sulfate; dil. to 100 ml with dist. water. Filter through glass fiber (or sintered) filter.

*7. *Hydrazine-copper reducing agent*[2]

[1] Fairly stable. Remake, if necessary.

[2] Make fresh for each run.

(make fresh, daily): into 50-ml vol. flask ⟨3⟩ transfer with 25-ml vol. pipet [3] 25 ml of stock hydrazine sulfate solution (sol. 6), and with 5-ml vol. pipet [4] add 5 ml of copper sulfate catalyst (sol. 4); *dil. to 50 ml* with dist. water.

8. *Sulfanilic acid solution* (stable): into 100-ml vol. flask with ca. 80 ml of dist. water, dissolve 0.30 g of sulfanilic acid; with 25-ml graduate add 12.9 ml of concd. hydrochloric acid; dil. to 100 ml with dist. water.

9. *1-naphthylamine solution*[1] (remake each 2–4 weeks): in 100-ml vol. flask ⟨8⟩ with ca. 80 ml of dist. water, dissolve 0.60 g of 1-naphthylamine hydrochloride (discard if not white); dil. to 100 ml with dist. water and 1 ml of concd. HCl.

10. *2 M sodium acetate solution* (stable): into 100-ml vol. flask with ca. 80 ml of dist. water, dissolve 27.2 g of hydrated sodium acetate; dil. to 100 ml with dist. water.

11. *Potassium nitrate standard stock solution* (stable): into 1,000-ml vol. flask ⟨9⟩ with some dist. water, dissolve 0.0722 g of potassium nitrate; dil. to 1,000 ml with dist. water.

12. *Acetone.*

Procedure

Advanced preparations:

1. Have reaction flasks rinsed and air dried (or prepared specially, cf. "Note" in "Phosphates," procedure 30).

2. *Collect water samples* in 250-ml polyethylene narrow-mouthed screw-capped bottles, and analyze promptly; hold cold for several hours or freeze at −20°C for weeks. Filter through Whatman filter paper before analysis.

3. *Warm samples* and standard solutions to room temperature (18–25°C).

4. With marine samples, *determine salinity* (either by titration or by salinometer, see project 10).

5. *Make up fresh* phenol sodium phenate *buffer* (sol. 3) (mix 25 ml of phenol solution and 8 ml of 1 N NaOH; dil. to 50 ml).

6. *Make up fresh hydrazine sulfate solution* (sol. 6): mix 0.48 g of hydrazine sulfate in dist. water; dil. to 100 ml.

7. *Make up fresh hydrazine-copper reducing solution* (sol. 7): mix 25 ml of fresh hydrazine sulfate solution with [5] ml of copper sulfate catalyst; dil. to 50 ml.

8. Check phenol solution (sol. 2) and naphthylamine solution (sol. 9).

9. *Prepare standard solution* (= 7.14 μg-at/liter) as follows: into 100-ml vol. flask ⟨4⟩ transfer with 1-ml vol. pipet [5] 1 ml of stock potassium nitrate standard solution (sol. 11), mix, and dil. to 100 ml with dist. water. If other dilutions are desired, see Table 2.

Analysis:

10. *Warm up Klett* with K54 green filter (or spectrophotometer at 543 mμ).

11. *Set out* sufficient *125-ml flasks for* water *samples* ⟨5⟩, 1(−6) for *standard* ⟨6⟩, and 1 for *blank* ⟨7⟩.

12. *Make up 41 ml of solution* in each flask as follows:

Table 2. Dilutions needed for preparation of standard curve for nitrate analysis

Flask	Concentration: μg-at NO_3-N/liter	Concentration: ppm NO_3	Dilutions (use 41 ml of each)
1	0.71	0.044	10 ml of sol. 4/100 ml
2	1.43	0.089	10 ml of sol. 5/100 ml
3	3.57	0.222	0.5 ml stock nitrate sol./100 ml
4	7.14	0.442	1.0 ml stock nitrate sol./100 ml
5	14.28	0.890	2.0 ml stock nitrate sol./100 ml
6	21.43	1.330	3.0 ml stock nitrate sol./100 ml
7	35.70	2.210	5.0 ml stock nitrate sol./100 ml

a. With 50-ml graduate ① measure out *41 ml of each water sample* and place in flask ◇5◇.
b. With 50-ml graduate ② measure out *41 ml of standard* solution (step 9, above) into standard flask ◇6◇.
c. With 50-ml graduate ③ measure out *41 ml of dist. water* into the blank flask ◇7◇.

13. *Read turbidity* of each sample against dist. water (in Klett with 4-cm path), and *return fluid to flask.*

14. With 2-ml vol. pipet [6] *add 2 ml of phenol sodium phenate buffer* (sol. ③ and step 5) into each flask.

15. *Swirl.* (If precipitate forms, remake buffer and repeat analysis.)

16. With 1-ml vol. pipet [7] *add 1 ml of hydrazine-copper reducing agent* (sol. 7 and step 7) to each flask.

17. *Mix thoroughly,* cover with aluminum foil cap, and *set aside in dark* at constant temperature *for 24 hrs.* (May be put in refrigerator, if necessary.)

Continue analysis the next day:

18. Warm up Klett with K54 green filter (or spectrophotometer at 543 mμ).

19. With 10-ml grad. pipet [8] fitted with bulb, *add 2 ml of acetone* (sol. 12) to each flask.

20. Shake, and let *stand* at least *2 min.*

21. With 2-ml vol. pipet [9] *add 2 ml of sulfanilic acid solution* (sol. 8) to each flask.

22. Swirl, and let *stand* at least *5 min.*

(The following steps (*) require exact timing):

*23. At intervals of 2 min, in batches of four, using 1-ml vol. pipet [10] *add 1 ml of naphthylamine* reagent (sol. 9).

*24. *Swirl,* and immediately *add* with 1-ml vol. pipet [11] *1 ml of 2 M sodium acetate* solution (sol. 10). Swirl.

*25. At a constant time of 15 min after adding the acetate, *read against dist. water blank.* (If repeated zero readings are found, remake naphthylamine, sulfanilic acid, and phenate stock solutions [sol. 9, 8, 3].)

Closing steps:

26. Turn off Klett, and remove and rinse cuvets; drain and air dry.

27. Wash glassware with 10–20 rinses of tap and dist. water, then drain to air dry.

28. Rinse pipets with tap and dist. water, then drain to air dry.

Calculations As indicated in the formula, divide each corrected (for turbidity, step 13)

Table 3. Sample data, calculation, and results for nitrate analysis involving salinity correction (f_s = 0.94) for brackish water (S = 5 ^{o}/oo)

Flask	Test	Readings (Klett units): Turbidity (E_t)	Readings (Klett units): Final (E)	Results: μg-at NO_3-N/liter	Results: ppm NO_3
1	Standard 7.14 μg-at NO_3-N/liter	–	114.5	–	–
2	Sample 1	27.7	124.5	5.71	0.35
3	Sample 2	23.8	168.5	12.05	0.74
4	Sample 3	41.6	210	15.18	0.94
5	Sample 4	28.4	246	21.69	1.35
6	Blank	–	57.1	–	–

Sample calculation for sample 1:

$$C_u = \frac{124.5 - 27.7}{0.94} - 57.1 \times \frac{7.14}{114.5 - 57.1} = 5.706\ \mu\text{g-at } NO_3\text{-N/liter}$$

C_u = ppm NO_3 = 0.062 × 5.706 μg-at NO_3-N/liter = 0.354 mg NO_3/liter

sample reading (extinction) value by a salt factor if marine samples are being analyzed and subtract the reagent error of blank (E_b).

$$C_u = \left(\frac{E_u - E_t}{F_s} - E_b\right) \times \frac{C_s}{E_s - E_b}$$

where C_u = concentration of sample (unknown) in μg-at NO_3-N/liter; C_s = concentration of standard; F_s = salinity correction (ignore for fresh water, where F_s = 1); E_u = extinction of unknown; E_b = extinction of blank; E_s = extinction of standard; and E_t = extinction of turbidity check (step 13). See Table 3.

Note For dark-colored solutions requiring dilution or a shorter light path, make corrections as indicated in "Spectrophotometry," project 14, involving factors V_a/V_o and P_o/P_a, where a = volume or path length actually used and o = original volume or path length required.

Conversions

μg NO_3-N/liter = 14 × (μg-at NO_3-N/liter)
μg NO_3/liter = 62 × (μg-at NO_3-N/liter)
ppm NO_3 = mg NO_3/liter = 0.062 × (μg-at NO_3-N/liter)
meq NO_3/liter = 0.016 × (mg NO_3/liter)

Ranges Inland waters: 0–10(–45) mg NO_3/liter (APHA, 1965: 195); marine: 0.1–43 μg-at NO_3-N/liter (Sverdrup, Johnson, and Fleming, 1942: 181) or 0.006–2.67 ppm NO_3.

Standard Curve Since reagents vary with time, a calibration curve should be made about once a month. Using special 250-ml flasks saved for standards, deliver the indicated volumes per Table 2. Plot on graph paper with extinction units on abscissa and concentration on ordinate (Figure 4).

Salinity Correction The intensity of color varies with salinity and can be obtained from the following curve (Figure 5).

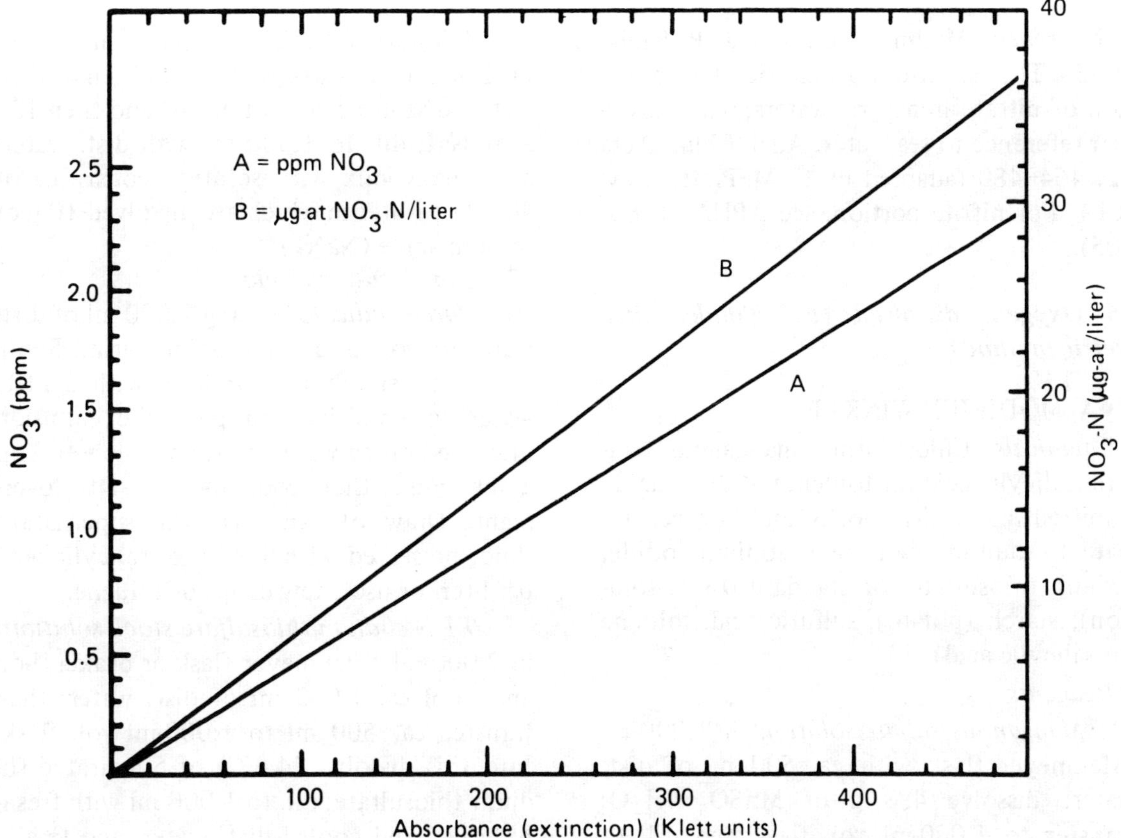

Figure 4. Sample calibration curve for nitrate analysis. (Data from M. E. Butcher, August 11, 1970.)

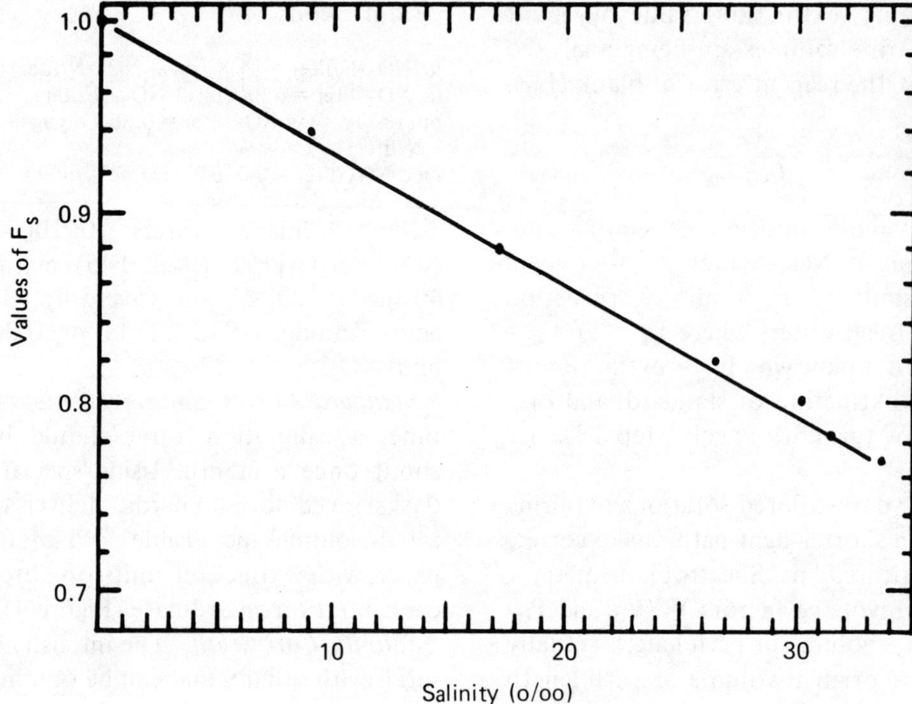

Figure 5. A sample salinity correction curve for nitrate analysis. (Data from D. M. Pratt, pers. comm.)

Reference Mullin, J. B., and J. P. Riley. 1955. The spectrophotometric determination of nitrate in natural waters, with particular reference to sea water. Anal. Chim. Acta 12: 464–480 (adapted by D. M. Pratt, Univ. R.I.). For nitrite portion, see APHA (1965: 205).

26. Oxygen, dissolved (by Winkler titrimetric method)

●A. MODIFIED WINKLER

Chemicals Chloroform, manganous sulfate, salicylic acid (or toluene), sodium azide (omitted in earlier works and for certain water), sodium hydroxide, sodium iodide, sodium thiosulfate (or standard 0.1 N solution), starch (potato), sulfuric acid, toluene (or salicylic acid).

Reagents

1. *Manganous sulfate solution:* in 1,000-ml Erlenmeyer flask with ca. 500 ml of dist. water, dissolve 480 g of $MnSO_4 \cdot 4H_2O$; transfer to 1,000-ml vol. flask and dil. to 1,000 ml with dist. water.

2. *Alkali-iodide-azide reagent:* in 1,000-ml Erlenmeyer flask with ca. 500 ml of dist. water, dissolve 500 g of NaOH and then 135 g of NaI; dil. to 1,000 ml with dist. water; and finally mix with solution consisting of 40 ml of water in which are dissolved 10 g of sodium azide (NaN_3).

3. *Concd. sulfuric acid.*

4. *Starch indicator:* bring 1,000 ml of dist. water to boil, and while boiling grind 5–6 g of potato starch in a mortar with a little water to emulsify and pour the emulsion into the boiling water. Stir, and allow to boil a few min.; then cool and let settle overnight. Draw off and use the supernatant fluid, preserved with 1.25 g of salicylic acid per liter, or use a few drops of toluene.

5. *0.1 N sodium thiosulfate stock solution:* in 2,000-ml Erlenmeyer flask or beaker, boil and cool ca. 1,000 ml of dist. water; then transfer ca. 500 ml to 1,000-ml vol. flask. Into this dissolve 24.82 g of 5-hydrated sodium thiosulfate; dil. to 1,000 ml with freshly boiled and cooled dist. water, and finally add 5 ml of chloroform as preservative.

6. *Standard 0.025 N sodium thiosulfate:* either dil. commercial standard 0.1 solution, or make your own by dil. 250.0 ml stock[3] 0.1 N solution to 1,000 ml with freshly boiled and cooled dist. water, and standardize and adjust it as indicated under "Standardizing."

Procedure Keep permanent 10-ml grad. (or automatic 1-ml) pipets in bottles in the field kit. Do NOT suck up alkali or H_2SO_4.

In the field:

1. Collect samples in Kemmerer water bottle and carefully drain, with tip of delivery tube below the water surface, into 250-ml gs bottle so as to avoid bubbles; then allow bottle to overflow several times.
2. Immediately add 1 ml of manganous sulfate solution (sol. 1) just beneath surface of water.
3. Add 1 ml of alkali-iodine-azide reagent (sol. 2) just beneath surface.
4. Insert stopper down side wall so as to avoid trapping bubbles.
5. Invert bottle several times to mix, then let settle half way, or stand 5 min, whichever is less.
6. Invert again to mix, and let settle half way, or stand 5 min.
7. Add 1 ml of concd. sulfuric acid (sol. 3), stopper, and invert to mix.
8. Allow to stand at least 5 min before continuing, but titrate within 6 hrs.

In the laboratory:

9. With 100-ml vol. pipet, transfer 100 ml of fixed sample into evaporating dish.
10. Record volume of 0.025 N sodium thiosulfate (sol. 6) in buret, and titrate, with stirring, to pale straw color.
11. Add 1–2 ml of freshly prepared starch indicator (sol. 4), giving strong blue color.
12. Continue titrating until blue color just disappears.
13. Record volume titrated.

[3] Use slight excess to facilitate adjusting.

Calculation

$$O = 2 \times V$$

or, when conditions are adverse:

$$O = \frac{(P - \mu) \times 0.678}{35 + t}$$

where O = dissolved oxygen (mg/liter); V = volume (ml) of sodium thiosulfate used in titration; P = barometric pressure (mm Hg); μ = saturation vapor pressure (mm Hg) at the ambient temperature; t = temperature (°C). (Correction factors for P, V, and t are given by Mackereth, 1963: 16.)

Conversions

$$\text{ml diss. } O_2/\text{liter} = (\text{mg diss. } O_2/\text{liter}) \times 0.698$$

$$\text{mg-at diss. } O_2/\text{liter} = (\text{mg diss. } O_2/\text{liter}) \times \frac{1}{32}$$

Ranges Fresh water: 0–14.6 ppm (APHA, 1965: 406) or 0–0.45 mg-at O_2/liter; marine: 0–7 ml/liter or 0–10 ppm (Sverdrup, Johnson, and Fleming, 1942: 209), 0–0.33 mg-at O_2/liter.

References APHA (1965: 406); Welch (1948: 207).

Notes For certain waters with ferrous iron, interference occurs and lowered readings are obtained. The Rideal-Stewart modification, if higher readings are obtained with it, should be used (see "Rideal-Stewart," below).

•B. RIDEAL-STEWART MODIFICATION OF THE WINKLER

To be used where ferrous iron interferes and higher results are obtained with the modification.

Chemicals Potassium oxalate (4-hydrated), potassium permanganate.

Reagents Those indicated for the Winkler method, above, plus the following.

1. *Potassium permanganate solution* (fairly

stable): in 1,000-ml vol. flask with ca. 500 ml of dist. water, dissolve 6.3 g of $KMnO_4$, and dil. to 1,000 ml with dist. water.

2. *Potassium oxalate solution* (remake frequently): into 100 ml of dist. water dissolve 2 g of 4-hydrated oxalic acid.

Procedure Collect water sample as for Winkler, then proceed as follows:

1. Cautiously add 0.70 ml concd. sulfuric acid just beneath surface (Winkler, sol. 3).
2. Add 1 ml of potassium permanganate solution (sol. 1, above).
3. Stopper and mix.
4. Let stand 5 min, and if color disappears sooner add a little more permanganate solution and finish the 5-min wait; but, if color persists, continue on.
5. Add 0.5–1.0 ml of potassium oxalate solute (sol. 2, above).
6. Mix well and keep dark until clear (2–10 min).
7. Add 2 ml of manganous sulfate solution (Winkler, sol. 1).
8. Immediately add 3 ml alkali-iodide-azide reagent (Winkler, sol. 2).
9. Stopper and mix, and allow to settle half way.
10. Mix thoroughly for 20 sec, and allow to settle half way.
11. Add 2 ml concd. sulfuric acid, and mix (Winkler, sol. 3).
12. In laboratory, proceed with titration as described for "Winkler," above.

References Modified from APHA (1965: 410); Welch (1948: 209).

•C. OXYGEN, PER CENT (AIR) SATURATION

Using Rawson's nomogram (Welch, 1948: 366, or Reid, 1961: 147), read per cent saturation at intersection of straight edge connecting water temperature and dissolved oxygen concentration of the sample. For saline waters, use nomogram, Figure 6, or table by APHA (1965: 409) to determine ppm at saturation, and calculate per cent from the formula below:

$$\% \text{ saturation} = 100 \times \frac{O_s}{O_c}$$

where O_s = ppm O_2 of sample, O_c = calibration value, i.e., the concn. of dissolved oxygen in ppm at saturation.

•D. OXYGEN, DISSOLVED, STANDARDIZING THE THIOSULFATE

The 0.025 N standard thiosulfate is not stable, and will need to be checked occasionally.

Chemicals Potassium biniodate, potassium iodide, sulfuric acid.

Reagents

1. *0.100 N potassium biniodate solution:* in 1,000-ml vol. flask with ca. 500 ml of dist. water, dissolve 3.249 g of the biniodate, and dil. to 1,000 ml.
2. *0.025 N potassium biniodate solution:* dil. 250 ml of stock to 1,000 ml with dist. water.
3. *Concd. sulfuric acid.*

Procedure

1. In 200-ml volumetric flask, place 100–150 ml of dist. water.
2. Dissolve in ca. 2 g of potassium iodide.
3. In a separate container (e.g., 50-ml graduate) measure out 9 ml of dist. water, and cautiously mix in 1 ml of concd. sulfuric acid. Add this solution to the flask (steps 2 and 2).
4. Add exactly 20.00 ml of 0.025 N potassium biniodate solution (sol. 2).
5. Mix and dilute to 200 ml with dist. water.
6. Transfer to a clean 500-ml Erlenmeyer flask.
7. Put the ca. 0.025 N sodium thiosulfate being standardized into buret, record volume, and titrate directly into the flask; titrate to pale straw.
8. Add ca. 1 ml of starch indicator, making strong blue color.
9. Titrate to end point (when blue color just disappears), and record volume.

Calculation Because exactly 20.00 ml of 0.025 N sodium thiosulfate should be re-

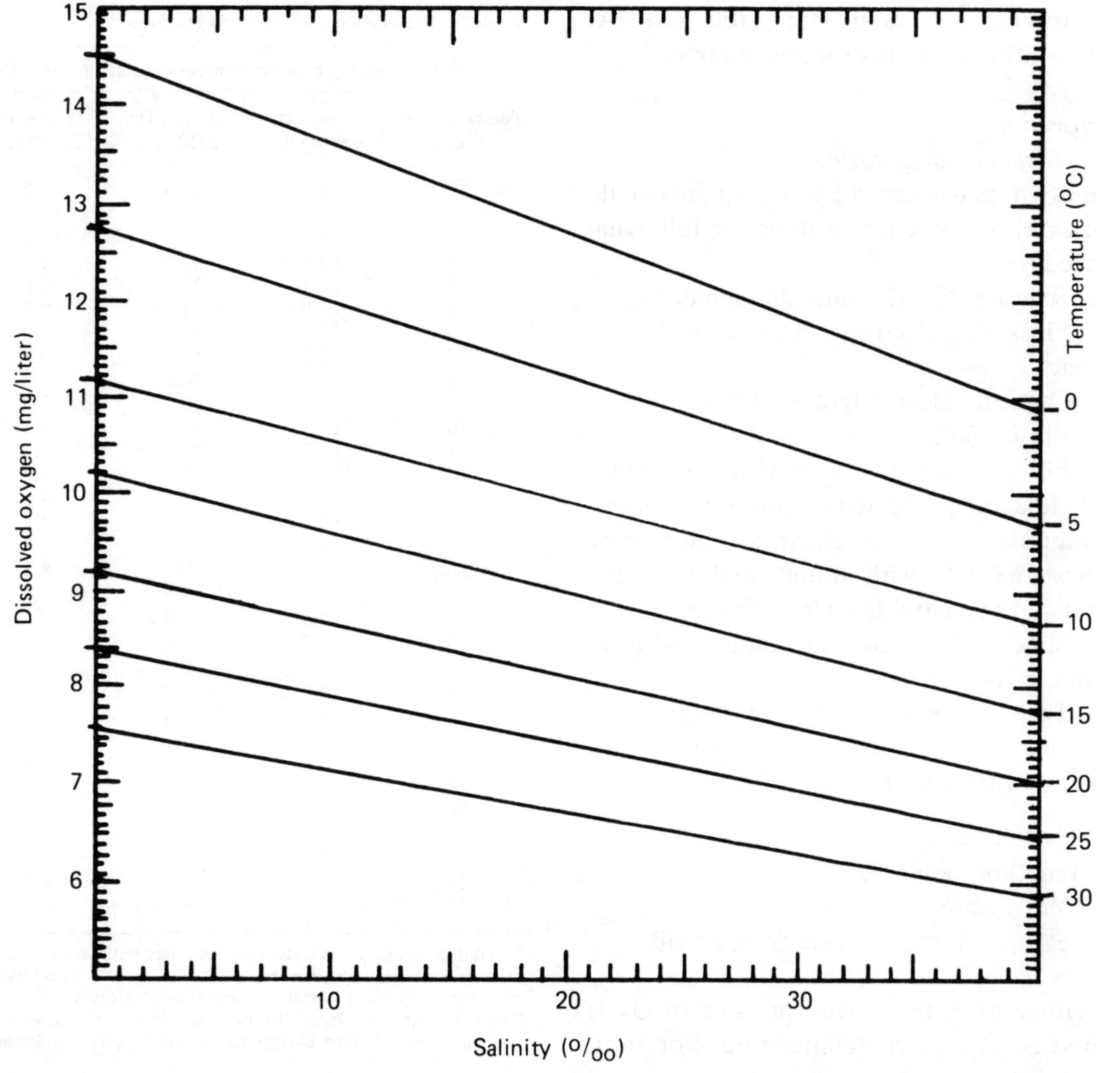

Figure 6. Dissolved oxygen at 100% saturation as related to salinity and temperature. *Directions:* From temperature (right) follow slope up to left to point directly above the salinity (bottom), then strike directly left and read dissolved oxygen concentration (left).

quired for 20 ml of 0.025 N potassium biniodate, then:

$$N = \frac{20 \times 0.025}{V} \quad \text{or} \quad N = \frac{0.5}{V}$$

where N = normality of the sodium thiosulfate, and V = volume of 0.025 N thiosulfate used in the titration. To adjust the thiosulfate solution:

$$V = \frac{0.025v}{N}$$

where V = volume of the thiosulfate needed; v = volume to which it is to be diluted, and N = normality on hand (must be greater than 0.025 N to work).

Reference APHA (1965: 407).

27. Oxygen, dissolved (by electrometric or polarographic method)

Necessary materials include oxygen meter (e.g., YSI[4] or Beckman oxygen analyzer), oxygen probe, Teflon membrane, recharging

[4] Yellow Springs Instrument Co. (Yellow Springs, Ohio).

electrolyte, and calibration table (APHA, 1965: 409) or YSI Instruction Booklet.[4]

Procedure

Advanced preparations:

If needed, as evidenced by inadequate needle response, recharge probe using the following procedure:

1. Remove "O" ring and old membrane.
2. Flush out electrode chamber with dist. water.
3. Carefully clean bright electrode.[5]
4. Flush again.
5. Fill, or cover electrode with electrolyte.
6. Hold up probe with tip upward, orient membrane on top of electrode, then draw down one side with thumb and then the other so as to avoid trapping bubbles.
7. Slide "O" ring over membrane and position it in its groove.
8. Trim off excess membrane. Keep moist, as in jar of dist. water, held in by two sides of a well fitting split cork.

Calibration:

Two methods are used:

1. Moist air
2. Saturated water (either fresh or salt)

In either case, the partial pressure of O_2 is the same at a given temperature. For saturated water, use clean water, shake vigorously, then allow bubbles to settle out.

1. Warm up instrument for 3–5 min.
2. Bring calibration water (or air) to same temperature as that to be tested.
3. Measure its temperature.
4. From Table 4 (for salt water, use special table, APHA, 1965: 409), determine the saturation concentration in ppm O_2 for that temperature.
5. Insert probe in water, move until needle stops creeping.
6. Set pointer to the saturated ppm O_2 value.

Table 4. Calibration table for oxygen meters[a]

	Oxygen saturation concentration (ppm O_2)		
Temperature (°C)	760 mm Hg sea level	700 mm Hg 2,000 ft	625 mm Hg 5,000 ft
0	14.6	13.4	12.0
1	14.2	13.1	11.7
2	13.8	12.7	11.4
3	13.4	12.3	11.1
4	13.1	12.1	10.8
5	12.8	11.8	10.5
6	12.5	11.5	10.2
7	12.2	11.2	9.9
8	11.9	10.9	9.7
9	11.6	10.7	9.5
10	11.3	10.4	9.3
11	11.0	10.1	9.1
12	10.8	9.9	8.9
13	10.5	9.7	8.6
14	10.3	9.5	8.5
15	10.1	9.3	8.3
16	9.9	9.1	8.1
17	9.7	8.9	7.9
18	9.5	8.8	7.8
19	9.3	8.6	7.6
20	9.1	8.4	7.5
21	8.9	8.2	7.3
22	8.8	8.1	7.2
23	8.6	7.9	7.0
24	8.4	7.7	6.9
25	8.3	7.6	6.8
26	8.1	7.4	6.6
27	8.0	7.3	6.5
28	7.8	7.2	6.4
29	7.7	7.1	6.3
30	7.5	6.9	6.1

[a]Solubility of oxygen in water (i.e., saturated with air) as related to temperature and air pressure (in equilibrium with air saturated with water vapor at the average corresponding altitudes), See also Figure 6. (Adapted from "Instructions for the YSI Model 51 Oxygen Meter," Yellow Springs Instrument Co., Yellow Springs, Ohio.)

Note For saturation by moist air, use same procedure except for omitting use of water (step 2).

Measuring:

7. Without altering calibrated unit, insert probe into water to be tested.
8. Move probe until needle stops creeping.
9. Read the dissolved oxygen in ppm.

28. Periphyton (Aufwuchs) analysis

The method of handling periphyton varies with whether the growth is on a plant host

[5] Though not totally recommended, a gentle rub with Ajax cleans Beckman electrode effectively.

which can be collected, on substrate which must be scraped, or on slides which can be processed in the laboratory.

Sampling

1. *On plant parts:* Use W-Z diver's sampler, submerge sampler, unstopper ends, slide tube over host and periphyton, stopper the ends, and return entire unit to laboratory. Keep sample cool, and analyze promptly.

2. *On substrate:* Work simultaneously with scraper and suction unit (e.g., plastic baster), scraping off and sucking up the material. Accumulate suckings in a jar, and handle as plankton.

3. *On slides:* Submerge Petri dish of suitable size; remove slide from support and place in Petri dish, cover, and return to laboratory for study. Keep sample cool, and analyze promptly.

Analyses

1. *Slides:* Dry the bottom and edges of slide, place in mechanical stage of microscope, examine wet under 100X. Add drops of water if drying occurs. Make strip analysis lengthwise, identifying (or recording code name for) each form. When new forms are no longer being met, make differential count along the lengthwise strip (strip count) if there are relatively few cells, or count one or more fields (field count) if cells are abundant (see "Phytoplankton analysis," in procedure 33). For vouchers, scrape off, thoroughly mix, preserve one half, and process other half for diatoms and/or as done for phytoplankton (see "Laboratory procedures" under "Notes," project 5). For diatoms, use ethanol-preserved (70% ethanol in water) material; allow diatoms to settle in centrifuge tube (or spin down if forms are not fragile types with spines, etc.), suck off supernatant fluid (save for checking for plankters); add concd. sulfuric acid of same volume as diatom material remaining; warm gently for 20 min (or allow to stand overnight), and add a few crystals of potassium dichromate; mix and allow to stand (or add a few more crystals) until it turns brown. Then suck off (using 10-ml grad. pipet with propipet bulb) the supernatant fluid, disperse the plug with a stiff jet of dist. water from a plastic wash bottle, and fill most of tube. Allow to settle overnight (or centrifuge down, if satisfactory), disperse and rinse as above, three more times until water is no longer acid; then mount with Hyrax[6](or clarite).

To mount in Hyrax, heat up hot plate; put drop of diatom material on clean coverslip, and stir with clean toothpick; with forceps transfer coverslip onto hot hot plate; allow to dry (if there is a question of the diatoms being adequately cleaned, heat for 20 min); center suitably sized drop of Hyrax on clean slide, invert hot coverslip onto the Hyrax, put slide on warm hot plate, bring up heat, and let Hyrax boil until bubbles slow down. Remove slide onto nonscorching surface (e.g., asbestos pad), and with toothpick press down coverslip working out the bubbles. The slide will harden promptly, and can be labeled and stored.

2. *Scrapings:* Quantitatively transfer scrapings to 50-ml Erlenmeyer flask and stir with magnetic stirrer (or shake vigorously to separate cells). Put drop of dispersed material on slide and study (project 4) by calibrated drop, or with Stempel pipet fill Sedgwick-Rafter counting chamber and proceed, in both cases, as for phytoplankton analysis (in procedure 33).

For biomass data, the scrapings can be caught on tared Millipore filter, dried, and reweighed.

3. *Plant periphyton:* Scrape off periphyton (and save host to recheck for possible remaining algae), and treat as scrapings (above) (Ref.: Hargraves and Wood, 1967: 57).

Vouchers: To make permanent record of findings, make slides as described, make drawings with aid of camera lucida (see

[6] Available from Custom Research and Development, Inc., Mt. Vernon Rd., Rt. 1, Box 1586, Auburn, Cal. 95603.

"Laboratory procedures" under "Notes," project 5), or take photomicrographs (see "Photomicrography," procedure 31).

29. pH

Two convenient units for measuring pH are Beckman's N-2 field pH meter and Leeds & Northrup's model 7401 line-driven pH indicator. As with all units, care is required in rinsing buffer from electrode and flushing electrodes between samples with new sample to remove residual ions. Both instruments can be temperature adjusted by a dial to accommodate solutions of different temperatures.

Procedure (with Beckman N-2)

Field use:

1. Stand unit erect, and carefully open both sides downward. Swing out electrodes.
2. Remove rubber cap from lower end of calomel electrode and open aspirator hole.
3. Lower tips of electrodes into dist. water in beaker.

Standardizing:

4. Fill beaker ca. 1 cm deep with buffer (pH 4 for low acid waters, pH 7 for neutral or alkaline waters).
5. Lower electrodes into buffer, and rotate beaker to mix.
6. Measure temperature of buffer with thermometer provided.
7. Set "temperature" knob to that value.
8. Turn main dial to "check" and allow unit to warm up.
9. Turn main range dial knob to red zone and note needle value on red numbers of dial.
10. Bring needle to pH of buffer by turning STD (standardizing) knob.
11. Return main dial to "check" position, and with "check" knob align "check indicator" with needle. (*Note:* The unit is standardized and will hold well; but, in case of drift, readjust needle with STD knob to check arm pointer.)

To measure pH:

12. Rinse down electrode thoroughly with dist. water, several times, wiping down with tissue each time.
13. Place sample in clean beaker and lower electrodes into sample, rotating beaker to mix.
14. Measure temperature of sample.
15. Set temperature dial to that value.
16. Turn main dial to acid, or to base range, if needle does not deflect properly.
17. Record pH on numbers of same color as dial setting.

To close up:

18. Turn main range dial "off."
19. Rinse down electrodes and dry with tissue.
20. Replace equipment in box, and especially replace rubber cap (with drop of dist. water inside) on calomel electrode and slide protector over breatherhole.
21. Swing in electrode unit.
22. Turn dial to "off."
23. Cautiously close and lock unit.

Laboratory use (with Leeds & Northrup 7401):

Operation is basically the same as above in standardizing and measuring, but note that the "function" switch is put on "manual," 5-min warmup is needed, and the zero-measure knob must always be on zero when electrodes are withdrawn from the solution.

Conversion See "Hydrogen ion concentration," procedure 17.

Ranges pH 1.7–12 (Reid, 1961: 159); inland water: mostly 6–9 (l.c., p. 159); marine water: 7.5–8.4; surface water mostly 8.1–8.3 (Sverdrup, Johnson, and Fleming, 1942: 194, 209), but may drop to 7.0 in stagnant basins (l.c., p. 210).

References APHA (1965: 225); Sverdrup, Johnson, and Fleming (1942: 210); also see instructions with unit.

30. Phosphates (inorganic soluble phosphates; orthophosphates)

Time required: ca. 20 min

Glassware To conserve time and glassware, and to facilitate general use of a detailed analysis, special glassware items needed in the procedure are set aside for each step. They are coded below by geometric symbols and numbered serially by use. When analysis is done, they need only to be carefully rinsed first with tap water, then dist. water, and returned to their special clamp or peg to air dry. (*Note:* If PO_4 contamination of glassware is suspected, rinse all items with hot dil. HCl, then with dist. water, then dry.)

Cylinders, graduated: one 25-ml ②; one 50-ml ①; three 100-ml ③ ④ ⑤
Pipets, graduated: two 10-ml [4] [5]
Pipets, volumetric: one 2-ml [2]; one 5-ml [3]; one 10-ml [1]
Flasks, Erlenmeyer: several 250-ml for samples ◇6; six 250-ml for standard ◇7; two 250-ml ◇3 ◇5; one 250-ml for blank ◇8
Flasks, volumetric: two 100-ml ◇2 ◇4; one 1,000-ml ◇1

Chemicals Ammonium molybdate, chloroform, hydrochloric acid, potassium dihydrogen phosphate (anhydrous), stannous chloride, sulfuric acid (sp. gr. 1.82 and low arsenic), tin (mossy).

Reagents (store in polyethylene containers):

1. *Ammonium molybdate solution:* in 100 ml of dist. water, dissolve 10 g of ammonium molybdate.

2. *50% sulfuric acid:* into Erlenmeyer flask place 50 ml of dist. water, and while mixing slowly add 50 ml of concd. sulfuric acid. Cool, transfer to 100-ml vol. flask, and dil. to 100 ml with dist. water.

3. *10% hydrochloric acid:* into 250-ml Erlenmeyer flask place ca. 50 ml of dist. water, and while stirring slowly add 10 ml of concd. hydrochloric acid. Cool, transfer to 100-ml vol. flask, and dil. to 100 ml with dist. water.

4. *Ammonium molybdate reagent*[7] (make fresh, not older than 2 weeks): into 50-ml grad. cylinder ① add 30 ml of 50% sulfuric acid (sol. 2), then with 10-ml vol. pipet [1] add 10 ml ammonium molybdate solution (sol. 1), mix, and pour into emptied and rinsed storage bottle.

5. *Stannous chloride:* preweigh out 0.20-g amounts and put in vials for use in sol. 6.

*6. *Stannous chloride solution*[8] (make fresh, daily): with 25-ml grad. cylinder ② measure out 25 ml of 10% hydrochloric acid (sol. 3) and pour into emptied and rinsed dropper bottle; then add 0.20 g stannous chloride (reagent 5) and *add a small piece of mossy tin;* mix.

7. *Standard potassium phosphate stock solution* (stable for many months): into 1,000-ml vol. flask ◇1 with some dist. water dissolve 1.361 g of potassium dihydrogen phosphate, dil. to 1,000 ml with dist. water, add 1 ml chloroform, store in dark bottle, dil. as required.

Procedure

Advanced preparations:

1. Have reaction vessels rinsed and air dried (or prepared specially, cf. "Note" at end of "Phosphates" section).

2. *Collect water samples* in 250-ml polyethylene narrow-mouthed screw-capped bottles, and analyze promptly.

3. *Warm up samples.*

4. *Make up fresh ammonium molybdate reagent* (sol. 4).

5. *Make up fresh stannous chloride solution* (sol. 6).

6. *Prepare working standard solution* as follows: into 100-ml vol. flask ◇2 with 2-ml vol. pipet [2], *add 2 ml of stock standard potassium phosphate solution* (sol. 7), and *dil. to 100 ml* with dist. water (may be transferred to special 250-ml Erlenmeyer flask ◇3 marked A); then into 100-ml vol. flask ◇4 with 5-ml vol. pipet 3 , *add 5 ml of*

[7] Fairly stable. Remake if necessary.

[8] Make fresh for each run.

the solution A just made, and dil. to 100 ml with dist. water (may be transferred to special 250-ml Erlenmeyer flask ◇5 marked B).

Analysis:

7. *Warm up Klett* with K66 filter (or spectrophotometer at 690 mμ).

8. *Set out sufficient 250-ml flasks* for samples ◇6, standard ◇7, and one for blank ◇8.

9. *Make up 100 ml of solution* in each flask as follows:

a. With 100-ml graduate ③ measure out *100 ml of thoroughly mixed sample* into each 250-ml sample flask ◇6, rinsing graduate with a portion of the next sample each time.

b. Into standard 250-ml flask ◇7 marked 0.8, using 10-ml grad. pipet [4], add *8 ml of standard dilution B* (step 6), and dil. with *92 ml of dist. water*. Mix. (Use dist. water cylinder ④.)

c. With 100-ml graduate ⑤ measure out *100 ml of dist. water* and add to "blank" 250-ml flask.

10. With 10-ml grad. pipet [5] add *1 ml of ammonium molybdate reagent* (sol. 4) to each flask. Swirl.

11. *Read turbidity* of each sample against dist. water (in Klett with 4-cm path and K66 filter). (*Note:* If possible, work from lowest to highest concentration.) Return sample to flask.

(The following steps (*) require exact timing):

*12. At intervals of 1 or 2 min, and in batches of four flasks, *add 4 drops of stannous chloride solution* (sol. 6). Swirl.

*13. At a consistent time of 7 min after adding the stannous chloride, *read against dist. water.* Continue with subsequent batches of flasks.

Closing steps:

14. Turn off Klett, remove and rinse cuvets, drain to air dry.

15. Wash glassware with 10–20 rinses of water and dist. water, drain to air dry.

16. Rinse pipets with water and dist. water, drain to air dry.

Calculations As indicated in the following formula, subtract reagent error in blank (E_b) and the turbidity correction (E_t), if any, from the reading of each sample (E_u):

$$C_u = \frac{E_u - (E_t + E_b)}{E_s - E_b} \times C_s \times F_s$$

where C_u = concentration of sample (unknown) in μg-at PO_4-P/liter; C_s = concentration of standard; F_s = salinity correction (ignore for fresh water, where $F_s = 1$); E_u =

Table 5. Sample data, calculation, and results for phosphate analysis of water sample with high salinity (S = 35 ‰) and salinity correction factor (F_s = 1.20)

Flask	Test	Readings (Klett units)		Results	
		Turbidity (E_t)	Final (E)	μg-at PO_4-P/liter	ppm PO_4
1	Standard 0.8 μg-at PO_4-P/liter	–	42	–	–
2	Sample 1	14	65	1.23	0.117
3	Sample 2	14	48	0.72	0.068
4	Sample 3	15	76	1.53	0.145
5	Sample 4	19	64	1.05	0.100
6	Blank	–	10	–	–

Sample calculation for sample 1:

$$C_u = \frac{65 - (14 + 10)}{42 - 10} \times 0.8 \times 1.20 = 1.23 \ \mu\text{g-at } PO_4\text{-P/liter}$$

$$C_u = \text{ppm } PO_4 = (1.23 \ \mu\text{g-at } PO_4\text{-P/liter}) \times 0.095 = 0.117 \text{ mg } PO_4\text{/liter}$$

Table 6. Volumes of phosphate solution B needed for preparation of standard curve for phosphate analysis

Flask	Concentration μg-at PO_4-P/liter	ppm PO_4	Add (to make up to 100 ml)
1	0.2	0.019	2 ml sol. B/100 ml
2	0.4	0.038	4 ml sol. B/100 ml
3	0.8	0.076	8 ml sol. B/100 ml
4	1.0	0.095	10 ml sol. B/100 ml
5	2.0	0.190	20 ml sol. B/100 ml

extinction of unknown; E_b = extinction of blank; E_s = extinction of standard; and E_t = extinction of turbidity check (step 11). A sample calculation can be found in Table 5.

Note For dark-colored solutions requiring dilution or a shorter light path, make corrections as indicated in "Spectrophotometry," project 14, involving factors V_a/V_o and P_o/P_a, where a = volume or path length actually used and o = original volume or path length required.

Conversions

μg PO_4-P/liter = 31.027 × (μg-at PO_4-P/liter)

μg PO_4/liter = 95.027 × (μg-at PO_4-P/liter)

ppm PO_4 = mg PO_4/liter = 0.095 × (μg-at PO_4-P/liter)

meq PO_4/liter = 0.0317 × (mg PO_4/liter)

Ranges Inland waters: 0–30 mg PO_4/liter (APHA, 1965: 230); marine: 0–2 μg-at PO_4 P/liter (Sverdrup, Johnson, and Fleming, 1942: 204) or 0–0.190 mg PO_4/liter.

Standard Curve Must be determined for each instrument, and for each new replacement lamp. Using special 250-ml flasks ⟨7⟩ marked STD and indicating the concentrations, deliver the indicated volumes of phosphate solution B (step 6) per Table 6. Plot on graph paper with extinction units on abscissa and concentration on ordinate (cf. Figure 4).

Salinity Correction Salinity influences the readings of phosphates, the effects varying somewhat for different waters. One set of corrections is given in Figure 7.

Note Newly involved glassware should be washed in concd. sulfuric acid, rinsed with

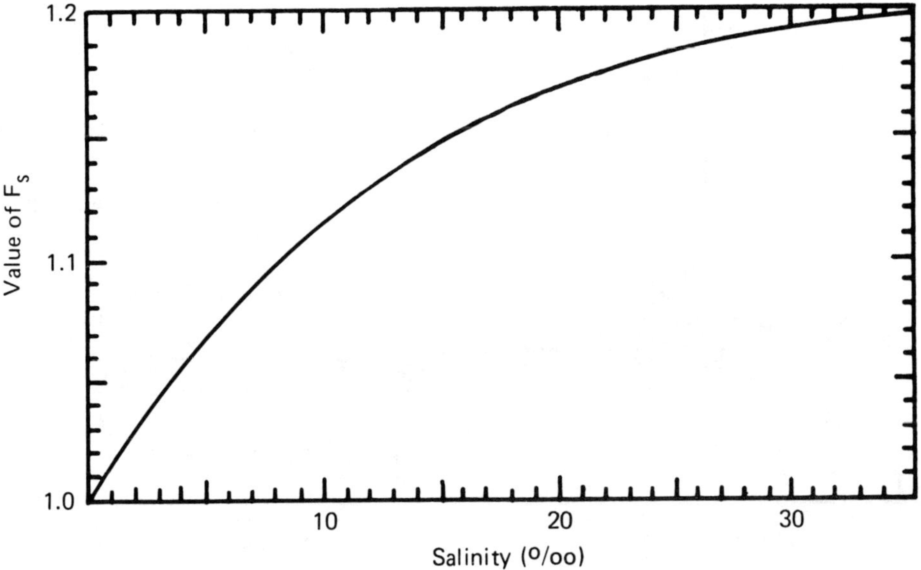

Figure 7. Sample salinity correction (F_s) curve for phosphate analysis. (Data from D. M. Pratt, pers. comm.)

0.1 N NaOH, 20–30 times with tap water, then dist. water, and drained to air dry. However, between analyses, glassware need only be rinsed abundantly with dist. water.

References

APHA (1965: 234).

Atkins, W. R. G. 1923. The phosphate content of fresh and salt waters in its relationship to the growth of algal plankton. J. Mar. Biol. Assoc. 13: 119–150.

Denigès, G. 1920 Réaction de coloration extrêment sensible des phosphates et des arséniates. C.R. Acad. Sci. 171: 802–804.

Wattenberg, H. 1937. Critical review of the methods used for determining nutrient salts and related constituents in salt water, 1. Rapp. Cons. Inst. Expl. Mar. 103: 5–26. (From adaptation by D. M. Pratt, Univ. R. I.)

31. Photomicrography

Phytoplankton can be satisfactorily photographed with a simple arrangement (or with specialized equipment) by using standard exposure times. Assemble the following: microscope with corrected lenses and adequate condensers; research-quality microscope lamp (capable of focusing and having iris diaphragm and filament bulb) (see Figure 8); 35mm camera or camera back (with removable lens and through-the-lens focusing viewfinder); and cable release. Microscope and lamp will need to be firmly attached to the table. For film, use a slow, fine-grained black and white film (e.g., Panatomic-X) and corresponding developer (Microdal-X). Darkroom facilities are desirable.

Procedure

To adjust for optimal (Koehler) illumination:

1. Position lamp ca. 15 in. from microscope, and aim beam directly at mirror. Work in very subdued light, and avoid looking into microscope (throw image onto white paper held ca. 12 in. above ocular).

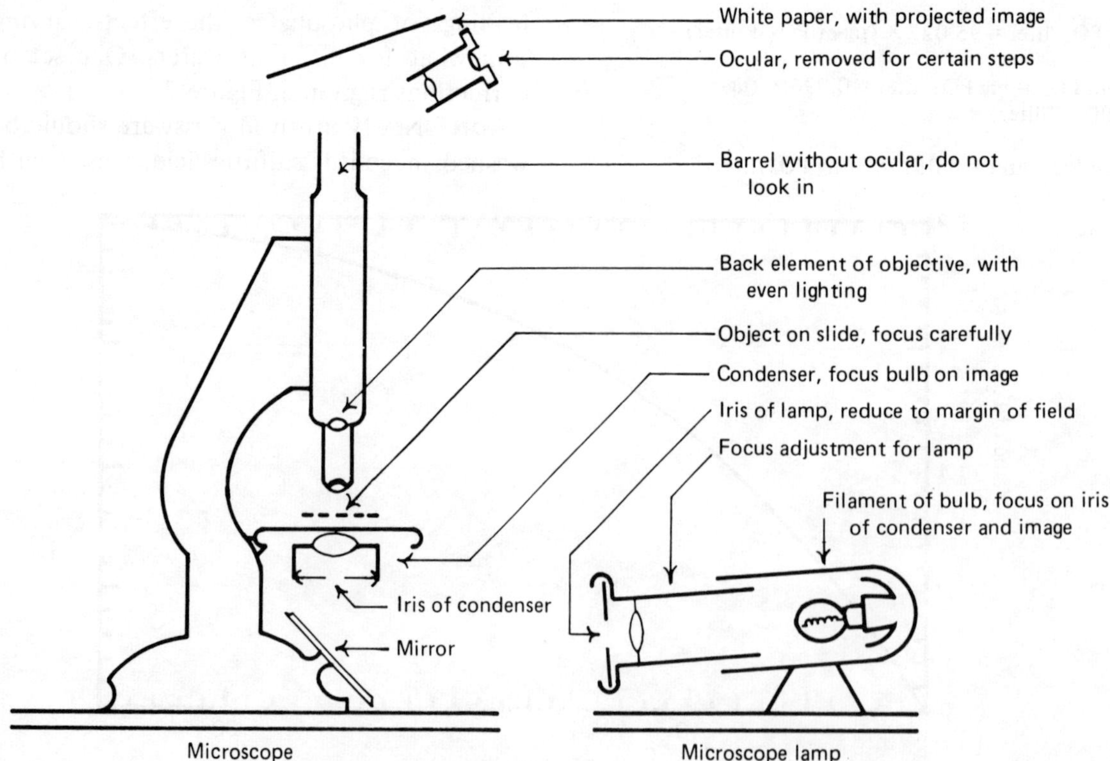

Figure 8. Diagram of setup described for photomicrography.

2. To adjust mirror (using flat side unless working without condenser), tilt until maximal light is obtained and is centered.

3. To adjust microscope focus, position good prepared slide on stage and focus microscope at low power.

4. To adjust condenser, open iris diaphragm of condenser and close down that of lamp, then raise or lower condenser until the lamp's iris is focused in the microscope. (*Note:* Be sure condenser is centered for all objectives.)

5. To adjust lamp focus, close down condenser iris diaphragm and open lamp's iris part way, then focus lamp (while watching condenser from below) until filaments of bulb are focused on the iris diaphragm (hard to see except in dark). (*Note:* Be sure filaments of bulb are centered relative to lamp lens.)

6. To adjust lamp iris diaphragm, remove ocular and project image onto white paper held above ocular. Then open or close lamp's iris diaphragm until the outer edge of the iris matches the outer edge of the back lens. (*Note:* Be sure back lens of objective is completely lighted. If not, condenser is probably inadequate for that lens and a suitable one is needed.)

7. To adjust iris diaphragm of condenser, open or close until the illuminated back lens of the objective is reduced 1/3 in area.

8. When adjustment is complete, replace ocular. From this point on, restrict adjustments to focusing of microscope; otherwise realignment will be necessary.

To determine exposure times:

9. Load camera with suitable film, be sure shutter is closed.

10. Position slide on stage; and, with camera removed, locate object to be photographed, center it, and replace camera.

11. Focus object in camera's viewer with microscope adjustments.

12. Take stepwise series of exposures, such as 1/100, 1/50, 1/25, 1/10, 1/5, 1/2, 1, 2, 4, 8, and 16 seconds. Record each carefully, and leave blank exposure at end of series.

13. Repeat for each different objective, or condenser system, that is to be used.

14. Develop film by rigorously standard procedure. Select time which gives the best exposure (as determined by an experienced photographer, or by which produces best prints).

15. Prepare a table or graph (see Table 7), giving optimum exposures for each film and lens-condenser combination.

Note 1 Once determined, always use same exposure times, film, and lens systems.

Note 2 The directions given here are for adapting generally available laboratory equipment. If special photomicrographic unit is to be used, follow spe-

Table 7. Sample exposure times obtained for Wild microscope and Panatomic-X film developed with 1:3 dil. of Microdal-X[a]

Accessories				Exposure time	
Objective	Ocular	Filter	Voltage	Best sec.	Next best sec.
10X	10X	–	5	1/25	1/50
10X	10X	10X phase	6	1	2
20X	10X	–	5	1/25	1/50
20X	10X	20/40 phase	6	1–1.5	2
40X	10X	20/40 phase	6	1–1.5	2
50X, oil	10X	50/100 phase	6	5	8
97X, oil	10X	50/100 phase	6	25	30

[a]Accessories included Wild camera and drawing tube. (Data by Carmelo Tomas.)

cific directions accompanying the instrument.

To take photomicrograph (work in subdued light):

16. Position slide on stage; and, with camera out of the way or removed, locate and focus desired subject.
17. Replace camera, and focus object in camera's viewfinder.
18. Select proper exposure time from the premade exposure table or graph, and make the exposure (use cable release unless vibrations blur pictures, in which case exposure can be made by turning lamp on and off for required time while camera shutter is held, e.g., at bulb, then closing shutter).
19. Carefully record photograph (date, exposure number, and subject), then advance film and proceed with further exposures.

To develop film:

Do your own developing if feasible, because commercial work tends to be too grainy. Use the following reagents (make up according to instructions on containers, and store in darkness):

1. *Water:* simply a bottle of tap water at room temperature.
2. *Developer* (e.g., Microdal-X) (remake monthly).
3. *28% acetic acid* (stable): 8 parts tap water and 3 parts glacial acetic acid.
4. *Short-stop* (make up for each use): ca. 1.75% acetic acid; mix 32 cc of 28% acetic acid (sol. 3) and 500 ml of tap water.
5. *Acid fixer* or hypo (quite stable, test with hypotester).
6. *Hypo clearing solution stock* (stable).
7. *Hypo clearing solution* (prepare as needed).

The procedure for developing black and white film is:

1. Using cleaned and dried developing tank, and working in total darkness, open developing tank and open film cassette (pop off one end); while holding film on edges only, feed film into spiraled track of developing tank and separate from spool. Close developing tank. Place on tray or pan.
2. Working on pan, pour adequate volume (ca. 250 for 35mm film in small tanks) of water (sol. 1), tap tank on table (to loosen bubbles), and spin film. Pour off water (or save for short-stop).
3. Pour in adequate volume of developer (sol. 2), spinning film immediately. Determine temperature (of water); select development time for that temperature from manufacturer's instructions. Spin film at 2-min intervals.
4. Prepare short-stop (sol. 4) (e.g., 16 ml of 28% acetic acid in 250 ml of water in graduated cylinder).
5. At end of developing time, pour off (or back) developer, and pour in newly prepared short-stop. Spin immediately.
6. After ca. 15 sec, pour off short-stop.
7. Add adequate volume of acid fixer (sol. 5), spinning immediately and then every 2 min for 10 min.
8. After 10 min, pour off (or back) the hypo.
9. Add adequate volume of hypo clearing agent (sol. 7). Spin immediately, and time for 1 min.
10. After 1 min, pour off hypo clearing agent.
11. Run water from faucet into center concavity of developing tank, and allow water to run at moderate speed through tank for at least 5(−30) min. (*Note:* If clearing agent is not used, water flow must be balanced so as to be at room temperature.)
12. Open developing tank, remove film (holding only at edges).
13. Take film strip by ends, and snap film up and down smartly, shaking off and spreading water drops.
14. Hang up in dust-free room, such as by a clamp clothespin, and clamp a second pin (weighted, if necessary) or lower end. Allow to dry thoroughly (e.g., overnight).

To print or enlarge:

Have this work done by, or under the direction of, an experienced photographer. Try to avoid routine commercial work, which tends to be disappointing.

References

Eastman Kodak Co. 1970. Photography through the Microscope. Publ. no. P-2. 5th Ed. Eastman Kodak, Rochester, N.Y. 68 p.

Eastman Kodak Co. 1974. Kodak Darkroom Dataguide. Publ. no. R-2. 5th Ed. Eastman Kodak, Rochester, N.Y. 28 p.

32. Phytoplankton analysis

Phytoplankton analysis, per cent composition: see "Plankton analysis," procedure 33.

33. Plankton analysis

Plankton counts should be both qualitative (flora) and quantitative (vegetation), and are conveniently made by using a combination of two methods, one on a concentrated sample (e.g., a net tow) and the other on unaltered water (raw sample). See also the sedimentation method, project 10.

Procedure

Net sample:

1. Using a net tow sample (see "Plankton net" for instructions), mix thoroughly by inverting 25 times.
2. Mount drop of mixed sample on slide, and cover with coverslip. (The volume of a drop can be found by counting drops required to reach 1 ml in a small graduated cylinder.)
3. Examine at 100X, recording each kind (by name or temporary code word) and the number of each kind (differential count) (APHA, 1965: 662); and, in case of new forms, sketch and measure size.
4. Scan from one side of coverslip to the other, identifying and tabulating number of algae.
5. Calculate per cent of each form.
6. Be sure to preserve a portion of each sample for future reference (4% formalin; 5% in seawater); and, in case of novel or excellent specimens, draw with aid of camera lucida or take photomicrograph. When drawing, always indicate scale by tracing a small part (e.g., two lines of smallest unit) of micrometer scale and write down its true length.

> ***Note*** To estimate cells/ml in the case of filamentous algae, record number of colonies, determine average number of cells/colony by checking cells in several filaments and averaging, and multiply number of colonies by cells/colony.

Raw water:

1. Using a natural water sample, mix thoroughly by inverting 25 times.
2. Pipet with Stempel pipet, or wide-mouthed pipet, 1 ml of mixed sample water into Sedgwick-Rafter chamber, stir with needle, cover cautiously (placing slantwise and closing up straight, and, if necessary, adding a drop or so of sample to avoid trapping air).
3. Count at 100X all the cells of large or distinct common forms which are found in one (or more) sweep(s) (strip count) (APHA, 1965: 663) made the full length of the chamber, being careful to focus up and down to see all algae; or, count 20 or more fields (field count) (APHA, 1965: 663).
4. Calculate number of cells per ml of the large, distinct forms; and, using the % composition values obtained from the differential count (see "Net Sample" above) calculate the number of cells of each form and summate to obtain the total count.

Calculations Sample calculation method:

Area of chamber = length X width (in mm)

Area of chamber counted = length X width of field (measured by micrometer scale), or area of fields (πr^2).

$$\text{Proportion of chamber counted} = \frac{\text{area of chamber counted}}{\text{area of entire chamber}}$$

Therefore, if four species were found, the per cent compositions by differential count were 20, 32, 12, and 10%, respectively, and 80.7 of species 1 were counted by Sedgwick-Rafter chamber in 20 fields having a field of view 1.35 mm wide; then:

Table 8. Sample computation of cell count

Species	% composition	Cells/ml
1	20	2,820
2	32	4,500
3	12	1,690
4	10	1,410
Others	26	3,660
Total count	14,080 or 14.1 × 10^6 cells/liter	

$$\text{Volume examined} = \frac{20 \times (\pi \times 1.35/2)^2}{20 \text{ mm} \times 50 \text{ mm}} \times 1 \text{ ml}$$
$$= 0.0286 \text{ ml}$$

80.7 cells of species 1 in 0.0286 ml = 2,820 cells/ml

From per cent compositions, the cell counts can be found (Table 8).

For estimating plankton volume, see project 10 (also see APHA, 1965: 658).

34. Plankton net
Attach jar to net securely. For qualitative sample, either draw through water at selected (or varied) depth, or pour pail(s) of water through net, then drain, and either remove jar and empty contents into bottle, or work jar backward up net and empty while still attached. For more quantitative samples, use plankton sampler; or, if using net, record distance (or rate and time) and net coefficient; or use volumetric net. For phytoplankton, use no. 25 mesh net (200 meshes/in.; and 0.004-mm pore size) (Welch, 1948: 355).

Reference Welch (1948: 232).

35. Plankton net coefficient
See "Net coefficient," procedure 24.

36. Plankton sample
For qualitative study, fix one half (4% formalin,[9] 5 % in seawater) and keep other half for study of living material. For quantitative work, record volumes of samples, preservatives, or dilutions, and other factors carefully throughout so that numbers/vol of original can be calculated accurately.

37. Plankton sampler
Take raw sample directly in 250-ml gs bottle, indirectly by messenger-activated Kemmerer, Van Dorn, or Nansen sampler, or by a quantitative plankton net such as the Clarke-Bumpus sampler, and transfer to bottle.

38. Plankton volume
See project 10.

39. Plant hook
See "Grapnel," procedure 16.

40. Range finder
A 100-ft photographic range finder, or yachtsman's Ordco range finder, can help—along with compass reading—to establish position in a pond. For more precise measurement, the surveyor's stadia and plane table alidade can be used, although this is considerably less convenient and more time consuming. At greater distances, other methods of fixing location are needed (see "Bearings," procedure 2, and "Sextant," procedure 48).

41. Redox (oxidation reduction potential)
Redox can be measured by either of the pH meters listed, but usually Beckman N-2 is more useful in the field.

Procedure

Set up platinum electrode:

1. Open pH meter carefully; swing out electrodes.
2. Slide back electrode lock and replace glass electrode with platinum electrode.
3. Immerse electrode tips in dist. water.
4. Set "temperature" knob to 29°C (regardless of the temperature).
5. Turn main knob to "check."
6. With STD knob, bring needle to read 7. Unit is ready for measurement of redox.

To measure E_7:

7. Lower electrodes into sample.
8. Turn main dial to 0–8 range (reversing direction of dial, if needle exceeds scale).
9. Record value.

[9] Better preservation of flagellates is reported with 1% formalin or Lugol's Iodine.

Calculation

$$E_7 = 60(7 - E_o) + 243$$

where E_7 = millivolts at pH 7; E_o = reading in pH; 60 = conversion constant for this unit; and 243 = emf of calomel electrode relative to hydrogen.

Note E_7 is + if E_o is in 0–7 range; but - if E_o is in 7–14 range.

$$\text{volts} = \frac{\text{mv}}{1{,}000}$$

Ranges Inland waters: +200 to +600 mv; sediments: -100 to +500 mv. Some common redox values are +500 mv for local ponds, -240 mv for decaying organic sediment. Marine waters: ?. (*Note:* In lakes, E_7 is mirror image of ferrous iron. Temperature has only slight direct effect on redox value, and can usually be ignored.)

References Reid (1961: 153); Ruttner (1963: 204).

42. Saturation, per cent

See "Oxygen, dissolved," procedure 27.

43. SCUBA (self-contained underwater breathing apparatus)

Equipment Tank, harness, regulator, face mask, exposure suit (in colder water), boots, hood, gloves, life vest, and weight belt.

Tanks are filled with medically pure air, untainted by exhaust fumes (check the supplier's equipment). Breathing is natural, but emergency loss of regulator or flooding of mask requires practice to overcome; and, on rising or sinking, internal lung and body pressures must be released by continuous breathing to avoid air embolism and potential death. Deaths have occurred in less than 10 ft from this cause. Vomiting or coughing underwater is dangerous. Only skilled workers can overcome these hindrances. The ubiquitous snorkel is easy to use, but has killed more local biologists than has SCUBA.

References CNCA (1959); Wood (1963).

44. Secchi disk (pronounced SEK-kee)

A Secchi disk is a 20-cm disk with alternating black and white quadrants.

Procedure

1. Lower disk into water until it disappears. Note depth.
2. Raise slowly until it just appears. Note depth.
3. Record average depth.

Calculation An approximate relationship useful in open water is:

$$\text{Extinction coefficient} = \frac{1.7}{\text{Secchi disk reading (m)}}$$

Range 0.10(–2–15)–30 m.

Note Under optimal conditions, this value approximates the depth at 5% transmitted light. Readings differ with variation of clouds, water surface, and shadows, as well as water color and turbidity.

References Welch (1948: 159); Poole and Atkins (1929) cited by Sverdrup, Johnson, and Fleming (1942: 82) relative to the extinction coefficient.

45. Sedgwick-Rafter counting chamber

See also "Raw water," in "Plankton analysis," procedure 33.

The Sedgwick-Rafter counting chamber consists of a chamber 1 X 20 X 50 mm on a slide with a special large coverslip. The area covered is ca. 1,000 mm^2, and the volume is ca. 1 ml.

Correction Variation is found among counting cells; and, to standardize cells, check area, measure internal dimensions of frame, and calculate area. Check volume by using 1-ml volumetric pipet, draining 1 ml of thoroughly mixed water sample into chamber, and covering all but one corner of cell with coverslip. Then, using 1-ml transfer pipet graduated to 0.01 ml, determine how much water needs to be added or removed to permit closing cell with no loss of water nor formation of bubble. Mark area and volume on each slide, e.g., with diamond pencil.

46. Sediment analysis

See "Sediment" section in "Notes," project 4.

47. Sediment samplers

Use Ekman dredge from boat. Divers should

use 1(−2)-in. diameter lucite tube (or W-Z diver's sampler) and take core (see also project 6) by forcing tube into substrate, withdrawing, and plugging ends.

48. Sextant

For establishing location in pond from a boat, an inexpensive plastic sextant (e.g., Mark III, Davis Instrument Corp., San Leandro, Cal.) is feasible. However, compass and range finder are often easier to use.

Procedure

1. Select three shoreline features or establish three tall, easily seen staffs (and establish their exact location) for sightings.
2. Holding sextant on its side, find one feature (or staff) in telescope, and move arm until image of second feature (or staff) comes into view; then line up images.
3. Read degrees and minutes on scale.
4. Similarly measure angle to third feature (or staff).
5. Later, working on a chart or map, and using a three-armed protractor (or transparent sheet with bearing lines drawn out), adjust protractor (or diagram) until the angles are correct, which will pinpoint the boat location.

Reference Chapman (1968: 352c).

49. Silicates (reactive silicates)

Time required: ca. 60 min

Glass- or Polyethylene-ware To conserve time and glass- or polyethylene-ware, and to facilitate general use of a detailed analysis, special items needed in the procedure are set aside for each step. They are coded below by geometric symbols and numbered serially by use. When analysis is done, they need only to be carefully rinsed with tap, then dist., water and returned to their special clamp, peg, or drain hole to air dry.

Cylinders, graduated, polyethylene: five 100-ml ① ② ③ ④ ⑤

Pipets, graduated: one 1-ml [2]; one 10-ml [4]

Pipets, volumetric: one 1-ml [10]; three 2-ml [3] [9] [11]; one 3-ml [5]; one 5-ml [6]; two 20-ml [1] [12]; two 50-ml [7] [8]

Flasks or beakers, polyethylene beakers: two sets of 100-ml, one for samples by the direct ⟨4⟩ and the second for samples by the indirect procedure ⟨7⟩; for marine work also one 100-ml for standard ⟨5⟩, and two 100-ml for blanks, one by direct ⟨6⟩ and the other by the indirect ⟨8⟩ procedure; a special set of five 100-ml for standard curve ⟨10⟩; one 400-ml ⟨1⟩

Flasks, volumetric: one 50-ml ⟨9⟩; three 100-ml ⟨2⟩⟨3⟩⟨4⟩; one 200-ml ⟨11⟩

Chemicals Ammonium molybdate, hydrochloric acid, oxalic acid, sodium chloride, sodium silicofluoride (Na_2SiF_6), stannous chloride ($SnCl_2 \cdot 2H_2O$), sulfuric acid, and Si-free glass-distilled water (freshly distilled and stored immediately in polyethylene).

Reagents (store all solutions in polyethylene containers):

1. *5% ammonium molybdate solution* (stable): in 100-ml vol. flask with ca. 80 ml Si-free dist. water, dissolve 5 g of ammonium molybdate and dil. to 100 ml with Si-free dist. water.
2. *1 N hydrochloric acid:* into 100-ml vol. flask with a 10-ml grad. pipet (equipped with a bulb) add 8.6 ml of concd. hydrochloric acid, mix, and dil. cautiously to 100 ml with Si-free dist. water.

*3. *Acid-molybdate reagent*[10] (make this 2:3 dilution just before use): into 100-ml polyethylene graduate ① with 20-ml vol. pipet [1] transfer 20 ml of ammonium molybdate solution (sol. 1), and pour into freshly emptied and rinsed storage container or 400-ml beaker ⟨1⟩; then, with another 100-ml polyethylene graduate ② measure out 30 ml of 1 N HCl (sol. 2) and add to the vessel, and mix.

4. *50% sulfuric acid* (stable): into 250-ml Erlenmeyer flask, using 100-ml polyethylene graduate, transfer 50 ml of Si-free dist. water, and with another 100-ml poly-

[10] Make fresh for each run.

ethylene graduate cautiously add (with swirling) 50 ml of concd. sulfuric acid; cool, transfer to 100-ml vol. flask, and dil. to 100 ml with Si-free dist. water.

5. *10% oxalic acid* (stable): in 100-ml vol. flask with some Si-free dist. water dissolve 10 g of oxalic acid, and dil. to 100 ml with Si-free dist. water.

6. *20% stannous chloride stock solution* (stable): into 250-ml Erlenmeyer flask, using 100-ml polyethylene graduate, transfer ca. 20 ml of Si-free dist. water, and with 10-ml grad. pipet (equipped with propipet bulb) cautiously mix in 25.8 ml of concd. HCl; cool, then transfer quantitatively to 50-ml vol. flask; dil. to 50 ml with Si-free dist. water; return mixture to the Erlenmeyer flask, and dissolve in 20 g of stannous chloride.

*7. *Stannous chloride reagent*[10] (make just before using): into 100-ml polyethylene graduate ③, using 1-ml grad. pipet [2] (with a propipet bulb), add 0.5 ml of stock stannous chloride solution (sol. 6), and dil. to 50 ml with Si-free dist. water.

8. *Silicate standard stock solution* (stable): into beaker with ca. 100 ml of Si-free glass-dist. water, dissolve 0.9060 g of dry, finely powdered sodium silicofluoride, stirring if necessary with nickel-stainless steel spatula; transfer quantitatively to 1,000-ml vol. flask, and dil. to 1,000 ml with Si-free dist. water (=5 μg-at Si/ml).

9. *Sodium chloride standard-diluting solution* (e.g., 3.5%): in 100-ml vol. flask with some Si-free dist. water, dissolve 3.5 g (or amount sufficient to give solution approximating salinity of sample) of sodium chloride; dil. to 100 ml with Si-free dist. water.

Procedure

Advanced preparations:

1. Have a recently prepared calibration curve (cf. "Standard curve," below).

2. Have all polyethylene and glassware rinsed with Si-free dist. water, drained, and air dried.

3. *Collect water samples* in 250-ml polyethylene narrow-mouthed screw-capped bottles.

4. *Make up fresh acid-molybdate reagent* (sol. 3).

5. *Make up fresh stannous chloride reagent* (sol. 7).

6. If marine samples are involved, prepare 3.5% sodium chloride diluting solution (sol. 9).

7. *Prepare standard* of approximate anticipated concentrations of the samples (e.g., 40 μg-at Si/liter for New England inland water), as follows: into 100-ml vol. flask ⟨2⟩ with 2-ml vol. pipet [3], transfer 2 ml of stock silicate standard solution (sol. 8); mix, and dil. to 100 ml with Si-free dist. water (call this solution X, contains 100 μg-at Si/liter). Then, into 50-ml vol. flask ⟨9⟩ or cylinder, transfer with suitable pipet (e.g., 20-ml vol. [12]) indicated volume (see "Standard curve," below) (e.g., 20 ml) of sol. X; mix, and transfer to polyethylene beaker for standard ⟨11⟩.

Analysis:

8. *Warm up Klett* with K66 filter (or spectrophotometer at 690 mμ) for use with round cuvets.

9. *Set out polyethylene beakers* for either of the following cases: a) for freshwater samples, set out sufficient beakers for water samples ⟨4⟩ for a standard ⟨5⟩, and one for a blank ⟨6⟩, but b) for marine samples, set up two sets of beakers, one set for the "direct" procedure including those listed above (a), and a second set for the "inverted" procedure, to include beakers for all the water samples ⟨7⟩, and for a blank ⟨8⟩.

For marine waters, run direct (10–19) and indirect (10′–19′) methods simultaneously.

DIRECT (fresh water)

10. With 3-ml vol. pipet [5] *add 3 ml of acid-molybdate reagent* (sol. 3) to each beaker (save pipet for step 12′).

11a. With 50-ml vol. pipet [7] (or cylinder (4)) *add 50 ml of Si-free dist. water* to "blank" beaker.

11b. With 50-ml vol. pipet [7] (or cylinder (4)) *add 50 ml of silicate standard dilution* (step 7) to "standard" beaker.

11c. With 50-ml vol. pipet [8] (or cylinder (5)) *add 50 ml of sample* to each sample beaker.

12. Wait 10 min.

13. With 5-ml vol. pipet [6] (from step 10′) *add 5 ml of 50% sulfuric acid* (sol. 4) to each beaker.

14. With 2-ml vol. pipet [9] *add 2 ml of 10% oxalic acid* (sol. 5) to each beaker.

15. Wait 5 min.

16. *Read* (turbidity check) *against dist. water* in Klett using K66 filter (or at 690 mμ) and 4-cm path. (*Note:* Be sure optical density of cuvet for blank does not exceed that of sample cuvet.)

17. With 1-ml vol. pipet [10] *add 1.0 ml of stannous chloride reagent* (sol. 7) to each beaker. *Swirl* (stir with rinsed and dried spatula).

18. Wait 20–40 min.

19. *Read against dist. water* (or against standard, see step 16, above) (use short-light path).

Record extinctions (optical densities) as E_u, E_b, and E_s for unknowns, blank, and standard.

INVERTED (needed, in addition to direct, for marine samples)

10′. With 5-ml vol. pipet [6] *add 5 ml of 50% sulfuric acid* (sol. 4) to each beaker (save pipet for step 13).

11a′. Do as in 11a. *Add 50 ml of Si-free dist. water.*

11b′. Do as in 11b. *Add 50 ml of silicate standard dilution.*

11c′. Do as in 11c. *Add 50 ml of sample.*

12′. With 3-ml vol. pipet [5] (from step 10) *add 3 ml of acid-molybdate reagent* (sol. 3) to each beaker.

13′. Wait 10 min, then do as in 13; *add 5 ml of 50% sulfuric acid.*

14′. Do as in 14. *Add 2 ml of 10% oxalic acid.*

15′. Wait 10 min.

16′. Do as in 16. *Read* (turbidity check) *against dist. water.*

17′. Do as in 17. *Add 1.0 ml of stannous chloride.*

18′. Wait 20–40 min.

19′. Do as in 19. *Read in Klett.*

Record extinctions (optical densities) as EI_u and EI_b for unknowns and blank.

Closing steps:

20. Turn off Klett, remove and rinse cuvets, drain to air dry.

21. Wash glassware with 5–10 rinses of tap and dist. water; drain to air dry.

22. Rinse pipets with tap and dist. water; drain to air dry.

Note If negative values are obtained, read standard but set at its extinction value for its known concentration based on calibration curve.

Calculations The best results are obtained with standard calibration curve, but an estimate can be obtained by calculation, especially when a standard is run which approximates the concentration of the unknown. The two formulas below are basically the same except that for marine samples the inverted procedure extinctions are included.

For freshwater samples, direct procedure only:

$$C_u = \frac{E_u - (E_t + E_b)}{E_s - E_b} \times C_s$$

For marine samples, including direct and inverted procedures:

$$C_u = ([E_u - (E_t + E_b)] - [(EI_u + E_b) - EI_b]) \times \frac{C_s}{E_s - E_b}$$

where C_u = concentration of unknowns in μg-at SiO_2-Si/liter; C_s = concentration of standard (can vary, but in our area 40 μg-at SiO_2-Si/liter is convenient); E_t = extinction (optical density or Klett units) of turbidity check for each sample (step 16) (or EI_t = turbidity check by inverted procedure (step 16′); E_u = extinction of unknown; E_s = extinction of standard; E_b = extinction of blank; EI_u = extinction of unknown by inverted procedure; and EI_b = extinction of blank by inverted procedure. A sample calculation can be found in Table 9.

Note For dark-colored solutions requiring dilution or a shorter light path, make corrections as indicated in "Spectrophotometry," project 14, involving factors V_a/V_o and P_o/P_a, where a = volume or path length actually used and o = original volume or path length required.

For example, if it were necessary to dilute the colored solution from 65 to 130 ml, then the new reading in the spectrophotometer would be entered into the formula as follows, and the entire sequence multiplied by 130/65 (here 130/65 is V_a/V_o):

$$C_u = \frac{337 - (3 + 4)}{107.5 - 4} \times 40 \times \frac{130}{65} = 255 \text{ μg-at } SiO_2\text{-Si/liter}$$

Table 9. Sample data, calculation, and results for silicate analysis of freshwater sample (do not involve the inverted procedure nor NaCl solution of standard)[a]

		Readings (Klett units)		Results	
		Usual procedure			
Flask	Test	E_t	E	μg-at SiO_2-Si/liter	ppm SiO_2
1	Standard 40 μg-at Si/liter	–	107.5	–	–
2	Sample 1	3.0	680	260	15.6
3	Sample 2	4.7	740	283	17
4	Sample 3	4.8	560	213	12.8
5	Sample 4	9.1	511	192.4	11.5
6	Blank	–	4.0	–	–

Sample calculation for sample 1:

$$C_u = \frac{680 - (3 + 4)}{107.5 - 4} \times 40 = 260 \text{ μg-at } SiO_2\text{-Si/liter}$$

$$C_u = 0.06 \times (260 \text{ μg-at } SiO_2\text{-Si/liter}) = 15.6 \text{ ppm } SiO_2$$

[a]Extinctions were read with Klett using 4-cm path for standard and the round cuvets for the sample and blank.

Conversions

$\mu g\ SiO_2$-Si/liter = 28.06 × (μg-at SiO_2-Si/liter)
$\mu g\ SiO_2$/liter = 60.06 × (μg-at SiO_2-Si/liter)
ppm SiO_2 = mg SiO_2/liter = 0.060 × (μg-at SiO_2-Si/liter)
ppm Si or mg Si/liter = 0.028 × (μg-at SiO_2-Si/liter)
ppm SiO_3 = mg SiO_3/liter = 0.076 × (μg-at SiO_2-Si/liter)
meq SiO_3/liter = 0.0263 × (mg SiO_3/liter)

Ranges Inland waters: 0–60 mg SiO_2/liter (APHA, 1965: 258); marine: 10–190 μg-at Si/liter (Sverdrup, Johnson, and Fleming, 1942: 244, 245) or 0.6–11.4 mg SiO_2/liter.

Standard Curve (Make up for each instrument, and for each new replacement bulb.) Make up silicate series in dist. water, or for marine analysis make up in NaCl sol. approximating the salinity of the sample.

Into 100-ml vol. flask ⟨4⟩ using 2-ml vol. pipet [11], transfer 2 ml of stock silicate standard solution (sol. 8) and dil. to 100 ml with Si-free dist. water (contains 100 μg-at Si/liter) (call this solution X). Into 50-ml vol. flask ⟨9⟩, using vol. pipet, transfer 1 ml of sol. X, and dil. to 50 ml (= 2 μg-at Si/liter); transfer 50 ml to specially marked beakers for standard curve ⟨10⟩. Continue, making solutions as indicated in Table 10, and transferring to beakers. Plot on graph paper with extinction units on abscissa and concentration on ordinate (cf. Figure 4).

Salinity Correction The effect of salinity on the silicate results are too uncertain to base on a simple numerical factor, and the correction is handled by using NaCl solutions in making the calibration curves, the standards, and blanks in analyzing marine samples.

Note 1 To prepare newly employed glassware, soak in potassium dichromate-acid cleaner, rinse thoroughly, then finally rinse with dist. water repeatedly and Si-free dist. water. Between analyses, rinse with Si-free dist. water as usual.

Note 2 This analysis detects only certain forms of silica, others not reacting with the silicomolybdate complex. The degree of polymerization of silica is also pH dependent. Thus, the amount of silica measured here estimates only that part which actually reacts, and is designated thus as "reactive silicate" (Strickland and Parsons, 1968: 65).

References

APHA. 1965. (See "References" in project 5).
Armstrong, F. A. J. 1951. The determination of silicates in sea water. J. Mar. Biol. Assoc. 30: 149–160.
Pratt, D. M. (pers. comm.) (Mimeographed instruction sheets issued, Narragansett Marine Laboratory).
Ruttner, F. 1963. (See "References" at the start of this project).
Strickland, J. D. H., and T. R. Parsons. 1968. (See "References" in project 5).
Sverdrup, H. U., M. W. Johnson, and R. H. Fleming. 1942. (See "References" in project 5).

50. Soil sieves

See project 4.

51. Solutes

See "Conductivity," procedure 8.

Table 10. Solutions needed for preparation of standard curve for silicate analysis

Flask	Concentration: μg-at SiO_2-Si/liter	Concentration: ppm SiO_2	Add (to make up to 50 ml)
1	2	0.12	1 ml sol. X/50 ml
2	8	0.48	4 ml sol. X/50 ml
3	20	1.20	10 ml sol. X/50 ml
4	40	2.40	20 ml sol. X/50 ml
5	60	3.60	30 ml sol. X/50 ml

See "Nitrates," procedure 25.
See "Phosphates," procedure 30.
See "Silicates," procedure 49.
See "Total filterable residue," procedure 56.

52. Specific conductance
See "Conductivity," procedure 8.

53. Submarine photometer
The unit consists of two photometers (the deck cell and the sea cell; the latter equipped with a supporting frame for lowering into the water) and the control unit.

Procedure

To assemble:

1. Attach wires of deck and sea cells to proper posts.
2. Turn dial to "deck" and "sea" alternately, to ensure that needle is on scale (if not, reverse wire for that cell).
3. Position deck cell on boat; suspend from bottom of sea cell a weight on a 1- to 2-ft line (to warn against hitting bottom), and lower sea cell on a graduated rope or line (do not use the electric wire).

To measure:

1. Lower sea cell to just below water surface; take deck cell and then sea cell reading, varying multiplier knob as needed to get a good reading.
2. Record meter reading, and "X" value of multiplier.
3. Lower sea cell at 1-m intervals, repeating readings at each depth; stop when you notice that the weight has hit bottom.
4. When done and sea cell is returned to deck, cover sensor plates at once.
5. When disconnecting cell wires, be sure to twist ends together (to prevent polarity).
6. Rinse off units (especially if used in salt water), and flush sea cell by running mild stream of water through the lateral openings just beneath the glass filter.

Calculation As the two cells frequently differ in sensitivity, results from the two cannot be compared until converted to the same units.

A calibration curve for each cell is needed with meter readings on the abscissa and light (ft-c) on the ordinate:

$$T = 100 \times \frac{L_d}{L_I}$$

where T = per cent transmittance, L_I = incident light (at surface), L_d = light at measured depth.

Note Where the two cells are not functioning properly, and when sunlight and surface conditions are constant, all readings can be taken with the sea cell alone.

Conversion As an approximation, lux = 10.76 × foot-candles.

Calibration Curve In full sunlight, clear of shadows, set up photometer and cells, together with a reliable light meter (e.g., Weston illumination meter); and, covering with several (e.g., five) layers of smoothly flattened cheesecloth, take readings of deck and sea cells and reference cell. Remove one layer of cheesecloth at a time, and repeat readings.

An alternative method is to work indoors using floodlight and voltage regulator to vary light intensity.

Plot photometer units on abscissa, ft-c on ordinate, and draw separate curve for each cell.

Coding (for Color of Water) See "Light quality," procedure 22.

Reference Welch (1948: 161).

54. Surveying
See project 6.

55. Temperature
See also "Electronic thermometer," procedure 12.

Take temperature by direct methods, using glass mercury chemical thermometer (with cork attached by long string to help locate if lost in vegetation) or armored thermometer; or by indirect methods, using electronic thermometer, probe (e.g., YSI [Yellow Springs Instrument Co., Yellow Springs, Ohio] oxygen meter), or reversing thermometer mounted on Nansen bottle; or measure temperature of water samples taken by Kemmerer or other samplers.

Precaution Units vary in accuracy as well as in speed of reaching temperature.

*56. **Total filterable residue** (or dissolved solids)*

Procedure Use scrupulously cleaned, and previously dried and cooled (in desiccator) lightweight beaker (e.g., 100-ml) or evaporating dish.

1. Weigh beaker to nearest mg (work rapidly to avoid moisture uptake, and handle with dry metal tongs), and return to desiccator.
2. Filter water samples through a rapid but hard-surfaced ashless filter paper (bottle may be inverted into ring support [Figure 9] low over funnel so that water feeds automatically).
3. To prepared beaker, add measured volume (e.g., 75 ml) of filtered sample selected to yield 25–250 mg of solids.
4. Evaporate over steam bath.
5. Transfer beaker to oven and dry to constant weight (usually overnight) at 103–105°C.
6. Transfer to desiccator, to cool.

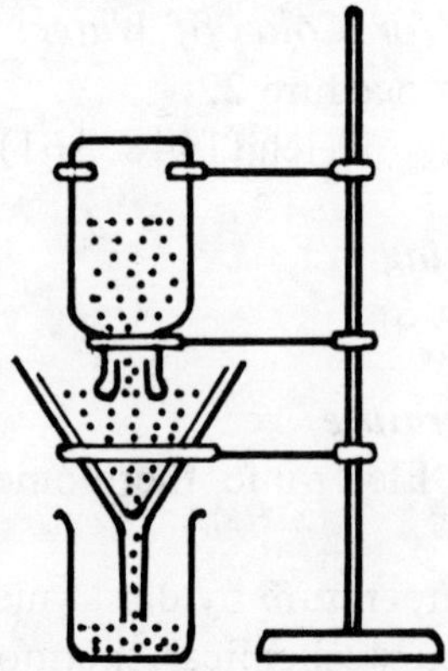

Figure 9. A convenient filtering setup for total filterable residue. Bottle is inverted into funnel, then slipped into open support rings until drained.

7. Reweigh to closest mg.
8. Subtract original weight from final weight for mg of solids.

Calculation

$$R_f = \frac{A \times 1{,}000}{V}$$

where R_f = total filterable residue (mg/liter); A = mg of solids obtained; and V = volume (ml) of water evaporated.

Range Inland fresh water: 10–1,000 mg/liter (APHA, 1965: 245); marine: not reported, incorporated in and approximates the salinity (35 g/liter).

Relation to Conductivity To obtain rough estimate of total filterable residue, measure conductivity (specific conductance), and then:

$$R_e = 0.6 \times C$$

where R_e = estimated total filterable residue (mg/liter); C = specific conductance (μmhos/cm at 25°C); and 0.6 is an approximate average of a variable empirical constant which ranges from below 0.55 with excessive acid or caustic alkali to well over 0.7 with high salinity (APHA, 1965: 37).

Reference APHA (1965: 37, 245).

*57. **Total solids*** (i.e., total dissolved solids) See "Total filterable residue," procedure 56.

*58. **Transect***
See project 3.

*59. **Vegetation***
Analysis procedures vary with nature of plants being sampled. A guide to information is given below.

Benthic macrophytes (macrophytobenthon): see projects 3 and 4.

Benthic algae (microphytobenthon): see "Periphyton analysis," procedure 28.

Plankton (phytoplankton): see "Laboratory procedures" under "Notes," project 5, and "Plankton analysis," procedure 33.

Periphyton (phytoperiphyton): see "Periphyton analysis," procedure 28.

Epibenthic algae (phytoepibenthon): using suction device (e.g., plastic baster), draw up the thin, colored layer that lies just on the surface of the bottom. Process as described for periphyton scrapings, procedure 28.

60. Vegetation analysis, per cent composition

For direct study of vegetation, as might be done by divers, see "Field operations" under "Notes," project 5, and for transect (project 3), for quadrat and biomass (project 4), and for phytosociology (project 8).

For indirect study, where grapnel drag or rough dredging is used, and the area covered cannot be accurately measured and the sampling is incomplete, absolute counts or biomass cannot be determined. Reporting on a 0–5 scale (where 5 is taken as very dense), and possibly on a per cent composition, can provide useful information.

Where sampling is complete, but area is not known, per cent composition is ideal.

1. Sort individuals by species.

2. Count number of individuals of each species; and, if desired, determine wet weight and dry weight of each species.

3. Summate to get total count (and perhaps weights), and calculate per cent composition:

$$\text{per cent} = \frac{\text{amount of one species}}{\text{total amount}} \times 100$$

where "amount" can be the number of shoots or unit of weight.

61. Water color

See "Color," procedure 6.

62. Water samplers

The convenient sampler will depend on conditions of operation—direct, indirect from boat, or by divers.

For direct sampling, wet 250-ml gs (or polyethylene) bottles and fill with water, or take from pail of water scooped from habitat.

For dissolved oxygen, or other gases whose equilibrium may be easily disturbed, use Kemmerer or W-Z sampler. Insert drain hose to bottom of bottle; keeping hose beneath the surface, add water slowly to avoid bubbles, and allow water to overflow one or more times the volume of the bottle.

For indirect sampling on line lowered from boat, use Kemmerer (or other make of) samplers. Nansen bottles are useful with oceanographic conditions.

For divers, a W-Z diver's sampler is ideal. Open both ends, slide the lucite tube through the water to desired place, stopper the ends, and on surfacing fill bottles as described for the direct sampling, above.

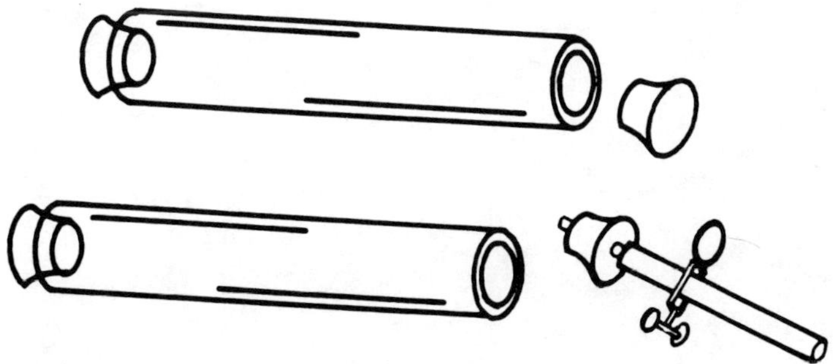

Figure 10. W-Z diver's sampler, and modification for use in obtaining samples for dissolved oxygen. These samplers are lucite cylinders cut from plastic pipe 5 cm in diameter, 4.5 cm bore, and 23 cm long, with no. 9 rubber or cork stoppers. The modification has rubber drain tube attached to short metal tube passing through one stopper, activated by pinchclamp. (*Note:* Because of limited volume of sample, Winkler will need to be run in smaller bottle, e.g., 100-ml gs bottle.)

63. W-Z diver's sampler

For underwater water sampling, as well as for periphyton work, an arrangement devised by the author and D. J. Zinn (ca. 1954) works well. This is simply a large, cylindrical, transparent tube equipped with cork or rubber stoppers. It was later perfected for periphyton (Hargraves and Wood, 1967: 56) (Figure 10). The addition of the drain hose is a further modification here suggested for taking water samples. To use, hold sampler erect, drain tube down. Remove upper stopper, and adjust pinch clamp for desired delivery.

Reference Hargraves and Wood (1967: 56).

PROJECT 6 Morphometry

OBJECTIVE

To prepare a hydrographic chart of a basin, and calculate the important parameters.

METHOD

Preparing a hydrographic chart involves two steps, the surface outline and the depth contours.

To Obtain a Surface Outline

1. Enlarge available surface map (topographic map, hydrographic chart, or aerial photograph):
   a. Pantograph
   b. Photographing, enlarging, tracing
2. In lieu of map, survey with plane table alidade:
   a. For small basin (500 ft or less diameter), use the one-base system, setting up a base point on the shore where the entire shoreline is visible. Have roving assistant carry stadia rod to points around shore. Measure distances by stadia reading (distance in ft = 100 X the part of stadia pole between upper and lower crosshairs seen in telescope); mark direction line on chart from base point toward stations, and indicate distance; and connect all shoreline marks and fill in irregularities of contours by inspection.
   b. For larger basin, use method of intersections. Select or mark (rags, stakes, etc.) stations around periphery. Select two (at least) suitable base points; set up plane table, carefully orient chart (by compass) at one station; draw direction line from base point toward each shoreline marker and to second base point. Send roving assistant to second base station, set up stadia rod, and determine distance in ft by stadia intercepts. Set up plane table at new station, carefully orient chart (by compass), draw direction line from second base point to each shoreline marker and base 1, connect intersecting point for each shoreline marker, and fill in irregularities by inspection. Trace rough chart onto final paper, using a subilluminated drawing box.

To Obtain Depth Contours

Using a recording fathometer on a powered skiff, run at uniform speed along straight transects between shoreline stations on opposite shores. Run boat directly inshore to about 3- to 5-ft depth, then put about (= turn around) and head directly to next site. Write information directly on the fathometer chart, e.g., starts and stops of each transect, transect numbers, base station numbers, and approximate distance from shore that turn is made.

DATA

A. Field data and calculations.
B. Hydrographic chart.
C. Table of parameters (e.g., length, mean breadth, area, volume, circumference, shoreline development, mean slope, area of shoal).

REFERENCES

Davis, R. E., and J. W. Kelly. 1942. Short Course in Surveying. McGraw-Hill, New York. 330 p.

Olson, F. C. W. 1960. Un systéme de morphométrie. Rev. Hydrogr. Int. 37: 151–170.

Reid, G. K. 1961. (See "References" in project 5).

Welch, P. S. 1948. (See "References" in project 4). (See pp. 5–50).

NOTES

Setting Up and Operating Plane Table Alidade

Set up tripod firmly at height so that the drawing board will be convenient for drawing and the alidade can be easily sighted. Screw on drawing board, tightening just snugly (avoid force). Holding alidade, place it in center of board, level the board until the bubbles are approximately centered, and gently lock the set clamps. Align board lengthwise with the basin, slack off on setscrew, perfect the leveling and tighten up setscrews snugly. Draw a north–south line on the chart. (*Caution:* Hold alidade throughout these leveling and orienting steps lest the drawing board tilt, causing the instrument to slip.)

Alidade is focused on subject (surveying rod) with the large knurled ring near the center rear of telescope; the crosshairs are focused with the small ring at the eyepiece; and the tilt of the crosshairs is adjusted by turning the triangular prism housing at the eyepiece.

Align alidade's straight-edged base on the base point, sight to subject, and then draw line from base point along the straight edge.

Recall: Distance, in ft, = 100 × distance (ft) along the stadia rod between the upper and lower stadia lines (crosshairs).

The procedure for making surface map by plane table alidade is outlined in Figure 1.

Soundings with Recording Fathometer

Work on a calm day. Run transects between stations across the width of the basin. Open fathometer housing to have access to chart, and mark each run directly on the chart, indicating transect number, stations joined, and stops and starts. Label chart clearly for later identification.

Connect fathometer to battery, turn on, and move boat into deeper water. If using a portable fathometer, hang transducer over edge with end just under water. When recording begins, vary sensitivity knob to get two distinct lines, the surface and depth lines. If more than one depth line is obtained, reduce sensitivity (to avoid repeated bouncing of soundings between bottom and boat). Nature of bottom is sometimes detectable by the clarity of the line, soft mud giving blurred and hard sediment giving clearer line.

Handling of boat while doing fathometry involves two difficulties, speed of run and turning around. Proper speed must be no faster than that at which accurate, clear soundings can be made (at even moderate speed either bubbles may develop under the sensor or the unit may be swept out of

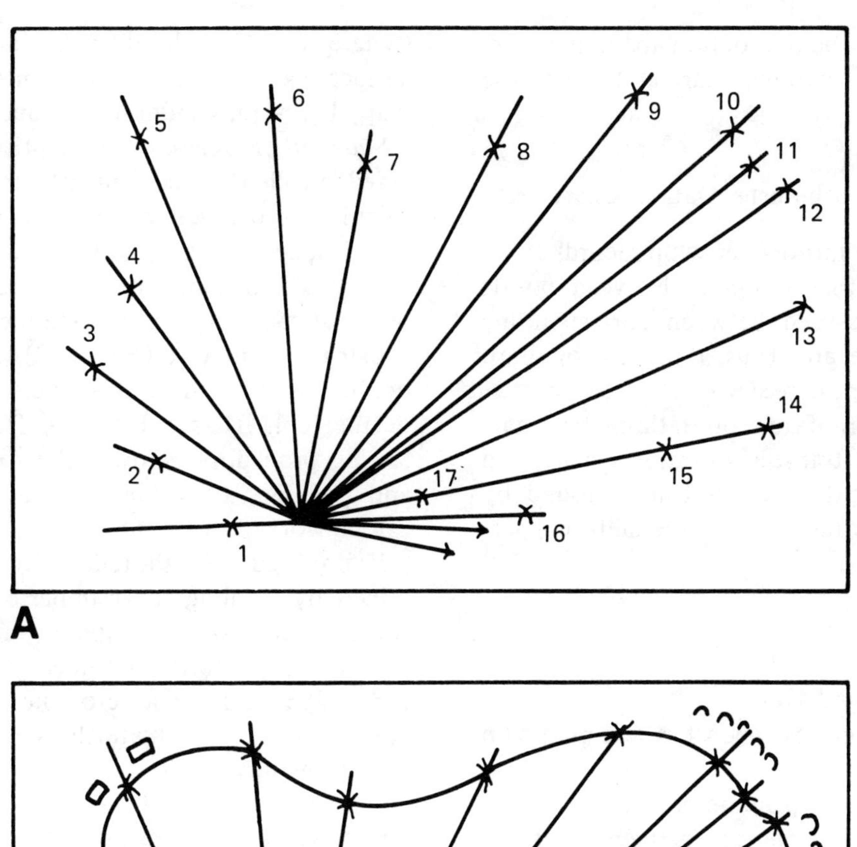

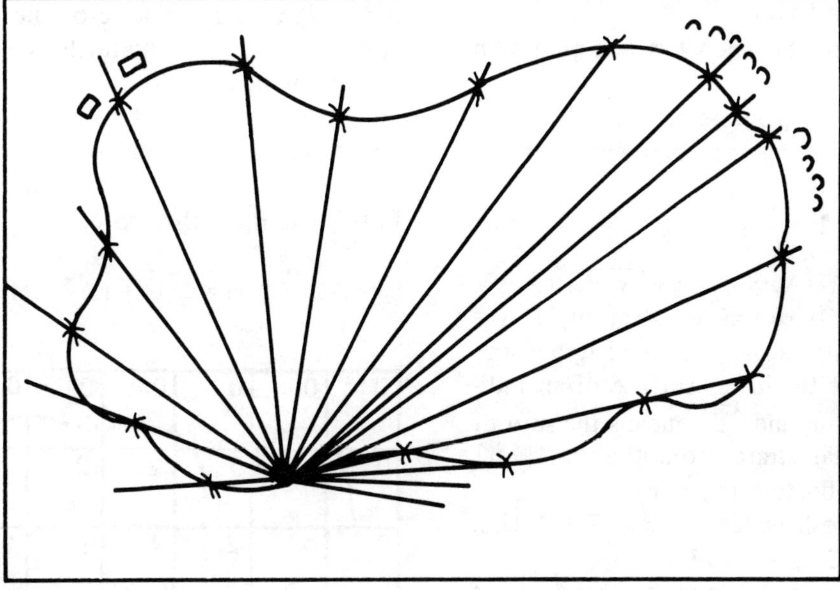

Figure 1. Steps in making surface map by plane table alidade. *A:* Plane table is lined up lengthwise with pond; base point is selected so that pond outline will fit on sheet. A scale is determined, and lines are drawn from the base point toward numbered stations. Distances are measured to each station by stadia and marked on lines. *B:* Shoreline is sketched in and outline is completed. Coastal details (e.g., houses, bluffs) should be added before moving the equipment. If depths are to be charted, keep stations intact.

vertical). A moderate trolling speed is often maximum effective speed.

At the end of each transect, approach shore to within a constant depth (perhaps 4 ft). Estimate (or measure with range finder) distance to shore, mark stopping point on the chart, put boat about smartly, and start next transect marking chart at the starting point.

Transferring Fathometer Data to Chart

Note that the fathometer whip records along an arc and that distances between points must be measured between corresponding points on the arc. Thus, the shape of sharp changes in depth are skewed.

Find length of run on fathometer chart and length of transect on outline chart, and points of depth intervals can be found by proportion (straight slide rule helps convert these directly).

Parameters

Formulas for Lakes

Length: distance between farthest points on shoreline = L

Area: measure by planimeter = A

Breadth: widest point perpendicular to length

Mean breadth: $\bar{b} = \frac{A}{L}$

Volume: $\sum^{1-n} \frac{1}{3}[(A_1 + A_2 + \sqrt{A_1 A_2})h] = V$ (where h = thickness of stratum; 1-n = number of strata; A_1 = area of upper and A_2 = area of the lower surface of an individual stratum; and $\sum^{1-n}$ means the sum of the individual strata from the top [1st] through the bottom [n] one)

Note For fresh water, 1 ft^3 = 7.481 U.S. gal = 3.782 kg = 8.337 lb

Note Volume can be estimated by shortcut method (see below)

Mean depth: $\bar{d} = \frac{V}{A}$

Maximal depth: greatest depth = D_m

Shoreline: (measure with cartometer [map measurer]) = S

Shore development: $SD = \frac{S}{2\sqrt{\pi A}}$

Mean slope: $\bar{S} = \frac{1}{n}(\frac{1}{2}L_0 + L_1 + L_2 + \ldots. L_{n-1} + \frac{1}{2}L_n)\frac{D_m}{A}$

(where L = length of each contour from surface L_0; n = number of contours in the map; D_m = maximum depth; and A = area)

Shortcut Procedure If depths are provided on chart, a convenient procedure for calculating parameters involves preparing a grid (make grid size equal a suitable unit, e.g., 1, 5, 10 ft or miles) and recording the depth at each intersection (see Figure 2).

Using the matrix (Figure 2), record the depth class (col. A) and frequency that each occurs (col. B) (see Table 1). Then, by following procedures shown, the total volume and per cent of volume above each depth can be worked out.

From Figure 2, shoreline (S) can be obtained by totaling the number of times the shoreline crosses the columns (vertical lines) and the rows (horizontal lines). Using a factor, 0.785, and the scale of the chart (here, grid = 2 miles), calculate the shoreline using the following equation:

$$S = 0.785 \times \text{scale} \times \Sigma \text{ changes}$$

In this example, therefore:

$$S = 0.785 \times 2 \text{ mi} \times \Sigma(14 + 13) = 42.4 \text{ mi}$$

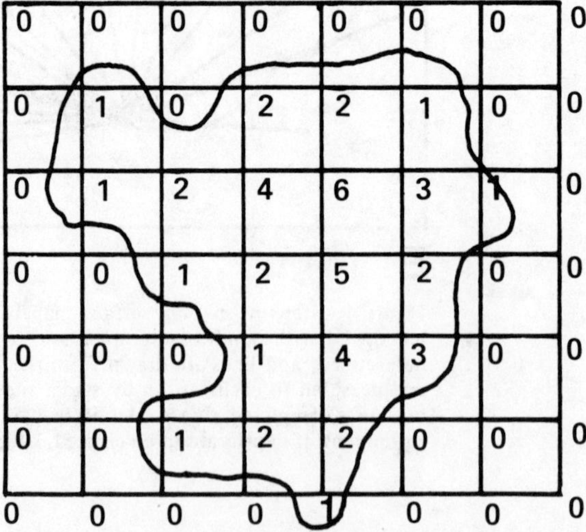

Figure 2. For a shortcut approximation of certain basin parameters, overlay hydrographic chart with transparent sheet with grid and record depths at intersections. Ignore outlying zeros in computation. Grid is 2 miles on a side.

Table 1. Tabulation and computation for a shortcut method of approximating certain basin parameters[a]

A	B	C	D	E	F	G	H	I
Depths	Frequency	A × B	B × a	C × a × 5,280²	ΣD	ΣE	% F	% G
1	8	8	32	8.92×10^8	32	8.92×10^8	38.1	16.7
2	7	14	28	16.73×10^8	60	25.65×10^8	71.4	47.9
3	2	6	8	6.69×10^8	68	32.34×10^8	80.1	60.4
4	2	8	8	8.92×10^8	76	41.26×10^8	90.5	77.1
5	1	5	4	5.58×10^8	80	46.84×10^8	95.2	87.5
6	1	6	4	6.69×10^8	84	53.53×10^8	100.0	100.0

[a]Data from Figure 1. *Directions:* Enter depths serially in col. A, tabulate frequency of each depth in col. B, and record product (A × B) in col. C; then, multiply B by a constant "a" (= area of each grid [here, 4 miles²]) and multiply C by "a" and by conversion factor (5,280²) to convert square miles to square ft. *Results:* Total area (last entry in col. F[84]) and that above each depth (col. F), total volume (last entry in col. G [53.53×10^8]) and that above each depth (col. G), % area above each depth (col. H) and % volume above each depth (col. I).

For mean slope, record in sequence from the upper left corner (Figure 2) the changes that occur in depth, recording first those in rows (horizontally) and then those in columns (vertically), as shown below. Divide the total number of ft by the number of changes.

Rows	Columns
1 1 2 0 1 1	1 0 1
1 1 2 2 3 2 1	2 1 1 1 1
1 1 3 3 2	2 2 2 1 1 2
1 3 1 3	2 4 1 1 2 1
1 1 0 2	1 2 1 1 3
1 1	1 1
42 ft in 28 changes	39 ft in 27 changes

$$\frac{42 + 39 \text{ ft}}{28 + 27 \text{ changes}} = \frac{81 \text{ ft}}{55 \text{ changes}} = 1.47 \text{ ft/2-mile step}$$

Mean slope = 0.735 ft/mile

Reference Saila, S. B. (pers. comm.; sheets issued for limnology course, Univ. R.I., after Olson, 1960).

Lead Line Throw ahead of boat, taking sounding as line becomes vertical. Bottom material often sticks to lead, giving evidence of substrate type. For deep water, use heavier lead and do not haul up between soundings (Ref.: Welch, 1948: 25).

Pantograph Lay out work on large drawing board or wood surface. Set intersecting arms to proper enlargement fraction at all four junctions. Tack down the support. Run pointer carefully along drawing; and, holding pencil down, gently sketch enlargement onto drawing paper.

Polar Planimeter See "Notes," project 4.

Range Finder Set up in advance, or select, a structure of known height such that it will be within range of operation of range finder (e.g., 0.5–6 ft at 35 yd, 1–10 ft at 50 yd, 29 ft at 1 mile); then, peering through eyepiece, turn dial on back until two images of the structure appear. Adjust until one is exactly above the other (no overlap); then read distance in yards or miles (n = nautical, s = statute) on scale, inserting decimal in the number where it obviously must be. See also "Range finder," in "Notes," project 5a.

Recording Fathometer See "Soundings with recording fathometer," above.

PROJECT 7 Vegetation of Polluted Waters

OBJECTIVE

To examine river for evidence of pollution and extent of the effects of wastes on vegetation and the use of vegetation. (*Note:* Pollution may be defined as additives which affect the intended use of the water.)

METHOD

1. Work your way from the source to the mouth of a river, or from one falls or ripple zone to the next, and record evidence of wastes or effects of pollution in terms of appearance of water, odor, and state of vegetation (emergent, floating, and submerged).
2. From the outfall point of suspected pollutant, working downstream, subdivide the stream into pollution zones (Table 1) (Ref.: Fjerdingstad, 1964 or 1962), and establish the approximate location of the beginning and end of each.
3. In each zone, examine the flora and vegetation of the benthon, neuston, periphyton, and plankton.
4. In each zone, measure important physical-chemical factors (especially temperature, total filterable residue, conductivity, pH, alkalinity, dissolved oxygen and its saturation, and possibly others such as phosphates, nitrates, and BOD).
5. In each zone, test for evidence of human sewage by the coliform count (cells/100 ml).
6. In an industrial area, a chemist of the company may be willing to provide analyses for suspected ions such as chromium, cop-

Table 1. Pollution zones of flowing water habitats

Terms	Synonyms	Vegetation
Zone of clean water	Caprozoic	(Green plants)
Zone of recent pollution (active decomposition or septic zone)	Polysaprobic	(No green plants)
Recovery zone (zone of strong pollution)	alpha Mesosaprobic	(Some surface algae)
Recovery zone (zone of mild pollution)	beta Mesosaprobic	(Some higher plants and surface algae)
Zone of clean water	Oligosaprobic	(Green plants)
Zone of water never polluted	Katharobic	(Green plants)

per, iron, zinc, and for such items as nonbiodegradable or biodegradable detergents. The upper limits of tolerance permitted for such ions has been set by the government (FWPCA, 1968). Refer to those values, if needed.

7. In reactor areas, obtain samples for and run counts for radioactivity (e.g., strontium 90).

DATA

A. Tabulate data (physical-chemical factors), tests for sewage (coliforms), suspected ions, radiation, etc., and flora (fauna) in each pollution zone.

B. Prepare a report covering:
   1. Source of pollution
   2. Nature and degree of pollutants (e.g., biological, chemical, thermal, radioactive, etc.)
   3. Effects on plants in the ecosystem
   4. Effect on other uses because of effects on green plants
   5. Possible use of plants or plant associations to indicate degree of the pollutant

REFERENCES

APHA. 1965. (See "References" in project 5).

Edmondson, W. T. (ed.) 1959. Fresh-water Biology. 2nd ed. (H. B. Ward and G. C. Whipple, eds., lst ed.) John Wiley & Sons, New York. 1248 p.

Fjerdingstad, E. 1962. Some remarks on a new saprobic system. *In* C. M. Tarzwell (ed.), Biological problems in water pollution, pp. 232–235. Third seminar. U.S. Dept. Health, Education and Welfare, Publ. Health Serv. Pub. No. 999-WP-25. 424 p.

Fjerdingstad, E. 1964. Pollution of streams estimated by benthal phytomicro-organisms. I. A saprobic system based on communities of organisms and ecological factors. Int. Rev. Hydrobiol. 49: 63–131.

FWPCA (Federal Water Pollution Control Administration). 1968. Water quality criteria. Report of the National Technical Advisory Committee to the Secretary of the Interior. Supt. of Doc., Washington, D.C. 234 p.

Gaufin, A. R., and C. M. Tarzwell. 1956. Aquatic macroinvertebrate communities as indicators of organic pollution in Lytle Creek. Sewage Indust. Wastes 28(7): 906–924.

IBP. 1969. (See "References" in project 5a).

Mackenthun, K. M. 1969. The practice of water pollution biology. U.S. Dept. Interior, Federal Water Pollution Control Administration. (Available from Supt. of Doc., Washington, D.C.). 281 p.

Millipore Corp. 1968. Microbiological analysis of water. Application Rep. AR-81. (Cat. No. LTARO81 BA). Bedford, Mass. 24 p.

Needham, J. G., and P. R. Needham. 1962. Guide to the study of fresh-water biology. Comstock Publ. Assoc., Ithaca, N.Y. 108 p.

Palmer, C. M. 1959. Algae in water supplies. Pub. 657. U.S. Publ. Health Service, Washington, D.C. 88 p.

NOTES

Vegetation

The vegetation typical of each pollution zone should be characterized by the species that are fixed in place, such as the rooted emergents, submerged, submerged trailing, or turf-forming benthic species. These might include, respectively, *Sagittaria, Callitriche, Potamogeton,* and *Eleocharis* or bryophytes such as *Fontinalis.* In addition, periphytic algae attached to these plants or to inanimate structures should be examined in terms of the species present and the relative abundance of each. By contrast, floating forms, such as unattached flowering plants or plankton, are less useful in streams than in pond work because they do not represent species capable of surviving existing conditions over periods of time as do the attached species and periphyton.

Table 2 lists species in our area which seem valuable as pollution indicators. The species are listed by the degree of pollution they can tolerate well.

Note In addition to the vegetation, invertebrates provide an excellent, and in fact the original (Gaufin and Tarzwell, 1956) criteria for pollution zones worked out for American streams. For a further listing, see Mackenthun (1969: 13).

Petrochemicals and Heavy Metals

Certainly, important polluters like petrochemicals and heavy metals should be investigated where pollution from industrial sources is indicated. New tests are currently being developed, and standard procedures generally require specialized laboratory facilities beyond the scope of the usual ecological laboratory. For this work, the cooperation of specialists is suggested. Some techniques are available in the handbooks by APHA (1965) and by IBP (1969).

Autoclave

Details for operation of one common type of laboratory autoclave follows.

Advanced preparations:

1. *Clean drain plug screen* at bottom of chamber, eliminating lint and sediment from the pores (*daily*).
2. Turn on exhaust faucet (at bottom) and *drain off water,* closing faucet as exhaust becomes predominantly steam.
3. *Turn "steam supply" valve* (lower valve in front between legs) on full.

Sterilizing:

4. *Open door* (spin wheel to left, thus disengaging locking bars), and pull door open.
5. *Prepare items for sterilizing,* and put into chamber.
   a. Keep items near front (for ease in removing).
   b. Remove lids of bottles, stoppers of flasks (or leave loose).
   c. Open pipet cassette (or leave vent open).
6. *Close door* (seating firmly against chamber, and turning dial to right, making sure that locking bars seat completely beneath the rim). Turn tight.
7. *Set timer* (usually 20 min).
8. *Set type of exhaust* (slow exhaust for

Table 2. Northeast species that are valuable as pollution indicators, arranged by the most contamination they tolerate

	Clean Water	Polluted Water	
		Mild	Strong
Angiosperms	Many species	*Callitriche*	*Sparganium*
		Eleocharis	*Typha latifolia*
		Pontederia	
		Potamogeton	
		Sagittaria	
Bryophytes	*Scapania*		*Fontinalis*
Charophytes	Most species	*Nitella flexilis*	
Periphytic algae	*Cladophora*	*Chlorella*	*Stigeoclonium*
	Ulothrix	*Chlamydomonas*	*Phormidium*
	Navicula	*Oscillatoria*	*Tabellaria*
		Mougeotia	*Fragilaria*
		Eunotia	*Schizothrix*
Surface "scum"	*Spirogyra*	*Mougeotia*	*Mougeotia*
Fungi			*Sphaerotilus*

cotton-plugged tubes and flasks; fast and dry for glassware, etc.).

9. If jacket pressure (right meter) indicates pressure of 17 (16) lb/in^2 has been reached (the pressurizing sound changes), *turn central knob* from *off* to *ster*(ilize).

Automatic cycling will follow. After the indicated time, the pressure will drop; the load is ready, and a buzzer will sound. Be ready to turn it off. (*Note:* During exhaust, a negative pressure exists.)

Time required for operation once action is initiated is about 20 min for sterilization and an additional 15 min for "dry." Therefore, *be ready to turn off buzzer* after 20 or 35 min from starting time.

10. When buzzer sounds, *turn main dial up to off* (buzzer will stop).

11. With asbestos gloves, or working very rapidly, *insert stoppers* in flasks and bottles, and close cassettes.

12. With asbestos gloves, *remove items* onto the table to cool.

13. When cool, seat stoppers and plugs to normal fit.

Closing up:

14. *Turn off "steam supply" valve,* lower valve in front, below chamber.

Reference See instruction sheet with autoclave.

BOD (Biochemical Oxygen Demand)

BOD is a test involving putting water sample in special 250–300-ml gs bottles, aerating the sample, inoculating with a "seed" of vigorous heterotrophic bacteria acclimated to the water, and after 5 days analyzing for dissolved oxygen. The mg of O_2/liter below saturation is the BOD. It is sometimes interpreted as a measure of organic matter.

For details of this somewhat involved procedure, which is more easily handled in microbiological facilities, see APHA (1965: 415).

Range 0 in totally oligotrophic (devoid of organic matter) waters, while 540–2,220+ where reported for the Toledo Harbor, Environmental Impact Statement, October 1972, with a mean of 1,500.

Coliform Count (Density)

Time required: ca. 2 hr first day and 10 min second day

Equipment Alcohol lamp, autoclave, binocular microscope, cassette (for sterile pipets), filter holder, special Millipore forceps, hot plate or burner, plastic Petri dishes, vacuum pump (Millipore), glass boiling beads, autoclave packaging of 47-mm filter with pads, tongs.

Chemicals 95% ethanol, potassium monohydrogen phosphate, MF-Endo broth (dehydrated).

Reagents

1. *Buffer stock solution* (stable): in 500-ml vol. flask add some dist. water, dissolve 34 g of K_2HPO_4, and dil. to 500 ml with dist. water.

2. *Buffer (diluting) solution*[1] (make up and sterilize as needed): into 1,000-ml vol. flask, using 5-ml grad. pipet, add 1.25 ml of buffer stock solution (sol. 1); mix, and dil. to 1,000 ml with dist. water.

3. *Broth* (MF-Endo broth)[1] (remake within 5 days, resterilize before use, and store in refrigerator): into 125-ml Erlenmeyer flask with cork stopper, add 49 ml of dist. water and 2.4 g of MF-Endo broth, 1 ml of 95% ethanol, and 3 boiling beads. With cork loose in flask, heat cautiously (to avoid initial foaming) on hot plate until boiling, and boil rapidly for just 3 min; then remove and stopper.

Procedure

Advanced preparations:

1. *Have equipment sterilized.*
    a. Collecting bottles, 250-ml gs bottles (with lids off, autoclave at 15

[1] Make up as needed.

lb/in^2 for 20 min. Replace stoppers after autoclaving).
b. Filtering unit (close both ends with aluminum foil, and autoclave [cf. step a]).
c. Pipets (assorted sizes, 1, 5, 10): place in cassette; and, leaving lid off or vented, autoclave (15 lb/in^2 for 20 min), and when cool, replace cover.
d. Autoclave package of Millipore filters (at 15 lb/in^2 for 20 min; note that label turns from black to green).
e. Autoclave test tubes for diluting fluid.

2. *Make up buffer* (sol. 2): in 1,000-ml vol. flask put *1.25 ml of buffer stock solution* (sol. 1); mix, and *dil. to 1,000 ml* with dist. water; and *autoclave* in units of 500 ml as working solution.
3. *Make up broth* (sol. 3).
4. *Determine volume* of volumes *required* to give counts of 20–200 colonies (see "Predetermining density range," below).
5. *Collect water samples* in sterile 250-ml gs bottles, inserting bottle neck down, then inverting to fill.

Analysis:

6. *Set out sufficient sterile Petri dishes* for one per sample and per dilution, and loosen cover.
7. *Prepare broth* (bring broth [sol. 3 and step 3] just to boil).
8. *Sterilize forceps* by dipping tips into ethanol, flaming, and letting flame burn out.
9. *Transfer pad from package to Petri dish,* one pad per dish. *Cover promptly.*
10. With sterile 10-ml pipet, *deliver 1.7–2 ml of broth onto each pad* (opening Petri dish carefully with one hand, using fingernail to pry). Cover promptly.
11. *Assemble filtering unit,* connecting a rubber tubing from pump to trap, and one from trap to filtering flask, and insert filtering unit in filtering flask.
12. Using sterile technique, and sterile forceps (step 8, above), carefully *place a gridded 47-mm, 0.8-μ pore Millipore filter onto the ground glass* by letting down one edge first and then slowly lowering rest onto support so as to avoid bubbles.
13. *Filter required volume of sample* (volume determined by prior run [see "Predetermining density range," below], the size ranges from 0.5 to 200 ml).
14. *Rinse with suitable volume of buffer* diluting solution (sol. 2), according to the schedule in Table 3.

Note Pour rinsing fluid around sides of funnel to ensure good washing.

15. Unlock apparatus and *remove filter with forceps.*
16. *Transfer filter onto pad* in Petri dish, lowering one side first, then cautiously rolling out filter so as to avoid bubble formation.
17. *Cover Petri dish* immediately.
18. *Label* with date, station, volume filtered.
19. *Incubate 18–24 hrs, upside down,* at 35 ± 0.1°C.

Table 3. Rinsing schedule to be followed in the coliform counting procedure for indicated sample size

Sample used (ml)	Vol. of buffer	Vol. of rinse (ml)	Technique
0.5	10 ml	100	Mix in sterile test tube, and filter
1	10 ml	100	Mix in sterile test tube, and filter
10	Direct	100	Add direct to filter
100, 200	Direct	200	Add direct to filter

Count next day:

20. *Open Petri dish,* remove filter, and dry for 1 hr on absorbent paper; then cover with 2 X 3-in. glass slides (hinged), and place on stage of *binocular microscope* at 10X.

21. Using 10X binocular microscope with overhead light, *count colonies showing metallic green sheen.*

Closing steps:

22. Wash funnel and filtering flask with hot water; then dry, inverted, on paper towel.

23. Rinse pipets with hot water, air dry, return to cassette, sterilize (step 1-c).

24. Remove filter from Petri dish, air dry under a weight, and mount in photo album under plastic cover.

25. Sterilize and discard Petri dishes—or, wash in alcohol (after removing paper) and air dry.

Calculation

$$C = N \times \frac{100}{V}$$

where C = coliform count/100-ml sample; N = number of colonies counted; and V = volume (in ml) of sample filtered.

Ranges Inland waters: 0–10,000; marine: 0–10,000 are common.

Predetermining Density Range Since a concentration to give 20–200 colonies per plate is needed, determine what volume of sample will do this:

1. Follow preparatory procedure (steps 1–12, above) for five samples.
2. In addition, set out two sterile test tubes.
3. Pipet a graded volume of sample, 0.5 ml into one tube and 1.0 ml into the other.
4. Add 10 ml of buffer diluting solution (sol. 2) to each test tube; mix.
5. Filter each, then rinse with 10 ml of buffer, and transfer filter to pad in Petri dish (steps 15–19, above).
6. Similarly, filter 10-, 100-, and 200-ml samples, rinsing with 200 ml of buffer each.
7. For each, transfer filter to pad in Petri dish (steps 15–19, above).
8. Incubate and count (steps 18–21, above).
9. Select volume which gives ca. 100 cells/plate, or those volumes which will produce at least one sample in 20–200-cell/100-ml range.

Standards These vary in different states, but an example is: drinking water (not more than 1 cell/100 ml); shell fishing (not over 200 cells/100 ml); swimming (not over 800 cells/100 ml).

PROJECT 8 Vegetation Analysis, Phytosociology

OBJECTIVE

To describe vegetation of region by phytosociological technique (e.g., tidal salt marsh).

METHOD

Field Work

1. Examine vegetation, noting distinct areas of uniform plant life (stands, or possible associations) and the lines or zones of separation (tension zone or ecotone).

2. List tentative associations, naming them on basis of most obvious species (to be changed later).

3. Determine minimum size of quadrat for a given association by setting out a 1-m^2 quadrat in a typical stand; then, beginning at one corner with a small (1-dm^2) quadrat, count number of species which occur; then, increasing quadrat size stepwise (by increasing length of side 1 dm at a time), count number of species at each size. Plot graph with area on abscissa and number of species on ordinate (Figure 1). Area above the size of onset of the plateau is adequate.

4. Lay out a series (ca. 10) of sufficiently large quadrats (e.g., ca. 1-m^2, but see step 3) in each association, and fill out association table: a) giving estimated per cent cover, b) giving list of species, c) grading each species on a 0,+,1–5 basis for abundance and on a 1–5 basis for sociability, separating the two by a period (e.g., +0.2 means a trace of the species, in small groups). (*Note:* An alternate method would be to lay transect perpendicular to associations, and make a series of quadrats in each association.)

5. It is desirable to prepare life form diagrams of each association now from direct

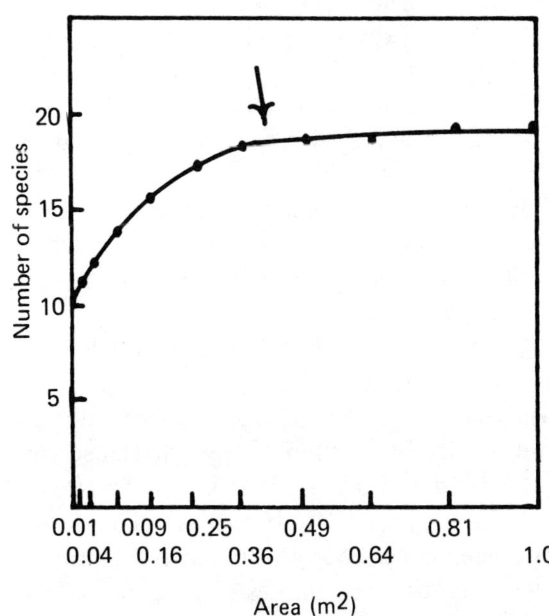

Figure 1. Species-area curve as used in phytosociology for determining minimum satisfactory quadrat size for a particular vegetation.

observation. (For quantitative work, use carefully measured quadrat, count number of shoots of each species/m^2, harvest, and obtain wet and dry weight; determine organic matter by obtaining ash weight.)

Important environmental measures are: a) to survey relative altitude of the upper and lower limits of each association, b) to take soil/sediment sample of each association for mechanical analysis, and c) to measure certain physical-chemical factors of the open water, such as temperature, pH, salinity, dissolved oxygen.

Laboratory Work

1. Prepare synthetic table compiling the data (averaged for each locality) for all the stands of an association, and determine constancy on a I–V basis.
2. Determine fidelity of the species, preferably ones with highest constancy.
3. Taking the one (or two) species with highest constancy and fidelity[1] as the characteristic species, rename the association (from tentative one given in the field):
   a. Add *-etum* to the root of the genus name.
   b. Express species epithet in the genitive.
   c. For combined names, end first genus with *-eto*, and link names with a hyphen.

For example, the *Spartina alterniflora* association becomes *Spartinetum alterniflorae,* while the *Bangia-Ulothrix* community becomes *Bangieto-Ulothricetum.*

4. Check to see if the association has already been described and named; and, if so, use that name (and cite reference), such as the works by Chapman (1960), Dansereau (1959), den Hartog (1959), Gehu (1961), and Tansley (1939). If the association has not been described, you may need to do it.

(If quantitative samples of plant materials, sediment, or water have been taken, complete the analyses.)

DATA

A. Phytosociological association table for each association, complete with legend. Note that the floristic list is included in table.
B. Table of quantitative data for each association, e.g., harvest, density, biomass, sediment analysis, altitude.
C. Alphabetical list of associations together with reference indicating source of basic description.
D. Summary table indicating the vegetation of the area by showing: a) distribution of the associations, and b) their relationship to various measured factors.
E. Life form diagrams of each association.
F. Voucher specimens.

REFERENCES

Braun-Blanquet, J. 1932. Plant Sociology. McGraw-Hill, New York. 439 p.

Chapman, V. J. 1960. Salt Marshes and Salt Deserts of the World. Interscience, New York. 392 p.

Coast & Geodetic Survey. Hydrographic charts. (Available from local agents).

Coast & Geodetic Survey. 1968. Surface Water Temperatures and Densities, Atlantic Coast, North and South America. 3rd ed. U.S. Coast & Geodetic Survey, Environmental Science Service Admin. Pub. 31-1. Supt. of Doc., Washington, D.C. 102 p. (See pp. 101, 102 for density-salinity conversion graph).

Dahl, E. 1960. Some measures of uniformity in vegetation analysis. Ecology 41: 805–808.

Dansereau, P. 1959. Phytogeographia Laurentiana. II. The principle plant asso-

[1] Other systems of phytosociology may use the dominant, or the most abundant, species for naming.

ciations of the Saint Lawrence Valley. Inst. Bot. Univ. Montréal, Montreal. 147 p.

Gehu, J. 1961. Les groupements végétaux du Bassins de la Sambre Française. Veg. Act. Geobot. 10(2-6): 69–372.

Goodall, D. W. 1952. Quantitative aspects of plant distribution. Bot. Rev. 27: 194–245.

Harvey, H. W. 1945. Recent Advances in the Chemistry and Biology of Sea Water. Cambridge Univ. Press, London. 164 p.

Knudsen, M. 1901. Hydrographical tables. (Reprinted as "The determination of chlorinity by the Knudsen method." Woods Hole Oceanographic Institute, Woods Hole, Mass. 63 p., 1946).

Miller, W. R., and F. E. Egler. 1950. Vegetation of the Wequetequock-Pawcatuck tidal marshes, Connecticut. Ecol. Monogr. 20: 141–173.

Stearn, W. T. 1966. (See "References" in project 2).

Strickland, J. D. H., and T. R. Parsons. 1968. (See "References" in project 5).

Taniguti, M. 1962. Phytosociological study of marine algae in Japan. Inoue & Co., Ltd., Tokyo. 129 p.

Tansley, A. G. 1939. (See "References" in project 3).

U.S. Coast & Geodetic Survey. 1968. (See Coast & Geodetic Survey, above).

Weaver, J. E., and F. E. Clements. 1938. Plant Ecology. 2nd ed. McGraw-Hill, New York. 601 p.

NOTES

Surveying Altitudes with Dumpy Level

Preparations:

1. Select spot for level within 100 ft from bench mark and from area to be surveyed.
2. Attach level loosely to the top of tripod.
3. Spread legs of tripod, seat firmly, adjust so that top is practically level, and tighten leg clamps.
4. Level the telescope by aligning scope with two opposite of the four leveling screws; then, screwing these two screws simultaneously in the same direction, cause the bubble to center.
5. Align telescope with the other two screws, and similarly center the bubble, and lightly tighten the screws.
6. Repeat steps 4 and 5 until no further adjustment is needed; then tighten screws snugly.

Surveying altitude difference:

7. Have surveying rod moved to bench mark, and stand rod on bench mark.
8. From level, sight to rod, and record exact position the crosshair crosses rod, reading to nearest decimal and estimating final decimal with vernier on target plate. Adding this value to known value of bench mark will give altitude of the telescope.
9. Move rod to upper or lower edge of association (or other object to be measured), and obtain similar reading, and similarly calculate altitude of the new object.
10. If the pole is not tall enough, extend pole. If object is too high, then determine altitude of an intermediate height object, move level to higher area, and readjust; again make sighting on rod and determine altitude of level; and, in turn, measure altitude of desired object (see Figure 2).

Association Chart (Table)

The association chart is made up in field according to instructions on chart (see Figure 3).

The entries for the association chart are % cover, estimated to closest 10%; abundance on a 1–5 basis, where 1 = very sparse, 2 = sparse, 3 = infrequent, 4 = abundant, 5 = very abundant; sociability, or grouping, on a 1–5 basis, where 1 = occurs singly, 2 = in tufts, 3 = in patches, 4 = extensive patches, 5 = continuous over area; and constancy on a I–V basis, where I = occurs in 1–20% of the

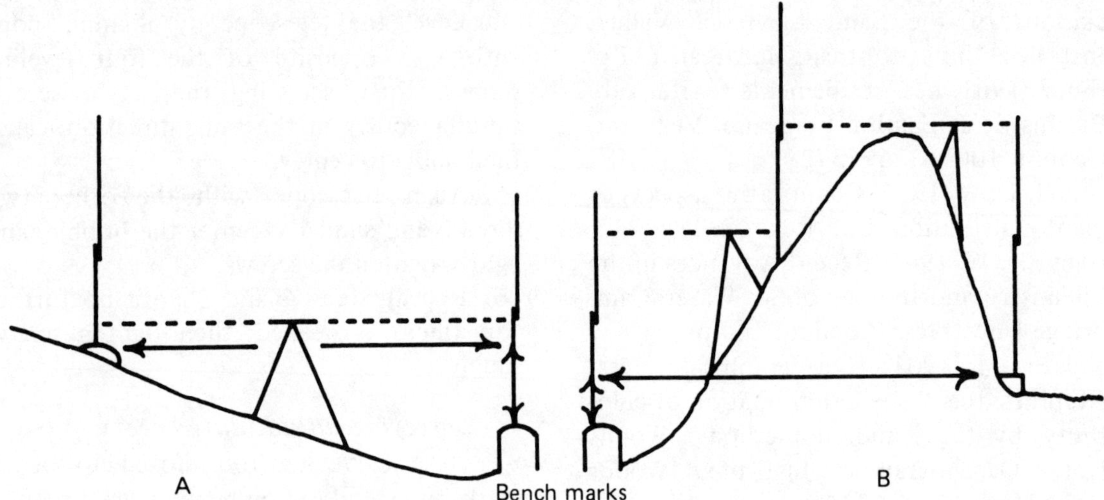

Figure 2. Surveying altitudes with dumpy level. *A* (to find altitude of object from bench mark): From bench mark of known altitude, read rod to find height of level, and subtract reading on object. *B* (to find altitude of object obscured from view [e.g., by ridge]): From known bench mark find height of level, move rod and establish height of ground at new station, move tripod and sight back to establish new altitude of level. Then, sight forward to new rod setting on final object. Add increments in altitude, and subtract decrement to find altitude of final object.

stands, II = in 20–40%, III = in 40–60%, IV = in 60–80%, and V = in 80–100% of the stands.

Note For a more complex association, the species may be listed in groups, such as herbaceous, seedling, moss layer, epiphytes, etc. (Braun-Blanquet, 1932: 69).

Association Chart, an Alternative Method

Taniguti's (1962) phytosociological charts differ from the classical one by emphasizing an environmental factor, in this case, altitude. A 10-cm grid, 50 cm wide and as high as needed, is adjusted to datum, as determined by predicted tide values; and species dominance is evaluated on a +, 1–5 scale, at each intersection (Table 1).

Phytosociological Terms

Abundance, plentifulness of a species and

Zosteretum marinae

Stand examined	1	2	3	4	5	6	7	8	9	10	Constancy class
Zostera marina	1.1	1.1	1.2	+.2	0.0	1.1	1.1	0.0	+.1	+.1	IV
Fucus vesiculosus	1.2	0.0	+.2	2.2	0.0	0.0	+.1	0.0	0.0	0.0	II

Legend

Stand data:

1. Mud flat, Bluffhill Cove, Pt. Judith, R.I., sandy mud, nearly flat, ca. 0.5 ft above datum, low tide, 67 ft WNW of drain outlet.
2. ibid., 50 ft W of stand 1.
3. ibid., 50 ft W of stand 2.

Figure 3. Sample association chart, as partly filled out in the field.

Table 1. Sample vegetation-altitude gradient table as used by Taniguti (1962: 24) for phytosociological analysis[a]

	(cm) =	0	50	100	150
Gloiopeltis furcata				1 1 1 +	
Myelophycus caespitosus			1	+	
Ishige okamurai			+	+	
Hizikia fusiforme			1 3 4 3	+	
Caulacanthus okamurai			+ + +	1	
Gigartina intermedia		1	2 1 + + 1		
Chondrus ocellatus		+ + 1 3	3 2 +		
Laurencia sp.		+ + 1 +			
Sargassum hemiphyllum		1 5 5 3 +			
Carpopeltis angusta		+			
Gelidium japonicum	+	1			
Sargassum ringgoldianum	1 1 1	+			
Eisenia bicyclis	5 5 3	1			

[a]Height might preferably be on vertical axis.

compactness of spacing on a +, 1–5 basis;–accidental species, species of very low fidelity, of 1, occurring sporadically;–association, plant community of definite floristic composition (note subassociation, and facies);–characteristic species, one of high fidelity, 3–5, and occurring almost exclusively in one association;–companion species, one of low fidelity, 2, occurring commonly with one and another association;–constancy, same as presence but is applied to a few limited stands;–cover, per cent of area covered by a species;–facies, a variation of an association having different relative densities of the same species;–fidelity, degree to which a species occurs in one association and not in others, on 1–5 basis where 3–5 are characteristic species, 2 are companion, and 1 is accidental species (see Braun-Blanquet [1932] for details);–presence, degree of persistence of a species in an association, in steps of 20% (comparable to constancy);–stand, segment of an association;–subassociation, a variation of an association with a distinctive characteristic species.

Quantitative Phytosociology

The original descriptive intent of phytosociology has been increasingly modified by occasional workers, and subjected to more mathematical interpretation (e.g., Goodall, 1952; Dahl, 1960).

Quantitative Quadrat

See project 4.

Salinity

Titrimetric method
(Time required: ca. 10 min)

Chemicals Potassium chromate, silver nitrate, standard seawater.

Reagents

1. *Potassium chromate indicator* (8 g of K_2CrO_4/100 ml of dist. water).
2. *Silver nitrate standard solution* (27.25 g of $AgNO_3$/liter of dist. water) (store in dark bottle).
3. *Standard seawater* (obtain from Copenhagen, or Woods Hole, suppliers).
4. *Substandard seawater* (collect clean seawater off shore).

Procedure

1. With 10-ml vol. pipet, transfer 10 ml of sample into evaporating dish (or wide-mouthed flask).
2. Add 6 drops of chromate indicator (sol. 1).

3. Titrate with silver nitrate standard solution (sol. 2), stirring continuously to break up the curd, titrating rapidly to first deep red flash lasting 10 sec.

4. Record volume titrated.

5. Repeat titration using substandard seawater of known chlorinity (i.e., previously titrated against standard seawater).

6. Rinse out carefully, and rinse silver nitrate from buret as soon as practical.

Calculation

$$C_u = \frac{V_u}{V_s} C_s$$

where C_u = chlorinity of unknown; V_u = volume required to titrate unknown; V_s = volume to titrate standard; and C_s = chlorinity of standard.

Convert chlorinity to salinity using Knudsen's (1901) tables or by the formula ($S = [1.805 \times Cl] + 0.03$).

Ranges Inland waters: not measured by this method, nor expressed in these units[2]; marine: 33–37 (5–40) ⁰/oo (Sverdrup, Johnson, and Fleming, 1942: 55).

Reference

Harvey (1945). Note that Strickland and Parsons (1968) give different values, especially a larger volume of a weaker chromate solution.

Salinity, by Salinometer

Using kit, or having available hydrometers of the ranges 1.000–1.010, 1.011–1.020, and 1.021–1.035, and a thermometer and cylinder:

1. Nearly fill cylinder with sample water.

2. Select hydrometer which matches the density of the water (use lower specific gravity salinometers first).

3. Gradually lower it by the stem into the sample, and read specific gravity at bottom of meniscus.

4. Measure water temperature.

5. With USC&G (1968) graph, convert the specific gravity to specific gravity at 15°C.

6. Use Knudsen's (1901) tables, or those in Strickland and Parsons (1968), to convert specific gravity to salinity.

7. Wash glassware.

Sediment Core

Force plastic or lucite tube into sediment, insert stopper into top, withdraw tube smoothly and plug both ends. Later, push out core, section crosswise to obtain desired parts, and study.

Sediment Moisture Content

Carefully weigh out sample of fresh sediment, place in preweighed pan, drain off excess water; dry at 105°F, cool, and reweigh; calculate % moisture loss of the original sediment weight.

Sediment Organic Content (Approximate)

Dry, pulverize, and mix sediment sample (cf. sediment mechanical analysis, project 4), place 0.5–1 g of sample in predried (in desiccator) and preweighed crucible, cover leaving a slight gap, combust in muffle furnace at 550°C for 6 hrs; cool, dry in desiccator, reweigh, and calculate % organic matter (loss in weight) of the original sample.

Synthetic Table

This table represents a synthesis of information about one association through its range

---

[2] Salinity for inland waters is considered the total ionic constituents expressed in mg or meq/liter (Hutchinson, 1957: 553), and involves largely chlorides, sulfates, carbonates, and possibly borates. Inland waters are usually measured by conductivity, and converted to salinity (1.c., p. 558), where in carbonate waters the conductivity (micromhos at 20°C) is usually 1.6 to 1.9 times greater than the salinity, the factor being high at salinities of 10.5 and low at salinities of 246.2 mg/liter. Inland waters range from low to 226,000 (1.c., p. 569); and, by the same units, seawater ranges from 33,000 to 40,000 mg/liter.

or over a wide range, and is made by taking the averages from each association table and compiling them into a composite one. This synthetic table is the basic table needed for establishing nomenclature for the association.

PROJECT 9 Vegetation of Intertidal Zone

OBJECTIVE

To investigate the intertidal algal vegetation or biota of a rock seashore.

METHOD

1. Obtain the predicted tide times and heights for the day; and, using the one-quarter–one-tenth rule, prepare a tide curve for the specific location for the trip. Use this to estimate the height of water at time of trip (for accurate altitude, survey from established bench mark).[1]
2. At the site, observe the horizontally oriented life zones.
3. Describe them in descriptive terms, such as black zone, green zone, balanus zone, brown, red, and Laminaria zone.
4. Differentiate into apparent associations.
5. Within each zone, collect and identify species of plants, and preserve vouchers; and, using quantitative quadrat and/or phytosociological techniques, analyze the vegetation of each zone.
6. Harvest a suitably sized quadrat from each zone for biomass analysis (wet and dry weight, and possibly chlorophyll content).
7. Establish datum (MLW) by surveying with dumpy level and rod to a fixed bench mark of known altitude, or by use of the tide curve (see "Tide Curve," below).
8. Using dumpy level or line level, determine the altitude of the top and bottom of each zone relative to the others, to MLW (or a fixed bench mark), and to the water level (record time).

8a. If time permits, determine altitude of zones for both seaward and landward (or sunny and shady) exposures.

9. By SCUBA, make comparable study of vegetation along a transect from low water down to a depth of 15–20 ft, or until zonation is obscured and vegetation becomes uniform. Describe vegetation, record depths, and obtain vouchers.

The above can be accomplished by dividing the group into three parties: vegetation study team, surveying team, and SCUBA team.

Vegetation Study Team

1. Using meter stick on line level, deter-

[1] A program developed with the author by Barbara Randall of the University of Rhode Island Computer Laboratory processes C&GS daily tide data, punched on cards, and plots the tide curve for that period. It is a Fortran IV program written for the IBM 360/40, and generates cards which are input to a Benson-Lehrner Delta Incremental Plotter. (Ref.: Randall, Barbara, pers. comm.)

mine relative altitude of each zone, and water level at a determined time.

2. List species in each zone, and gather comparable examples for voucher specimens (enough for everyone).

3. Make vegetation analysis (quantitative or phytosociological).

4. Harvest areas for biomass analysis (wet and dry/m^2).

5. Study both leeward and seaward, or N- and S-facing slopes. Also, estimate per cent cover, and make life form diagrams.

Surveying Team

1. Set up dumpy level.

2. Establish telescope height from a permanent marker.

3. Establish height distance below telescope level of upper and lower margin of each zone *and* water level at a determined time.

4. Leapfrog the tripod and survey rod to a bench mark, and from this determine altitude of each zone.

SCUBA Team

Equipped with depth gauge, thermometer, bug bag, small plastic bags, as well as SCUBA gear, begin at water level and work downward along the bottom recording: a) depth at each observation, b) bottom type, c) vegetation, and d) obtain voucher specimens.

DATA

A. Tide curve for the day and area, marked with lines indicating critical (Doty, 1946) tide levels: HHW, HLW, HHHW, LLLW, LHW, LLW, MSL, MLW (datum), and MHW. Add to one side a diagram of algal zones indicating their proper altitudes.

B. Pictorial sea-view diagram of intertidal zones (see Lewis, 1957; Lewis and Powell, 1960: 57) as seen from the ocean (Figure 1).

C. Floristic list of intertidal region (Smith, 1950; Taylor, 1957; Zim and Ingle, 1955).

D. Vegetation analysis of each zone by association table (den Hartog, 1959), or quantitative quadrats.

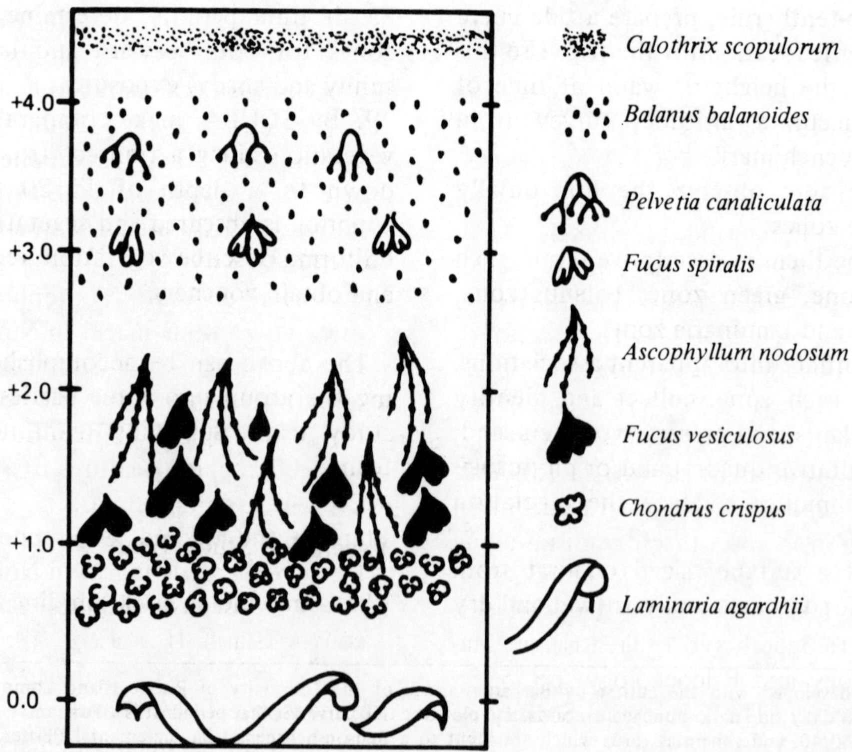

Figure 1. Sea-view diagram of intertidal vegetation. (Modified form Lewis and Powell, 1960: 57.)

E. Table of biomass data.

F. Table of altitudes (above or below datum) of limits of each zone (Lewis and Powell, 1960: 56).

G. Three-dimensional pictorial diagram of intertidal zonation (see Stephenson and Stephenson, 1949, 1950, 1952, 1954, 1961), but in addition indicate actual altitudes and the tide levels.

H. If data are available from a bisect of the estuary when studied on the oceanographic trip, compile them with data from the present study, and make a bisect to indicate the spacial distribution of biomass across the basin diagram by variation in cross hatchings or shadings.

I. If data are adequate, use a vegetation-altitude gradient table, as done by Taniguti (1962) (see Table 1, chapter 8).

J. Life form diagram of each association.

K. If time permitted obtaining the data, make diagram of the effect of exposure on altitude of algal zones (see Doty, 1957: 563; Chapman, 1964: 34).

REFERENCES

Chapman, V. J. 1964. Coastal Vegetation. Macmillan, New York. 245 p.

Chapman, V. J., and C. B. Trevarthen. 1953. General schemes of classification in relation to marine coastal zonation. J. Ecol. 41: 198–204.

Coast & Geodetic Survey (C&GS). 1969, etc. Tide tables, east coast North and South America including Greenland. Coast & Geodetic Survey, U.S. Dept. Commerce. Supt. of Doc., Washington, D.C.

Doty, M. S. 1946. Critical tide factors that are correlated with the vertical distribution of marine algae and other organisms along the Pacific coast. Ecology 27: 315–328.

Doty, M. S. 1957. Rocky intertidal surfaces. *In* J. W. Hedgpeth (ed.), Treatise on Marine Ecology and Paleoecology, pp. 535–585. Mem. 67, The Geological Society of America, New York. 1296 p.

den Hartog, C. 1959. The epilithic algal communities occurring along the coast of the Netherlands. Wentia 1: 1–241.

Hedgpeth, J. W. (ed.) 1957. Treatise on Marine Ecology and Paleoecology. Mem. 67, The Geological Society of America, New York. 1296 p.

Lewis, J. R. 1957. Intertidal communities of the northern and western coasts of Scotland. Trans. Roy. Soc. Edinburgh 63: 158–220.

Lewis, J. R., and H. T. Powell. 1960. Aspects of the intertidal ecology of rocky shores in Argyll, Scotland. I and II. Trans. Roy. Soc. Edinburgh 64(3,4): 46–100.

Northcraft, R. D. 1948. Marine algal colonization on the Monterey Peninsula, California. Amer. J. Bot. 35: 393–404.

Ricketts, E. F., and J. Calvin. 1952. Between Pacific Tides. 3rd ed. Stanford Univ. Press, Stanford, Cal. 502 p.

Smith, G. M. 1944. Marine Algae of the Monterey Peninsula, California. Stanford Univ. Press, Stanford, Cal. 622 p.

Stephenson, T., and A. Stephenson. 1949. The universal features of zonation between tide-marks on rocky coasts. J. Ecol. 37: 289–305.

Stephenson, T., and A. Stephenson. 1950. Life between tide-marks in North America. I. The Florida keys. J. Ecol. 38: 354–402.

Stephenson, T., and A. Stephenson. 1952. Life between tide-marks in North America. II. Northern Florida and the Carolinas. J. Ecol. 40: 1–49.

Stephenson, T., and A. Stephenson. 1954. Life between tide-marks in North America. III A. Nova Scotia and Prince Edward Island: description of the region. III B. Nova Scotia and Prince Edward Island. The geographical features of the region. J. Ecol. 42: 14–45, 46–70.

Stephenson, T., and A. Stephenson. 1961. Life between tide-marks in North America. IV A. Vancouver Island, I. IV B. Vancouver Island, II. J. Ecol. 49: 1–29, 227–243.

Stephenson, T. A., and A. Stephenson. 1972. Life between tidemarks on rocky shores. W. H. Freeman, San Francisco. 425

p. (Includes most of the preceding papers by these authors; paperback).

Taniguti, M. 1962. (See "References" in project 8).

Taylor, W. R. 1957. Marine algae of the northeastern coast of North America. 2nd ed. Univ. Michigan Press, Ann Arbor. 509 p.

Taylor, W. R. 1960. Marine Algae of the Eastern Tropical and Subtropical coasts of the Americas. Univ. Michigan Press, Ann Arbor. 870 p.

Womersley, H. B. S., and S. J. Edmonds. 1958. A general account of the intertidal ecology of South Australian coasts. Aust. J. Mar. Freshw. Res. 9: 217–260.

Zim, H. S., and L. Ingle. 1955. (See "References" in project 1).

NOTES

Altitude

Locate fixed bench mark near the seashore, find number and date stamped on plate, check with area engineer or send data to Coast & Geodetic Survey for altitude. From this base, survey down with dumpy level, and establish a convenient nearby temporary bench mark (Figure 2). From it, determine datum (MLW); and, using values in Tide Tables (see table of corrections), find height of mean sea level (MSL). These need to be verified with current observations.

Critical Tide Factors

See "Tide factors," below.

Datum

Datum in NE is defined in the Tide Tables (C&GS) as = mean low water; but, on hydrographic charts, upland details are surveyed from MHW. Inland surveyors use MSL on topographic maps.

Dumpy Level

See project 8.

Line Level (2 Meter Sticks, String, and Line Level)

Hang line level in center of string between one level (or meter stick standing on it) and meter stick standing at lower level. Holding string taut and firmly at upper level, raise string along other stick until bubble is centered. Altitude is read on lower meter stick, or difference between readings on two sticks (Figure 3).

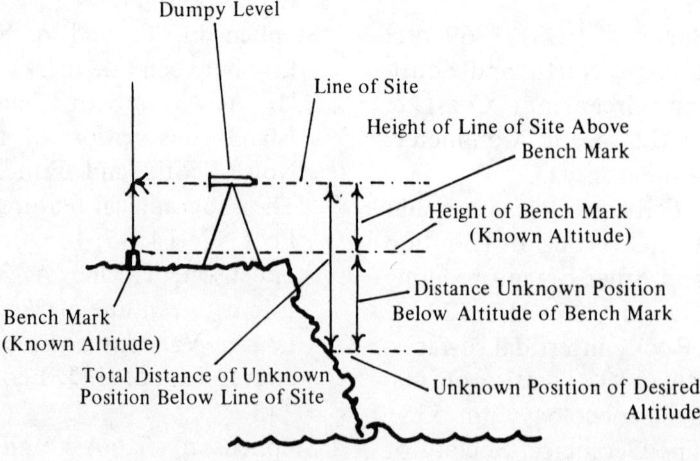

Figure 2. Dumpy level for finding altitude of life zone from bench mark.

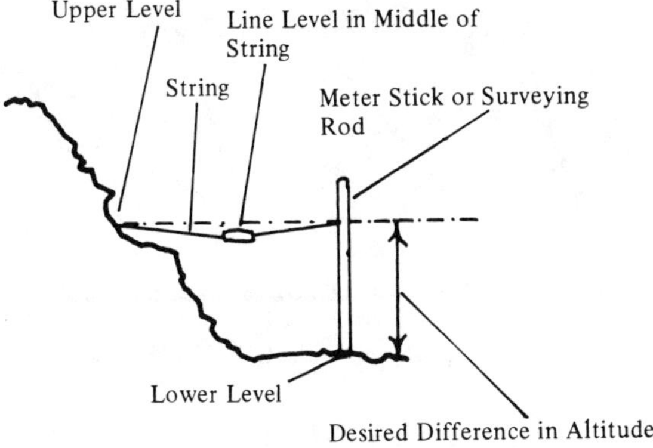

Figure 3. Use of level (at midpoint of string) to find height of alga or rock above the lower terrace. Height is read on vertical meter surveying rod.

Quantitative Quadrat

Number of individual shoots of each species/m^2, usually accompanied by estimate of per cent cover.

Three-Dimensional Diagram

See Figure 4.

Tide Curve (One-Quarter–One-Tenth Rule) (Figure 5)

1. Obtain times and heights of tide for the day from the Tide Tables, for the nearest main recording station.

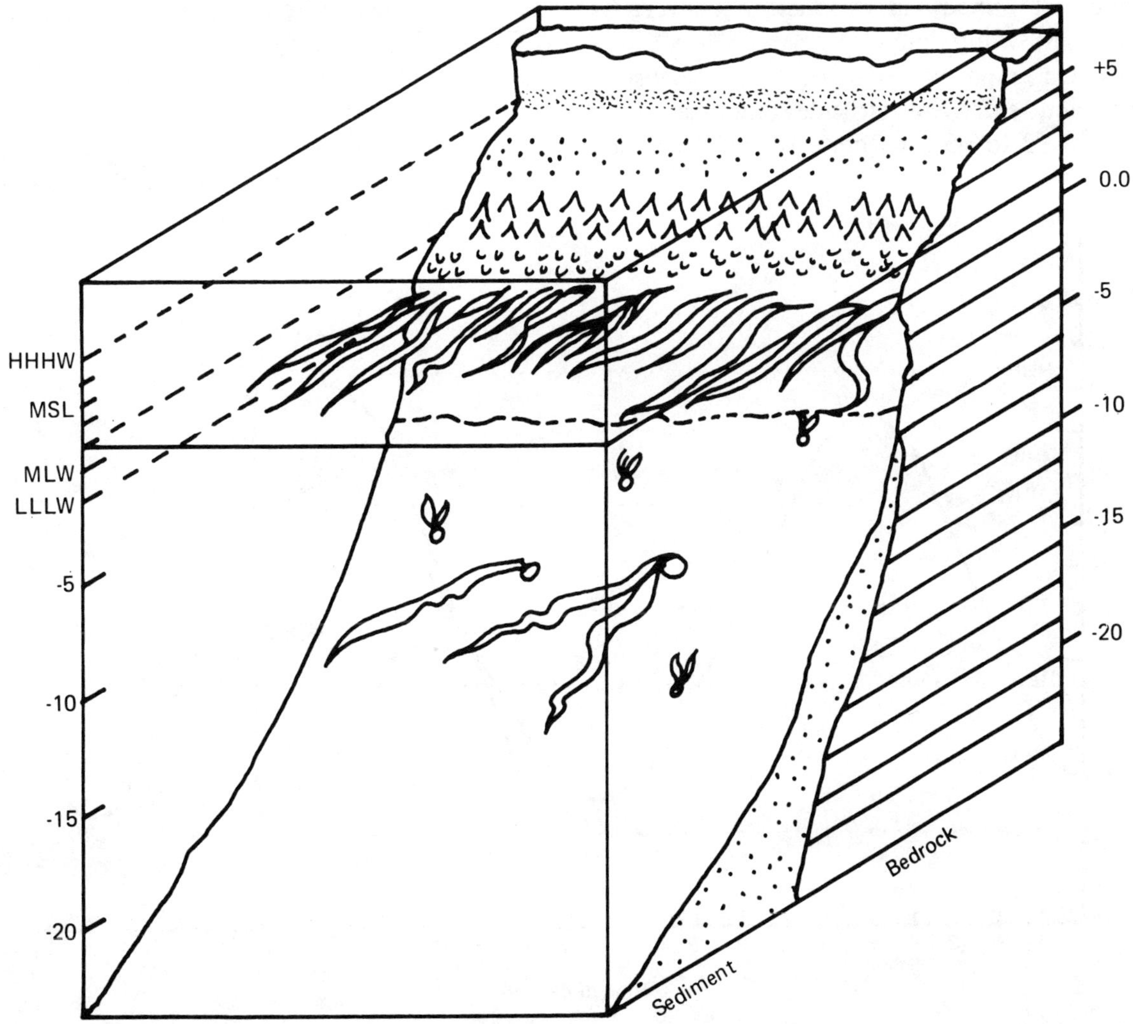

Figure 4. Sample three-dimensional diagram of marine shoreline. Zones are communities of *Calothrix, Balanus, Fucus, Chondrus, Laminaria* (the *Laminaria* fringe), and a few stands of *Rhodymenia.*

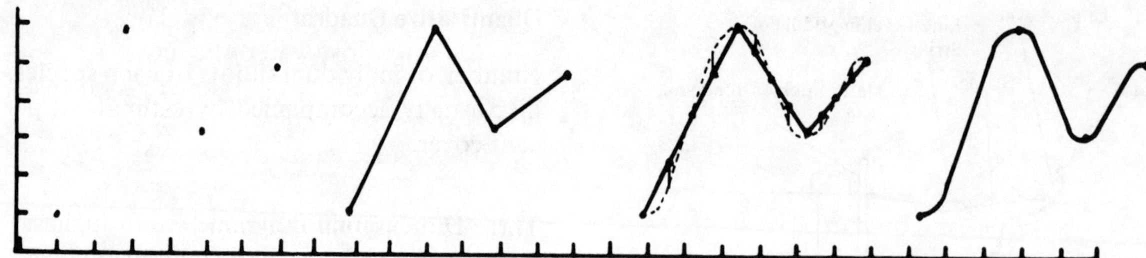

Figure 5. Example of a day's tide curve by using the 1/4–1/10 rule. (From data published in the C & GS "Tide Tables.")

2. Correct these figures for times and heights, using the corrections given in the back of the Tide Tables.

3. Correct for daylight saving or standard time. Tide Tables are reckoned in standard time; add 1 hr between last Sunday in April and last Sunday in October to convert to daylight saving time.

4. On graph marked with 24 hrs on abscissa, and sufficient altitude (e.g., ca. 7 ft [from −2 to +5 for Rhode Island]) on ordinate:

a. Mark points for the corrected tide points.
b. Connect successive points with straight lines.
c. Take measurement of each line, divide into 4 parts, and mark each interpoint line at the quarter points (i.e., at middle, and half way between center and each end).
d. Take 1/10 of the line length, and run a line vertically that length

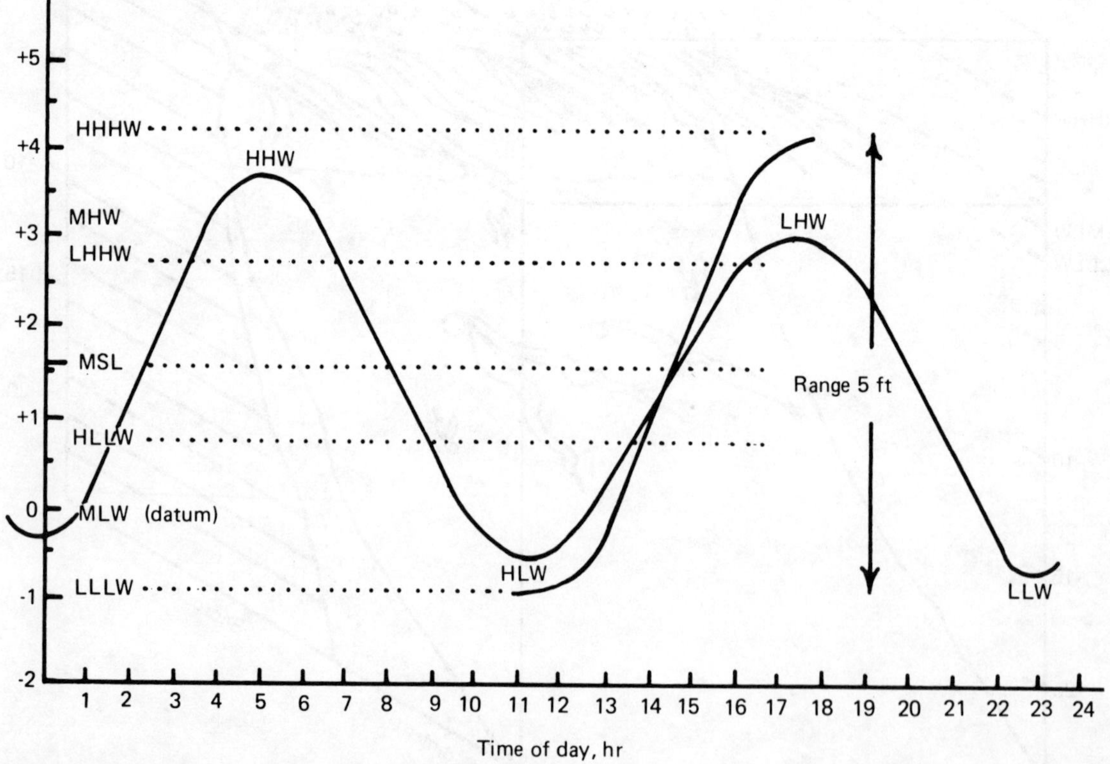

Figure 6. Sample plot of predicted tide curve for Harbor of Refuge, Point Judith, R.I., November 8, 1969, together with extreme spring (HHHW and LLLW) and neap (LHHW and HLLW) and maximum normal (i.e., non-storm-induced) tide range for the location (41°22′ N Lat., 71°29′ W Long.).

upward from the upper quarter point and downward from the lower quarter point of each line.

e. Connect the key points with a straight line, rounding off at the extremes of the tides.

Figure 6 is an example of a predicted tide curve.

Tide factors

HHW: the higher high water of a day
HHHW: the highest spring tide of a year (extreme high-water spring)
HLW: the higher low water of a day
LHW: the lower high water of a day
LLW: the lower low water of a day
LLLW: the lowest spring tide of a year (extreme low-water spring)
MLW: mean low water
MSL: mean sea level
Spring tides: semimonthly period of highest and lowest tide (approximately at full and new moon)
Neap tides: semimonthly period of minimum tides (at the quarter moons)
Equinoctial tides: the greatest spring tides of a year, usually around the time of the equinoxes (ca. March 22, September 22)

PROJECT 10 Oceanographic Hydrobotany

OBJECTIVE

To investigate the benthic and planktonic vegetation off shore using oceanographic techniques, thus extending the indirect sampling procedures beyond the limits of depth and conditions convenient by inshore (limnological) methods.

METHOD

1. Aboard an oceanographic research vessel equipped with hoist, davit, winch, cable, tachometer, and fathometer, make transect of samplings of benthic vegetation using scallop, or similar, dredge; take plankton samples at intervals of depth using 1-ft plankton net (20-mesh), calibrated meter wheel, inclinometer, and if available a Clarke-Bumpus quantitative plankton net. Also, at a selected station, take vertical water samples and temperature at intervals of depth using the Nansen water bottle and with reversing thermometer. Use samples for dissolved oxygen, salinity, alkalinity, and plankton.

2. For dredging, lower scallop dredge on steel cable by power winch swung by boom hoist or davit, and drag at known depth (fathometer) for known period of time. Record depth, speed, time, and width of dredge. Hoist dredge and dump onto deck. Record species and numbers of individuals, or record presence on a 1–5 basis. Record location of dredging.

3. For plankton work, lower net to a predetermined depth and drag at known speed for known period. Record net diameter, net coefficient of efficiency, and time of haul, as well as location. Raise, drain sample into bottle, rinse down with a little additional seawater. Divide sample into equal halves, and fix one immediately by adding sufficient neutralized (with borax) 38% formalin to make 5% solution of it in seawater[1]. Save other half for examination while alive (keep cool and in dark until examined).

4. In the laboratory, study live net plankton under coverslip, note the different kinds, determine the species as far as possible, and tabulate occurrence to determine per cent composition by species. Using Sedgwick-Rafter counting chamber, count number of individuals per ml of most common and easily recognized species. On basis of your earlier per cent composition data, determine number per ml of each species; summate the total number of phytoplankton cells per ml.

For further investigation, sediment 25- or 50-ml raw water samples in special cylinders using the Utermöhl (1931) method, as follows. Fill cylinder, add sufficient formalin to constitute 4%, cover with special coverslip, and allow to settle overnight. Count with inverted microscope, reporting numbers per square or per field, and then calculating the

[1] Hexamine, 1%, is currently recommended.

proportion of the area (and thus of total volume) of bottom of cylinder. Counts can also be made with a Sedgwick-Rafter chamber.

Exceedingly difficult organisms or structures can be studied well by using phase contrast.

5. For biomass measure, determine the average size of a number of cells of each species. Also, from a formula for the geometric shape approximating the shape of the cell, determine a constant for volume of cell size for each species. Knowing the average cell size, the cell volume, and the number of cells of each species/ml, calculate the volume of phytoplankton cells/ml. Convert to mg of phytoplankton per m^3. Finally, knowing this for several depths, plot a biomass-depth gradient curve; and, from it, estimate the total volume of phytoplankton in the water column above an area of bottom of 1 m^2. This is phytoplankton biomass per m^2. (If the nannoplankton/net plankton ratio is known, add correction for nannoplankton.)

6. Water samples should be analyzed as in previous projects. Take oxygen sample and fix at sulfuric acid stage in the field, using unmodified Winkler. The density should be obtained at once on another sample with salinometer, recording temperature and specific gravity. Samples for alkalinity and phytoplankton are taken for processing in the laboratory.

7. In the laboratory, titrate water sample for dissolved oxygen by Winkler titration; analyze for salinity by silver nitrate titration (see project 8) and for alkalinity (both phenolphthalein and total) as done in project 5a. Convert density readings to density at 15°C, then by tables to salinity and chlorinity.

DATA

A. Floristic list of phytoplankton and phytobenthon.

B. Table of numbers of cells of each kind (species) per unit (ml, liter, or m^3).

C. Estimated relative phytobiomass/m^3 and absolute biomass/m^2 of the plankton.

D. Floristic list of phytobenthon.

E. Table of chemical-physical factors data.

F. Summarize the data in the form of a bisect diagram of the transect, stippling or cross hatching different densities to indicate relative biomass per unit volume of unit area.

REFERENCES

APHA. 1965. (See "References" in project 5).

Harvey, H. W. 1945. (See "References" in project 8).

Lohmann, H. 1908. Untersuchungen zur Festallung des vollständigen Gehaltes des Meeres an Plankton. Wiss. Meeresunters. 10. Kiel.

Nauwerck, A. 1963. Die Beziehungen zwischen Zooplankton und Phytoplankton im See Erken. Symb. Bot. Upsaliens. 17(5): 1–163. (cell volume measurement).

Pratt, D. M. 1959. Periodicity of phytoplankton of Narragansett Bay. Limnol. Oceanogr. 4: 425–440.

Smayda, T. J. 1957. Phytoplankton studies in lower Narragansett Bay. Limnol. Oceanogr. 2: 342–359.

Strickland, J. D. H., and T. R. Parsons. 1968. (See "References" in project 5).

Sverdrup, H. U., M. W. Johnson, and R. H. Fleming. 1942. (See "References" in project 5).

Utermöhl, H. 1931. Neue Wege in der quantitativen Erfassung des Planktons. Verh. Int. Ver. Theor. Angew. Limnol. 5: 567–597.

Welch, P. S. 1948. (See "References" in project 4).

Wood, R. D., and J. Lutes. 1967. Guide to the phytoplankton of Narragansett Bay, Rhode Island. (Available from Bookstore, Univ. R.I., Kingston). 65 p.

NOTES

Clarke-Bumpus plankton sampler (Welch, 1948: 250): deep-water quantitative volume net-accessory equipment which, by a propellor, measures water entering net. Unit is lowered to desired depth, started by messenger slid down line, and when done a second messenger sent down closes unit.

Davit: a small crane used aboard ship.

Dredge: see "Scallop dredge."

Fathometer: see project 6.

Inclinometer: a protractorlike unit which, when suspended on plankton net line, will, together with length of line out, permit determination of depth of sampling.

Nansen bottle (APHA, 1965: 645, Figure 45): a heavy, deep-water unit comparable in principle to the Kemmerer water sampler.

Plankton: see also project 5a.

Reversing thermometer (Welch, 1948: 278): a mercurial thermometer with a large bulb at one end, a small bulb at the other, and a coiled restriction just above the large bulb. Lowered with large mercury reservoir down, temperature expands mercury past the coil according to temperature. At the desired depth, when the unit is reversed suddenly by action of the messenger, the mercury column separates at the coil, trapping some mercury above the coil and which part flows into the small bulb at the opposite, graduated end of the tube where it is read (in reversed position) like an ordinary thermometer. A small auxiliary thermometer provides temperature at the time the reading is taken, and the expansion of mercury caused by warming up (if any) can be corrected. Now largely replaced by electronic equipment.

Salinometer: see project 8.

Scallop dredge: a heavy, chainlike dredge with frame and cutting bar across front.

Tachometer: an instrument which records revolutions per min of motor. Pilots of research vessels make tables to convert (with due consideration for wind and current) rpm to knots; otherwise, speed can be determined by timing craft over known distance (such as 1-mile ranges) and correcting for drift (current or wind) (Chapman, 1968: 353 ff.).

PROJECT 11 Diel Periodicity

OBJECTIVE

To measure diel (24-hr) changes in environmental factors in a given aquatic habitat during a solar day (comprising both diurnal, daytime, and nocturnal, nighttime).

METHOD

Using standard methods (see especially project 5a) for taking and analyzing samples of water, determine values for indicated factors. For a minimal study, record changes in temperature, light intensity, pH, dissolved oxygen and its saturation at 4-hr intervals at one depth.

1. Select area for investigation. If station is in isolated area, use transceivers to maintain contact with base station.
2. Establish schedule for sampling (e.g., each 2 or 4 hrs).
3. Establish pattern of running tests so that the time between successive repeats of each test will be nearly constant.
4. Enter raw data directly as obtained into a raw data table (see Table 1) specifying time of starting and finishing.
5. Convert raw data to final form, and enter into final table (see Table 2).
6. Prepare parallel graphs, one for each factor, all on one time axis; and select a suitable ordinate scale to give vertical amplitude of each factor a similar appearance (see Figure 1; also Reid, 1961: 149).
7. Examine curves, and note which factors are obviously correlated, either positively or negatively. (If facilities are available, correlation coefficients can be obtained [Figures 2–4] by computer to give a measure of degree of correlation; while factor analysis computations can help determine the relative importance among the factors.)

DATA

A. Table of final data.

B. Set of parallel graphs on same time scale.

C. Conclusions and inferences from the data and curves, such as:

1. Which factors are directly related (correlated), inversely correlated, or exhibit no obvious correlations?
2. Where two or more methods are used to measure the same parameter, what percentage error is found? Of the methods, which is the more or most reliable?
3. In what ways do your results agree or disagree with the literature or theoretical explanations of diel variations?

REFERENCES

APHA. 1965. (See "References" in project 5).

Table 1. Sample of raw data table for diel periodicity

Schedule time	Time		Light (ft-c)					Temperature (°C)				Dissolved O_2 (ppm)		Redox (pH units)	Alkalinity (ppm)		Conditions
	Start	Finish	Sea cell	X	Deck cell	X	Illumination meter	Glass Air	Glass Water	Elect. water	pH	Elect.	Winkler		Ph-th	MO	
1600	1600	1712	0.4	1	1.61	10	50	26.8	17.6	16.5	7.3	8.8	7.0	4.4	0	12.6	Sunset
1800	1800	1845	–	–	–	–	–	25.0	17.5	17.3	7.25	9.0	7.2	4.2	0	11.7	Dark
2000	2000	2115	–	–	–	–	–	26.0	18.0	17.7	7.4	8.5	7.0	4.7	0	11.6	Dark
2200	2200	2300	–	–	–	–	–	26.0	18.0	17.8	7.6	7.4	6.8	4.7	0	11.9	Dark
2400	2400	0120	–	–	–	–	–	17.5	21.3	17.3	7.2	8.0	7.2	4.5	0	11.5	Dark
0200	0200	0235	–	–	–	–	–	20.0	17.0	17.0	7.1	7.4	6.0	4.6	0	11.4	Dark
0400	0400	0520	–	–	–	–	–	20.5	17.5	16.9	7.14	7.3	6.4	4.6	0	11.7	Dark, clear
0600	0600	0710	–	–	–	–	–	18.0	16.3	16.5	7.02	7.2	6.8	4.5	0	12.5	Dark, clear

Table 2. Sample final data table for diel periodicity

Time		Light (ft-c)			Temperature (°C)				Dissolved O_2			Alkalinity (ppm)		Redox (pH units)	CO_2 (ppm)	Conditions
Start	Interval	Sea cell	Deck cell	Illumination meter	Glass Air	Glass Water	Elect. water	pH	(ppm) Elect.	(ppm) Winkler	% Saturation	Ph-th	MO			
1600	72	5	50	50	26.8	17.6	16.5	7.3	8.8	7.0	70	0	126	+399	14	Sunset
1800	45	0	0	0	25.0	17.5	17.3	7.25	9.0	7.2	71	0	117	+411	13	Dark
2000	70	0	0	0	26.0	18.0	17.7	7.4	8.5	7.0	73	0	116	+381	12	Dark
2200	60	0	0	0	26.0	18.0	17.8	7.6	7.4	6.8	70	0	119	+381	13	Dark
2400	80	0	0	0	21.3	17.5	17.3	7.2	8.0	7.2	74	0	115	+395	14	Dark, foggy
0200	75	0	0	0	20.0	17.8	17.0	7.1	7.4	7.0	62	0	114	+387	17	Dark, foggy
0400	80	0	0	0	20.5	17.5	16.9	7.14	7.3	6.4	65	0	117	+387	18	Dark, clear
0600	70	0	0	0	18.0	16.3	16.5	7.02	7.2	6.8	68	0	125	+393	25	Dark, clear

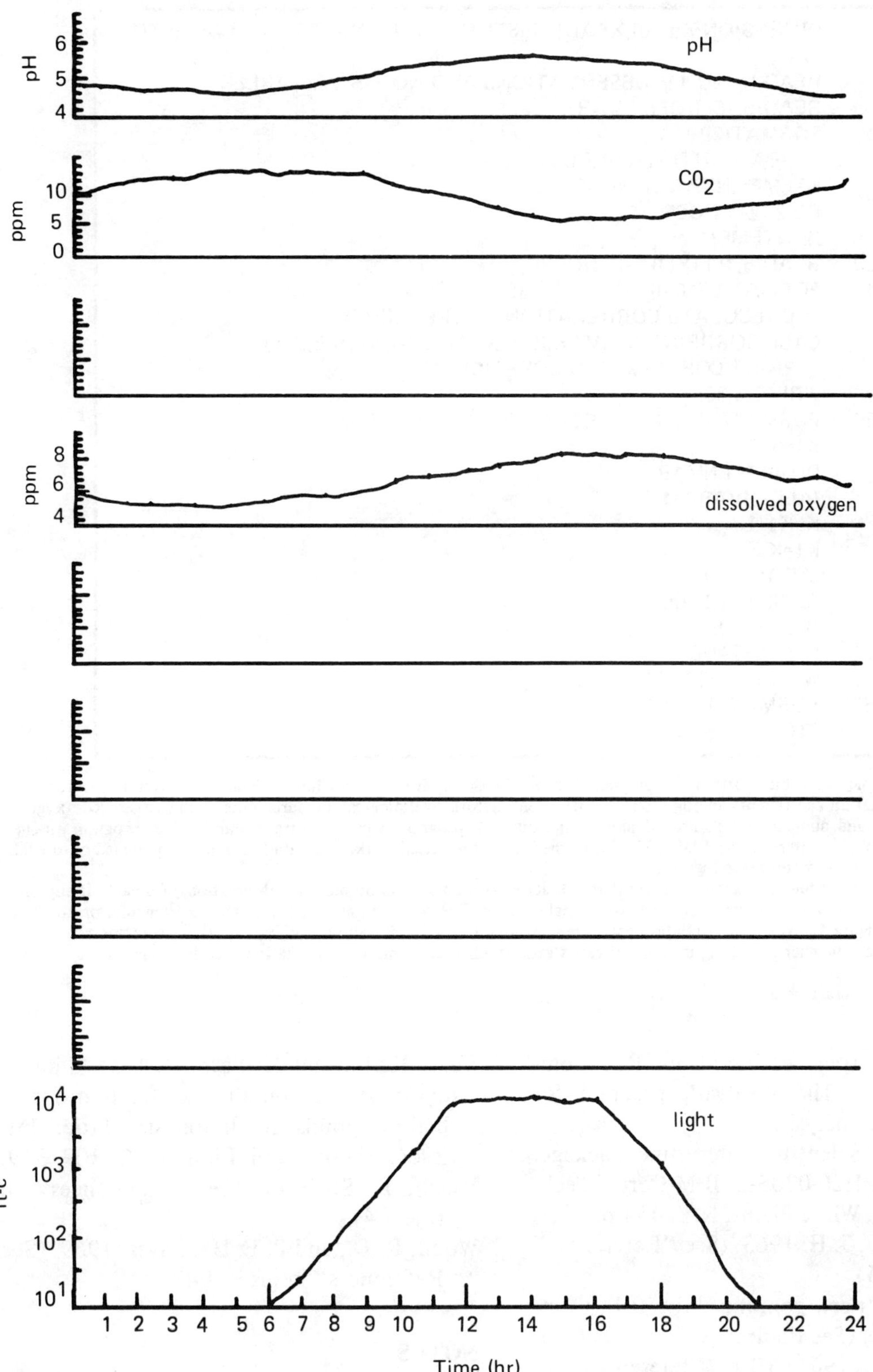

Figure 1. Sample parallel graph plot for multifactor recording of data, with data for four variables entered onto chart.

```
      DIMENSION X(500),XBAR(10),STD(10),RX(100),R(55),B(10),D(10),T(10)
      I0-1
C     READ IN NO. OF OBSERVATIONS AND NO. OF VARIABLES
      READ(5,10) NOBS,NVAR
   10 FORMAT(2I5)
C        READ  IN DATA CARDS
      NTEMP=(NVAR-1)*NOBS
      DO 20 I=1,NOBS
      I2=NTEMP+I
   20 READ(5,15) (X(J),J=I2,NOBS)
   15 FORMAT(8F10.0)
C        CALCULATE CORRELATION COEFFICIENTS
      CALL CORRE(NOBS,NVAR,I0,X,XBAR,STD,RX,R,B,D,T)
C        PRINT CORRELATION COEFFICIENTS
      WRITE(6,36)
   36 FORMAT('1',40X,'CORRELATION COEFFICIENTS'/)
      K1=0
      DO 40 I=1,NVAR
      IALL=NVAR-I+1
      K=K1+I
      K1=K
      IADD=I-1
      DO 30 L=1,IALL
      D(L)=R(K)
   30 K=K+L+IADD
   40 WRITE(6,35) I,(D(J),J=1,IALL)
   35 FORMAT(/I3,3X,10F7.3)
      STOP
```

Figure 2. Sample workable Fortran IV program for use in the University of Rhode Island Computer Laboratory to calculate correlation coefficients among a series of different factors, or biological measurements, such as dissolved oxygen, light intensity, and number of cells/liter of phytoplankton. This program is called Corre, a standardized program on file with IBM computer centers (Ref.: IBM, 1966: 32), which does the actual work. The data first must be punched onto IBM cards in a very special pattern (see Figure 3).

This program as written can handle no more than 10 factors (variables) and 50 records (observations) for each. If any one entry is missing, the gap must be filled with a reasonable value. The data will appear (output) as a triangular printout of numbers (see Figure 4) giving the correlation coefficients among the different factors and biological measurements.

Note The exact manner of setting up control cards varies with each computer installation. See its programmer for the proper setup.

Ref.: Randall (pers. comm.).

Carney, E. J. (pers. comm., Univ. R.I., Computer Lab.). The Aardvark program for multifactor analysis.

IBM. 1966. Scientific subroutine package. Tech. Pub. H20-0205-2, IBM Corp., Tech. Pub. Dept., White Plains, N.Y. 454 p.

Mackereth, F. J. H. 1963. (See "References" in project 5).

Randall, B. (pers. comm., Univ. R.I., Computer Lab.). (See Figure 2).

Reid, G. K. 1961. (See "References" in project 5).

Snedecor, G. W. 1956. Statistical methods. Iowa Univ. Press, Ames. 534 p.

Vaas, K. F., and M. Sachlan. 1955. Limnological studies on diurnal fluctuations in shallow ponds in Indonesia. Proc. Int. Assoc. Theor. Appl. Limnol. 12: 309–319.

Welch, P. S. 1948. (See "References" in project 4).

Wood, R. D., and P. E. Hargraves. 1969. (See "References" in project 4).

NOTES

Alkalinity

See project 5a.

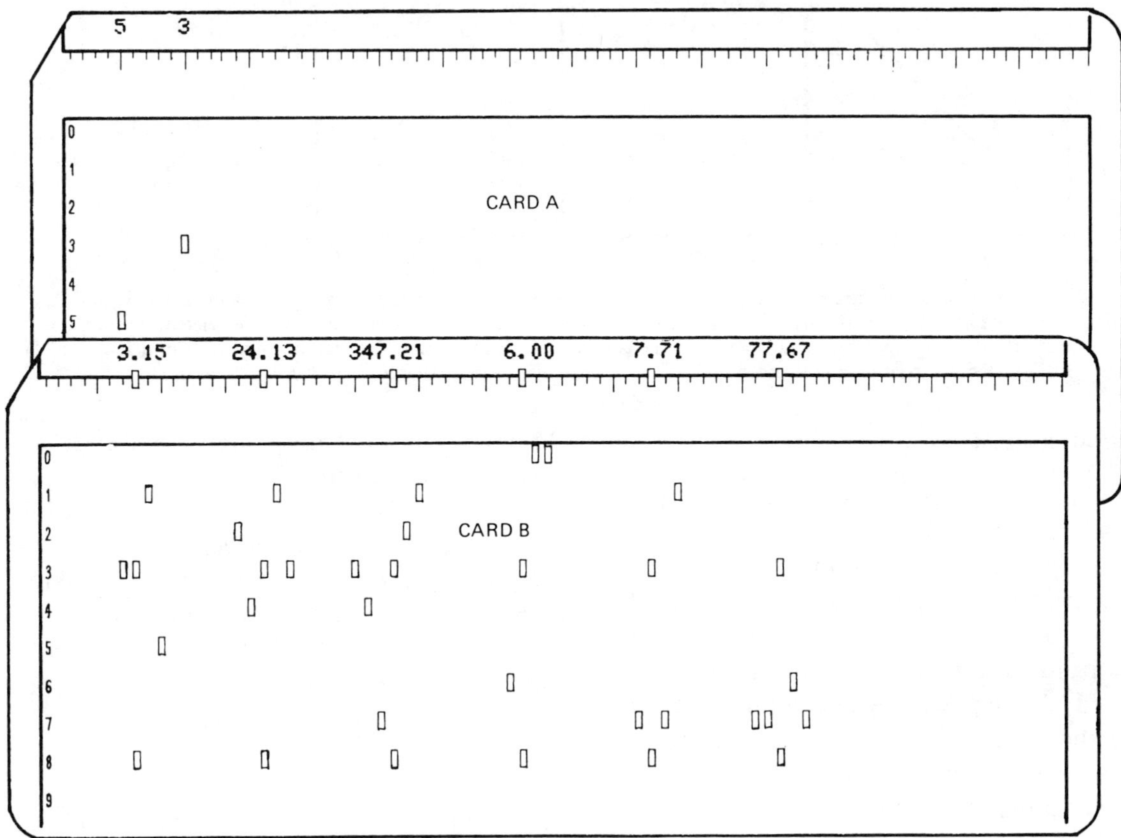

Figure 3. The two necessary types of cards for providing data from the correlation coefficient program (Figure 2) to the computer. Card *A* gives the number of observations made on each factor (typed within columns 1–5 of the card, ending at 5 [i.e., right justified], and the number of factors [variables] [typed within columns 6–10] ending at 10 [i.e., right justified]). Card *B* gives the figures from the observations, taking one row at a time, and typing the entire row on one (or more, if necessary) card. Each entry must be typed within 10 columns, right justified. If more than one card is necessary, complete the entries for the row of data, but start a new card for each new row of data (see Table 2).

	CORRELATION COEFFICIENTS		
	1	2	3
1	1.000	−0.602	0.662
2	1.000	−0.867	
3	1.000		

STOP
END OF JOB.

Figure 4. Sample output from correlation coefficient program (Figure 2). The first line gives correlation between the first factor and each of the others, e.g., –0.602 is the correlation coefficient between the first and second factors, while 0.662 is between the first and third factors. The second line gives the correlation between the second factor and the others, e.g., that between the second and the third. Note that the vertical columns are read on a slope (top right to lower left), such that factor 3 at the top right is correlated with factor 2 at the middle right. The 1.000 values are ignored because they are merely the relation of a number with itself.

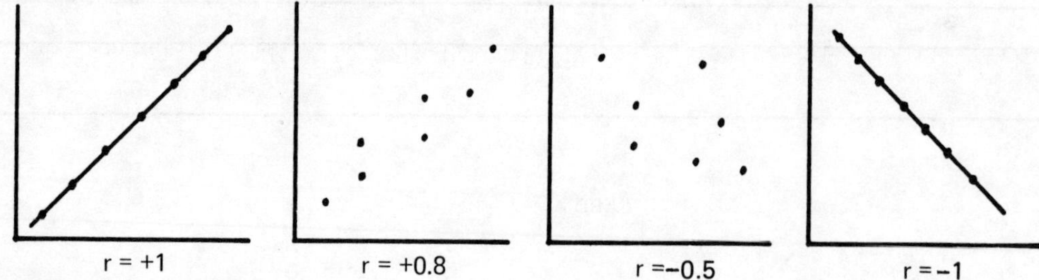

Figure 5. Diagram illustrating correlation. Values of one variable (vertical axis) are plotted in terms of the other variable (horizontal axis), and the pattern of points shows how closely the two are related. Perfect correlation is a straight line, and the poorer the correlation and the greater the scatter. (Modified from T. M. Little. 1966. Correlation and Regression. Univ. Calif. Agr. Ext. Serv., Davis, Cal. 62 p.)

Computer Analysis

Correlation coefficients, like other computations, can be easily obtained by computer once the data cards are punched and a program has been written (Figure 2) which will handle the cards, direct the computation, and print out (Figure 4) the information desired. Arrange with your computer laboratory the exact manner in which data should be punched (Figure 3). Also enquire about library programs available for analysis of data such as Corre, and the newer programs such as Aardvark for multifactor analysis (Carney, pers. comm.).

Correlation

Correlation is the degree (measured on a basis of 0.0–1) to which the line best described by one set of measurements falls on or close to the line described by another set of measurements, where two parallel lines have the maximum correlation (r = 1.0) (see Figure 5).

Illumination Meter

Use a standard, good quality meter (e.g., Weston Sunlight Meter) with filter which matches the spectral qualities of sunlight, and readable over a scale of 0–10,000 ft-c. To operate, remove probe from case, lay on flat surface (or turn toward light source in some cases), turn control dial carefully from range to range until reaching one which brings needle just onto meter and does not exceed scale. Read ft-c directly, on proper scale. Turn dial to off, return probe to case, and close unit. (*Note:* Keep sensor out of bright light except for brief periods of taking readings. Also, ft-c = ca. 10.76 lux, and bright sunlight is ca. 10,000 ft-c or 107,600 lux.)

Light Intensity

See "Submarine photometer" in project 5a, but see also "Illumination meter," above.

Oxygen, Dissolved

See project 5a.

Oxygen, Dissolved, Per Cent Saturation

See project 5a.

Per Cent Error

Per cent error is the size of error by one measure compared to that of another in terms of percent, usually:

$$\text{Per cent error} = \frac{\text{range of results by instrument with smaller deviation}}{\text{range of results by instrument with larger deviation}} \times 100$$

A more acceptable expression is based on standard deviation. The program (Figure 2) uses Corre, which can compute many things including standard deviation, and the programmer can modify the program to have this done without having to punch any new data cards.

pH

See project 5a.

Radiation

Using a recording radiometer, obtain data of radiation in g-cal/cm^2/min (sometimes expressed in Langleys, mg-cal/cm^2 as Langleys/min, but the effort is to eliminate them by using watts) (Ref.: Eppley Co., pers. comm., Newport, R.I.).

Redox

See project 5a.

Transceiver (Walkie-Talkie)

At least two units (e.g., Lafayette's Dyna Com 3a) are needed, unit 1 (or base unit) and unit 2. Method of calling, use of citizen band, and available channels are defined by law (FCC Rules and Regulations, Vol. VI, Part 95); and units can only be operated under an authorized license.

1. Extend antenna, cautiously, so as not to damage.
2. Turn on by turning "volume" knob (on top) clockwise until at about 10-o'clock position.
3. Check battery meter on top. If sufficiently charged, needle will move into green zone.
4. Select channel as previously agreed upon (button on right side).
5. Raise "squelch" dial clockwise until background noise is just eliminated.
6. Depress large button on left side (opens channel), and make call in following manner (using your own call number, e.g., KCR 0167):
   a. "KCR 0167, unit 2 calling unit 1, over." Release button, and await response. If none, repeat call. If response is received, it should be:
   b. "KCR 0167, unit 1 to unit 2, I read you, over."
   c. Make conversation brief and businesslike.
   d. On closing state: "KCR 0167, unit 2 clear with unit 1."
7. Then turn "volume" knob counterclockwise to "off."
8. Check "battery check" to be sure meter shows unit is off.
9. Carefully collapse antenna.

If batteries check out as weak, unscrew and remove back panel, remove battery cartridge, remove batteries, and replace with 10 new transistor batteries making sure they are replaced in the *exact* orientation indicated in the cartridge.

PROJECT 12 Algal Culture

OBJECTIVE

To culture algae suitable for laboratory or ecological investigation, and to use the cultures to test algicidal properties or for detecting limiting factors of a water.

METHOD

Algal work needs to be done in a laboratory well equipped for that purpose and maintained by personnel cognizant of the problems and procedures.

Initiating Culture

1. Select a medium suitable for culturing the alga (Bristol's is a broad application medium).
2. Prepare stock solutions from high purity chemicals in glass-distilled demineralized water, and store stocks in clean Pyrex glass containers.
3. Pour a little of each stock solution into a separate chemically clean beaker; and, using a clean pipet for each one, transfer the indicated volume into a volumetric flask containing at least half of the total required volume of water; dissolve, make up to volume, and mix.
4. Dispense approximately equal volumes of medium into clean culture containers (test tubes, bottles, flasks, Petri dishes); stopper with nonabsorbent cotton (or cover with caps).
5. Autoclave for 15 min at 15 lb/in^2.
6. Inoculate with cultures or, if beginning with wild cultures, select algal cells under dissecting microscope, pipet into sterile dist. water in watch glass, rinse through several passes of sterile dist. water, then introduce into culture medium.
7. Grow under suitable illumination, temperature, and aeration. A commonly used regime is 12 hrs of light at 20°C and 12 hrs of darkness at 15°C in growth chamber, possibly on shaker for aeration.
8. When culture has become established (1–2 weeks), conditions can be varied to promote optimal growth.

Testing Algicidal Properties of a Toxicant

1. Prepare medium in a series of flasks.
2. Mix in amount of toxicant to provide a stepwise concentration series (e.g., 0, 1, 5, 10, 100, 1,000 mg/liter, or in increments of micromoles).
3. Inoculate each with uniform volume of well mixed stock culture.
4. Label flasks.
5. Arrange at random on shaker, or shelf of culture chamber.
6. Daily, or after growth has developed, measure relative growth by one of several methods (e.g., optical density with a spectrophotometer, manual cell count with hemo-

cytometer or Sedgwick-Rafter counting chamber, or cell count with Coulter counter).

7. Plot graph with concentration of toxicant on abscissa (possibly on semilog paper) and relative growth on the ordinate.

8. Report concentration at which 50% of the growth occurs compared to that of the control, or 50% cell count was found, and report this as TL_{50} (concentration at 50% tolerance limit).

Evaluating Eutrophic Potential of Water

Compare growth of a test alga in the water against the growth in a standard medium (e.g., PAAP media; see EPA, 1971: 12).

1. Filter-sterilize (with 0.4-μ pore Millipore filter) several liters of the water after pretreatment with 50 ml of dist. water (discard).

2. Put equal volumes (e.g., 30 ml in 125-ml flasks) of the water in some and of a standard medium in other of a set of plugged and sterile flasks.

3. Inoculate with uniform amount of test alga (e.g., 1 ml of 7-day-old culture of *Selenastrum capricornutum* Printz, available through the Environmental Protection Agency, Corvallis, Oregon 97330.

4. Grow at 25 ± 1°C at 400 ft-c of continuous white fluorescent light.

5. Check density each day as a measure of growth.

6. Compare growth rates in the water and in the standard medium.

Detecting Limiting Factor in Natural Water

Grow test alga in samples of the water of which certain flasks are augmented with one of four essential elements, and others have combinations of the elements; compare growths.

1. Set out 12 or 16 125-ml sterile flasks, with 30 ml of filter-sterilized test water.

2. Using sterile technique, add a fixed amount of stock solution for N, P, Fe, and Mg to a given flask; and with other flasks add the same amounts but in all combinations, such as N + Fe, P + Fe, N + P + Fe, N + P + Fe + Mg.

3. Inoculate each by sterile technique with uniform volume (e.g., 1 ml) of 7-day-old *Selenastrum capricornutum.*[1]

4. Daily, or at intervals, check growth rate by increase in optical density, cell count, or ^{14}C uptake.

5. Flasks giving marked increases over controls contain supplemental elements limiting in the water.

DATA

A. Record of cultures initiated giving code number, name of organism, source, media, date, and name of isolator.

B. Table of results of toxicant evaluation and the TL_{50} value.

C. Table of information on eutrophication potential and apparent limiting factors.

REFERENCES

Brunel, J., G. W. Prescott, and L. H. Tiffany. 1950. The Culturing of Algae. A symposium. Charles Kettering Foundation, Antioch, Ohio. 114 p.

EPA. 1971. Algal Assay Procedure, Bottle Test. National Eutrophication Program,

[1] Note: For rough work with macronutrients, one can use aliquots of algal culture as described, but for critical work it is necessary to remove all possible traces of carryover nutrients. To do this, the cells from the stock culture should be centrifuged and the supernatant should be discarded. The sedimented cells should be resuspended in an appropriate volume of glass-dist. water containing 15 mg of $NaHCO_3$/liter and again centrifuged. The sedimented algae should again be resuspended in the water-bicarbonate solution and used as the inoculum. The concentration of cells used at the start of a bioassay culture should be checked to be ca. 10^3 cells/ml.

Environmental Protection Agency, Corvallis, Ore. 82 p.

Fogg, G. H. 1965. Algal Cultures and Phytoplankton Ecology. Univ. Wisconsin Press, Madison, 126 p.

Goldman, C. R. 1960. Primary productivity and limiting factors in three lakes of the Alaska Peninsula. Ecol. Monogr. 30: 207–230.

Goldman, C. R. (ed.). 1965. (See "References" in project 4).

JI/GTFE. 1969. Provisional algal assay procedure (PAAP). Joint Industry/Governmental Task Force on Eutrophication, P.O. Box 3011, Grand Central Station, New York. 62 p.

Margalef, R. 1963. Succession in culture flask. *In* E. P. Odum (ed.), Ecology, pp. 79, 80. Holt, Reinhart & Winston, New York. 152 p.

Odum, E. P. 1963. Ecology. Holt, Reinhart & Winston, New York. 152 p.

Pringsheim, E. G. 1951. Methods for the cultivation of algae. *In* G. M. Smith (ed.), Manual of Phycology, p. 347–357. Ronald Press, New York. 373 p.

Smith, G. M. (ed.). 1951. Manual of Phycology. Ronald Press, New York. 373 p.

Starr, R. C. 1964. The culture collection of algae at Indiana University. Amer. J. Bot. 51: 1013–1044. (Revised and reissued several times.)

Stein, J. R. (ed.) 1973. Handbook of Phycological Methods: Culture Methods and Growth Measurements. Cambridge Univ. Press, Cambridge. 448 p.

Trainor, F. R. 1973. (pers. comm.).

Trelease, S. F., and H. M. Trelease. 1935. Micrometabolic elements used in culture. Amer. J. Bot. 22: 520–542.

NOTES

Autoclaving

See Project 7.

Cleaning Glassware

Various methods are recommended for cleaning glassware, but the one recommended by EPA (1971: 15) for algal bioassay is representative and adequate for most purposes. Wash glassware with detergent or sodium bicarbonate (others prefer Ivory soap and hot water), scrub with test tube brushes, etc. Rinse with 10% HCl, and let items stand for a few moments exposed to the acid. Flush thoroughly with tap water, 10 times is adequate, then flush five times with dist. (or deionized) water, and finally rinse (I prefer several times) with glass-dist. water. Air dry in inverted position (or at 105°C in oven), then cover with aluminum foil caps or keep in dust-free cabinet. The EPA (l.c., p. 16) recommends conditioning the glassware before use by autoclaving, rinsing with the medium to be used, then draining for 20–30 min in inverted position.

Filter Sterilizing

Assemble filtering unit, including the 47-mm Millipore filter holder, filtering flask to accept the filter holder, a second filtering flask as trap, suitable flexible pressure tubing connections, and a sturdy clamp to cut off suction to filtering flask when desired. Sterilize, by autoclaving, the entire unit, together with 47-mm, 0.4-μ pore size, Millipore filters. Attach unit to suction pump, insert sterile filter into holder, turn on pump to moderate suction, pour water to be filtered onto the filter, and draw through at moderate speed. When filtering is completed, cut off suction to filtering flask by clamping tightly on its exhaust hose then releasing suction at the suction pump (thus preventing air from being drawn into the filtration flask). Handle filtered water with sterile technique.

Measurable Features of Mixed Algal Culture Progress

Flora: list of species (N = number of species)

Vegetation: number of individuals of each species

$$\text{Species diversity} = \frac{N}{\log N}$$

$$\text{Pigment ratio} = \frac{Y}{G} = \frac{E_{430}}{E_{665}}$$

(where E is optical density)

Biomass = mg dry wt/liter

Productivity = mg C fixed/g dry wt/hr

Reference Margalef *in* Odum, 1963: 79, 80.

Obtaining Algal Cultures

One may need to run experiments with algae with reference to a given habitat, and there may be the option of whether it could be a test organism, a selected species from the local environment, or if it must be the natural algae of the habitat.

The most practical option is to use a test alga. Strains can be obtained from biological supply companies, algal culture collections, or special agencies such as the Environmental Protection Agency in Corvallis, Oregon, which is involved in algal bioassay techniques. Among the algae recommended by that agency are *Selenastrum capricornutum* Printz, *Microcystis aeruginosa* Kütz. emend. Elenkin (= *Anacystis cyanea* Drouet and Daily), and *Anabaena flos-aquae* (Lyngb.) De Brebisson. These are usually obtained on shipment in fluid medium, and an aliquot can be transferred to sterile medium.

The second option, using a selected local strain, is not at all easy, and should be redefined to use available stock algae if possible. If a local strain is absolutely essential, getting these isolated is a task one should leave to a skilled algal culture expert. For techniques for isolation, and references to other useful works, see Stein (1973). Among the methods for achieving this are: 1) to streak wild algae onto agar-stabilized medium with platinum transfer needle, as is done in bacteriology; 2) to make serial dilution of the raw water and inoculate agar plates with a bit from each dilution, hoping to get a unialgal culture from some dilution; and 3) to use aspiration, as done by Trainor (pers. comm.), in which a bit of raw fluid is drawn up in a sterile capillary tube, and a vapor is created by blowing across the tube with a sterile, Pasteur pipet with air filter, the fog being directed over an agar plate. When successfully executed, it is possible for algal cells to settle separately and develop virtually pure colonies. Good-looking colonies are then picked with a sterile platinum needle and transferred to fluid medium; or the colony can be touched with a capillary tube, drawing up a bit, then that portion of the tube broken off into a test tube with sterile medium. By one of these methods, preferably the last, one may obtain a unialgal culture. Suppression of bacteria can be achieved at times as described by Stein (1973: 62) by repeated centrifugation and resuspension in clean medium, by cleaning with ultrasonics, or by treatment with antibiotics such as penicillin and streptomycin. Potassium tellurite is a useful bacteriostatic agent which may permit the alga on agar to outgrow the bacteria, then permitting the technician to pick the clean algae and get a bacteria-free (axenic) culture. Germanium dioxide represses growth of diatoms, and may enable isolation of desired algae from those contaminants.

If the natural plankton community is essential, raw water samples are taken with nontoxic samplers and kept cool, aerated, and suitably lighted (avoid direct sunlight). The difficulties include a wide variety of aspects, and basically the wild population includes protozoans, worms, bacteria, parasites, algae, and others, in unknown densities. As soon as the sample is enclosed in a container, some of these begin to die, others begin to thrive, and rapid changes can be expected. Thus, any test run on algae of a raw water sample will require extreme caution to approach reliability and should have the very shortest possible test time to reduce the degree of change that must be anticipated. Raw water culture work should be avoided if at all possible.

Maintaining Cultures

It is well to maintain cultures in such a way as to minimize the work yet keep organisms in good condition. *Selenastrum* survives well on Bristol's agar. Trainor's (pers. comm.) method of slanting the medium in ordinary 3-oz flat-backed medicine bottles works well. The algae, streaked over the surface and allowed to grow into a distinct line under optimal conditions, can then be held in storage in dim light with the bottle lid screwed down tight. These have lasted over a year, and show every potential of continuing vigor under these conditions. When cultures are desired, the stock is opened, some algae transferred to fluid medium with needle using sterile technique, and within 2 weeks a healthy, rich culture is obtained.

More delicate species may need to be subcultured at regular intervals, and some will require soil extract or organic supplements to keep them active.

Media

Table 1 contains the recipe for preparation of two useful media for algal culture for ecological use, Bristol's (Ref.: Starr, 1964: 1037) and PAAP media. The media should be mixed in considerable amounts of water, then diluted to 1-liter volume.

For enriched seawater medium, add 9 parts of filtered seawater to 1 part of Bristol's solution.

For enrichment for growing difficult species, add 1/10 to 1/2 volume of soil extract.

For agar medium, add 1.5% agar by weight, warm medium carefully until the agar disperses just before boiling (caution to avoid foaming!); stopper, and autoclave.

Table 2 contains the recipe for Trelease and Trelease (1935) solution for a micronutrient supplement for culture media, to be mixed in considerable amounts of water, then diluted to 1-liter volume.

Other Media

Bristol's medium and the algal assay procedure medium described here are just two of

Table 1. Recipe for preparation of two useful media for algal culture for ecological use, Bristol's and PAAP media[a]

Chemical to be used	Stock solution (g/liter)	Bristol's medium (ml of stock/liter)	PAPP medium[b] (ml of stock/liter)
$NaNo_3$	25	10	3.4
$MgCl_2$	19	–	1.0
$MgSO_4 \cdot 7H_2O$	7.5	10	6.54
NaCl	2.5	10	–
$CaCl_2 \cdot 2H_2O$	2.5	10	5.87
$NaHCO_3$	50 (mg)	–	1.0
$FeCl_3$	10	1 drop	0.032
K_2HPO_4	7.5	10	0.46
KH_2PO_4	17.5	10	–
EDTA-$Na \cdot 2H_2O$	300	–	1.0
Trelease nutrient solution	(see Table 6)	2	2

[a]To be mixed in considerable water, then diluted to 1-liter volume.
[b]Recommended for use at one third strength.
[c]PAPP requires 1 ml of a special recipe which is fairly similar to the Trelease solution, but results with Trelease are acceptable.

Table 2. Recipe for Trelease and Trelease solution for a micronutrient supplement for culture media[a]

Chemical to be used	Individual stock solutions g/liter	g/800 ml	Working solution (ml of stock/ liter)
$ZnSO_4$	2.5	2	8.06
Na_2SiO_3	2.5	2	7.5
$Al_2(SO_4)_3 \cdot 18\ H_2O$	10	8	7.5
KI	0.615	0.5	1.5
H_3BO_3	2.5	2	8.7
$CuSO_4 \cdot 5H_2O$	0.5	0.4	1.3
$NiCl_2 \cdot 6H_2O$	1.25	1	2.3
NaCl	2.5	2	8.2
LiCl	1.25	1	1.7
As_2O_3	0.615	0.5	1.5
$CoCl_2 \cdot 6H_2O$	1.25	1	2.3
$MnSO_4 \cdot 4H_2O$	2.5	2	12.5

[a]To be mixed in considerable water, then diluted to 1-liter volume.

the numerous algal media available. An excellent review of these is given by Stein (1973), and she lists a number of authors on pp. 23 and 48–50, including works by Hutner et al. (1966), Pringsheim (1946), Provasoli and Pintner (1960), and Starr (1964) for freshwater algae, and Guillard and Ryther (1962), Provasoli (1968), and Provasoli et al. (1957) for marine forms. In addition to Stein's book, Starr's (1964, 1971) papers are readily available general coverages of the topic.

Sedgwick-Rafter Counting Chamber

See "Plankton analysis," project 5a.

Spectrophotometer

See project 14.

PROJECT 13 Primary Productivity: Light and Dark Bottle

OBJECTIVE

To determine comparative primary productivity rates of plankton (and/or nannoplankton), and of a given macrophyte, under defined condition.

METHOD

Use two bottles with comparable plankton samples, one exposed to light and the other kept in complete darkness (or, in the case of macrophytes, similar samples in two bottles together with blanks, a total of three or five bottles) for a suitable period of time at controlled light and temperature. Then measure the dissolved oxygen of the waters of all samples and blanks; then calculate the oxygen change, and in turn the productivity in g of C fixed/unit/hour.

DATA

Table giving necessary supporting figures, and final results as:

A. Relative assimilation, as g or μg of C/hr/$10^{12}\mu^3$ or ml of plant or plankton material.

B. Absolute assimilation, as g or μg of C/hr/m^3 or liter of water or m^2 of basin bottom.

REFERENCES

Doty, M. S., and M. Oguri. 1957. Evidence for a photosynthetic daily periodicity. Limnol. Oceanogr. 2: 37–40.

Elster, H. J. 1965. Absolute and relative assimilation rates in relation to phytoplankton populations. *In* C. R. Goldman (ed.), Primary Productivity in Aquatic Environments, pp. 77–103. Univ. California Press, Berkeley. 464 p.

Goldman, C. R. (ed.). 1965. (See "References" in project 4).

Odum, E. P., and H. T. Odum. 1959. Fundamentals of Ecology. 2nd ed. W. B. Saunders, Philadelphia. 546 p.

Reid, G. K. 1961. (See "References" in project 1).

Ruttner, F. 1963. (See "References" in project 5a).

Strickland, J. D. H., and T. R. Parsons. 1968. (See "References" in project 5).

Wetzel, R. G. 1965. Techniques and problems of primary productivity measurements in higher aquatic plants and periphyton. *In* C. R. Goldman (ed.), Primary Productivity in Aquatic Environments, pp. 251–267. Univ. California Press, Berkeley. 464 p.

NOTES

Productivity Measurements

Phytoplankton Use the two-bottle system, one covered and one uncovered.

Procedure

1. Assemble two 250 (or 300 BOD)-ml gs bottles for each test, lightproof sack or aluminum foil, arrangements for measuring dissolved oxygen concentration (Winkler is preferred), growth chamber, and plankton samples. Hold plankton water in dark growth chamber for several hours to precondition.
2. In subdued light, mix plankton to uniformity, fill both bottles to top, stopper carefully to prevent trapping bubbles, and cover one bottle to exclude light.
3. Put bottles into lighted growth chamber, 300 ft-c, at suitable temperature (e.g., 20°C), and record time of start.
4. After 6 hrs (or other time if indicated by a pretrial), remove bottles and determine dissolved oxygen directly on the contents in the bottle using twice the usual amount of reagents (i.e., use 2 ml each of $MnSO_4$, KOH-KI, and H_2SO_4 solutions). Remove 100-ml sample to titrate in the normal manner for Winkler analysis.

Calculation

$$p = (O_L - O_D) \times \frac{1}{t}$$

where p = photosynthesis, as mg O_2/liter/hr; O_L = dissolved oxygen concentration in light bottle; O_D = dissolved oxygen in dark bottle; and t = time of incubation (in hours).

Conversions

$$P_r = p \times 0.375$$

where P_r = relative productivity, in mg C fixed/liter/hr, and 0.375 is a factor to convert mg dissolved oxygen to mg C.

To convert from mg to ml of dissolved oxygen:

$$\text{mg diss. } O_2 \times 0.698 = \text{ml diss. } O_2$$

Ranges Not known, but values up to 1.0 mg of C/hr/m^3 are reported for the sea (Ref.: Doty and Oguri, 1957) and 11(–29) for inland water (Ref.: Elster, 1965: 82, 90).

Macrophytes For macrophytes, such as seaweeds and other nonvascular aquatics, use the four-bottle system, two covered and two uncovered with one each as control (or the two-bottle system if membrane-filtered water is used). For vascular aquatics, the same systems are used; but special concern must be given to avoid involvement of gases in the aerenchyma.

Procedure

1. Assemble four or two 250–300-ml gs or BOD bottles for each test, together with other items listed above for phytoplankton.
2. Fill all bottles with comparable water (preferably membrane-filtered). In subdued light, place a good-sized piece of acclimatized (see above) plant in each of two of the bottles; the plant pieces should be of similar size and about as long as the bottle is high. Also, place one small, wetted rubber stopper in each action bottle to help mix in later steps.
3. Cover dark bottle (with plant) and one blank, and leave uncovered the second plant-containing bottle and a blank.
4. Incubate under controlled conditions for 10–30 min (a preliminary run will help determine appropriate time). Record exact time of incubation (t).
5. Mix thoroughly by inverting (driving stopper around inside). Then measure oxygen directly (with oxygen electrode) or remove plant cautiously and run Winker analysis directly in bottle using double volumes (i.e., 2 ml of each of the basic three reagents).

Note Oxygen electrodes are subject to leveling off of readings at supersaturation; thus, excess oxygen must be avoided by using an appropriately short incubation time or using previously partly deaerated water. Such deaerated water can be obtained by sucking with vacuum pump at ca. 10–15 lb/in^2 for 2–4 min with continued shaking, until first flush of bubbles appears, at which time usually 2–4 ppm of dissolved O_2 remain; then cautiously siphon this into the bottles.

6. Determine volume of water (V_L, etc.) contained in each action bottle by filling with water and adding plant and the small rubber stopper of known volume, stoppering bottle, then pouring water into graduated cylinder. Record volume of water.
7. Determine dry weight of each piece of plant (m_1 and m_2).

Calculations
Derivation:

$$P_r = 0.375 \times \frac{1}{t} \left\{ \frac{\left(\left[O_L \frac{V_L}{1,000}\right] - \left[O_W \frac{V_W}{1,000}\right]\right) - \left(\left[O_{BL} \frac{V_{BL}}{1,000}\right] - \left[O_W \frac{V_W}{1,000}\right]\right)}{m_L} + \frac{\left(\left[O_W \frac{V_W}{1,000}\right] - \left[O_{BD} \frac{V_{BD}}{1,000}\right]\right) - \left(\left[O_W \frac{V_W}{1,000}\right] - \left[O_{BD} \frac{V_{BD}}{1,000}\right]\right)}{m_D} \right\} \quad (1)$$

Reducible to the following by replacing V in ml/1,000 ml values as V in liters:

$$P_r = \frac{0.375}{t} \left[\frac{(O_L V_L - O_{BL} V_{BL})}{m_L} + \frac{(O_{BD} V_{BD} - O_D V_D)}{m_D} \right] \quad (2)$$

where P_r = productivity in mg C/g/hr, and 0.375 is conversion factor from mg O_2/g/hr to mg C/g/hr; t = time, in hours; m_D = mass of alga in dark vessel, in g (dry or wet) weight; m_L = the same for alga in light vessel; O_{BD} = dissolved oxygen concentration in water blank in light (at end of run); O_{BL} = the same for water blank in dark; O_D = the same for vessel in dark with macrophyte; O_L = the same for vessel in light with macrophyte; O_W = the same for water at start of run (in equation 1 only); V_{BD} = volume of water in liters (ml in equation 1) in water blank in dark; V_{BL} = the same for water blank in light; V_D = the same for water in vessel with macrophyte in dark; V_L = the same for water in vessel with macrophyte in light; and V_W = the same for water in water blank (equation 1 only).

Conversion To convert to ml O_2, delete the 0.375 factor to get p, then:

ml diss. O_2 = 0.698 × mg diss. O_2

Ranges Not known, but values up to 3.2 mg C fixed/g dry wt/hr are reported (R. T. Hartman and D. L. Brown, ined.(?) quoted by Wetzel *in* Goldman, 1965: 257).

Productivity Techniques and Terms

Absolute Productivity Productivity per unit area, or per unit volume of water (Ref.: Elster *in* Goldman, 1965: 79).

Aquatic Macrophytes Wetzel (1965: 254) reported that aquatic macrophytes involve difficulties caused by oxygen metabolism of contaminating organisms in the water surrounding the plant and by the internal oxygen metabolism of the aquatic plant. The latter is especially true because of accumulation of oxygen in the lacunal system of vascular plants, and the gradual release of oxygen on demand. Thus, considerable oxygen may be stored, instead of being released, during photosynthesis in an action chamber.

Wetzel found the ^{14}C uptake method more consistent, and presumably better for studies of vascular (aerenchymatous?) aquatics. One possible suggestion would be to inject the aerenchyma completely with water. To do this, cut off ends of plant structure, immerse in water in stoppered filtering flask, and subject plant to strong suction until aerenchyma is full (5–15 min).

Compensation Point Light intensity (thus also depth) at which photosynthesis equals respiration can be measured by a series of light and dark bottles at intervals along a line suspended in the water for 3–6 hrs in bright sun on a calm day. Determine light intensity with submarine photometer.

Critical Light Intensity Light intensity (thus also depth) at which accumulated photosynthesis equals respiration over 24-hr periods can be measured as is done for "compensation point," but use larger jars (liter or 1-gal) for 24-hr period on a calm day. Average critical light intensity would require measurements over a variety of days to establish minimal, maximal, and average values.

Gross Primary Production Total photosynthesis that occurs during a given time. The formulas, above, calculate gross primary production. (See also "Net primary production.")

Net Primary Production Total photosynthesis that occurs during a given time, less the respiration and metabolic processes that reduce the oxygen released. To obtain this, revise the formulas above to get only the increase in oxygen in the light (i.e., do not add respiration from the dark period).

Relative Productivity Productivity per unit weight or volume of plant material (Ref.: Elster *in* Goldman, 1965: 77).

Volume of Plankton Can be estimated by Whipple method or by calculating from a formula approximating the cell shape. For the former, use a Whipple gridded ocular scale, and estimate area of organism in relation to a grid square; then, using Whipple's table, convert the value into volume (e.g., see Whipple's graph in Welch, 1948: 294; or APHA, 1965: 659). For the other method, a formula can be developed for each organism or particle, and the total volume is obtained by summating the number of each kind of organism and multiplying by the average volume determined from the formulas.

PROJECT 14 Primary Productivity: Pigment Analysis

OBJECTIVE

To determine chlorophyll concentration in plankton and benthon as an estimate of rate of primary production.

METHOD

Since, on the average, primary production in the ocean bears a fairly constant relation to the chlorophyll content, measurement of these pigments is used widely as an index of productivity.

For phytoplankton, filter a known volume (0.5–4 liters) of water and catch the plankton on a membrane or glass-fiber filter, stabilize with magnesium carbonate, grind it with 90% acetone, clarify the extract, and then measure the concentration with a spectrophotometer at specified wavelengths (UNESCO advises 663, 645, 630, and perhaps 650 and 750 mμ). Using empirical formulas (Richards and Thompson, 1952, as modified), calculate the concentration of certain chlorophylls (a, b, c) and summate to obtain the total chlorophyll. Express as mg or μg chl/liter or per m^3. Similar results can be obtained by measuring the pigment concentration with a Klett using the K66 filter and expressing directly as mg or μg chl/liter or per m^3.

For macrophytes, obtain adequate sample, determine wet (fresh) and dry weight, dry at 85°C, grind with 80–90% acetone and sand, drawing off the extract; stabilize, clarify, measure extinctions (as for phytoplankton); calculate by empirical formulas or a constant, and express as mg or μg chl/g dry or wet wt of alga. If the biomass is known, this can be converted to chl/m^2.

The rate of productivity can be roughly estimated from these pigment values using the empirical constant of 2 (μg C fixed/liter/hr = 2 × μg chl/liter) (Ref.: Yentsch, 1965: 337).

DATA

A. Table of sample values and results of extraction and analyses.

B. Pigment concentration values.

C. Estimated productivity calculated from pigment values.

REFERENCES

Albert, L. S. (pers. comm.). (See "Spectrophotometry" in "Notes," below).

Findenegg, I. 1965. Factors controlling primary productivity, especially with regard to water replenishment, stratification, and mixing. *In* C. R. Goldman (ed.), Primary Productivity in Aquatic Environments, pp. 105–119. Univ. California Press, Berkeley. 464 p.

Goldman, C. R. (ed.). 1965. (See "References" in project 4).

Johnson, J. M., T. O. Odlaug, T. A. Olson, and O. R. Ruschmeyer. 1970. The potential productivity of fresh water environments as determined by algal bioassay technique. Bull. 20. Water Resources Center, Univ. Minnesota, Minneapolis. 79 p.

Nauwerk, A. 1963. (See "References" in project 10).

Odum, H. T., and E. P. Odum. 1955. Trophic structure and productivity of a windward coral reef community on Eniwetok Atoll. Ecol. Monogr. 25: 291–320.

Richards, R. A., and T. G. Thompson. 1952. The estimation and characterization of plankton populations by pigment analysis. II. Spectrophotometric method for the estimation of plankton pigments. J. Mar. Res. 11: 156–172.

Ryther, J. 1956. Primary production and its measurement. Limnol. Oceanogr. 1: 72–84.

Strickland, J. D. H., and T. R. Parsons. 1968. (See "References" in project 5).

Yentsch, C. S. 1965. The relationship between chlorophyll and photosynthetic carbon production with reference to the measurement of decomposition products of chlorophyll pigments. *In* C. R. Goldman (ed.), Primary Productivity in Aquatic Environments, pp. 323–345. Univ. California Press, Berkeley. 464 p.

NOTES

Productivity Measurement, by Acetone Extraction

Phytoplankton

Chemicals Acetone (best analytical quality), hydrochloric acid (cp.), magnesium carbonate ("Levis"-grade analytical quality), anhydrous sodium carbonate, sodium thiosulfate.

Reagents

1. *90% acetone* (freshly diluted from stock solution).

2. *Acetone, stock solution:* distill over 1% of acetone's weight of each of anhydrous sodium carbonate and sodium thiosulfate, and collect at 56.5°C; store in tightly stoppered dark bottles, or use good quality acetone shaken with anhydrous sodium carbonate (Ref.: Strickland and Parsons, 1968: 188).

3. *50% hydrochloric acid:* dil. 50 ml of concd. HCl to 100 ml with dist. water.

4. *Magnesium carbonate suspension:* add 1 g of finely powdered "Levis"-grade analytical quality magnesium carbonate to 100 ml of dist. water; shake vigorously before use.

Procedure A Based on prior tests, determine volume (usually 4–5 liters of offshore seawater or 0.4–0.5 liters of inshore, estuarine, or inland waters) of sample needed to contain 1 μg chl/liter.

1. Collect water sample; keep it cold and analyze it as soon as possible.

2. Decide on volume to be filtered (enough to contain ca. 1 μg of chlorophyll), based on prior test.

3. Filter through coarse (ca. 0.3-mm mesh) nylon net to reduce zooplankton.

4. Set up filtering equipment (e.g., Millipore), and use 47-mm membrane with 0.8-μ pore size, or 45-mm glass-fiber filter (Gelman, or Whatman GF/C).

5. Thoroughly mix sample, then invert sample bottle onto funnel and simultaneously begin suction.

6. Adjust suction rate to obtain ca. 1 liter/7 min (be especially cautious if using glass filters).

7. Suck filter nearly dry, and squirt 2–3 drops of magnesium carbonate suspension (sol. 4) to cover the plankton.

8. Disassemble equipment, remove filter, and place on numbered piece of paper in vacuum desiccator (with silica gel).

9. With vacuum pump, suck air from desic-

cator; turn off suction and seal lid simultaneously.

10. Dry for 6 hrs at coldest available temperature (in freezer, or next to freezing unit in refrigerator).

11. Remove and warm up desiccator until air valve can be opened, and then get out filter.

12. Trim away excess outer rim of filter; roll filter with plankton inside, and insert to bottom of 15-ml graduated centrifuge tube.

13. With propipet-equipped 5-ml grad. pipet, transfer 5 ml of 90% acetone (sol. 1) so as to run over plankton into the centrifuge tube.

14. Tightly stopper with aluminum or plastic cap; shake vigorously until filter is dispersed.

15. Let stand 18–24 hrs in dark at room temperature, shaking vigorously again at end of 1st hr.

16. If not clear, centrifuge 3–10 min at 2,500 rpm; if clear, proceed.

17. Cautiously pour or draw off fluid and transfer to graduated 15-ml centrifuge tube; allow contents to warm up, and dil. to 10 ml with 90% acetone (sol. 1), and mix (if color is too dark, dil. quantitatively with 90% acetone to density suitable for spectrophotometry [see "Spectrophotometry," below]).

18. Pour extract into spectrophotometer (or Klett) cuvet, and read in spectrophotometer at 630, 645, and 663 mμ. If phaeophytins are desired, also read at 665 and 750 mμ (or in Klett using K66 filter), comparing with 90% acetone as blank (see "Spectrophotometry," below; or "Klett colorimeter," in project 5a). (Use long-light path, e.g., 10 cm.)

19. If phaeophytins are sought, add 2 drops of 50% hydrochloric acid (sol. 3); mix.

20. Remeasure at 665 and 750 mμ after 5 min.

Procedure B SCOR/UNESCO procedure for phytoplankton, a rapid technique (cf. "Phytoplankton," above, for details).

1. Use water containing ca. 1 μg of chl; decide on volume by prior test. (*Note:* chl in μg/liter = ca. 1/2 of productivity in μg/liter/hr.)

2. Assemble filter unit, using glass-fiber (Gelman, or Whatman GF/C) or membrane (Millipore, 0.8-μ pore) filter.

3. Filter with low suction.

4. Cover plankton with magnesium carbonate suspension (sol. 4).

5. Analyze immediately, or store in dark over silica gel at 1°C up to 2 months.

6. Fold filter (plankton inside) twice, and insert to bottom of 15-ml glass tissue homogenizer tube.

7. Add 2–3 ml of 90% acetone (sol. 1), and grind at reduced speed (ca. 500 rpm) using power unit with a slip-clutch attachment (a short tygon tube connection may suffice) for 1 min.

8. Transfer grindings to a conical centrifuge tube, rinsing homogenizer tube 2–3 times with a little 90% acetone (let stand for 10 min).

9. Centrifuge 10 min at 4,000–5,000 g's (if still turbid, add a few drops of 100% acetone; mix, and recentrifuge). (See "Centrifuge force and velocities" at end of "Notes" section, for g's values.)

10. Cautiously pour off, or draw out and transfer, fluid into graduated centrifuge tube.

11. Dilute to a convenient volume (e.g., 15 ml) with 90% acetone; mix.

12. Read in spectrophotometer (or Klett with K66 filter) against 90% acetone, as given above at wavelengths of 630, 645, 663, and 750 mμ.

(Ref.: UNESCO. 1966. Monographs on oceanographic methodology. Cited and modified by Strickland and Parsons, 1968: 195.)

Calculations With spectrophotometer readings, calculate using Richards and Thompson's (1952) empirical formulas as modified by SCOR/UNESCO (Strickland and Parsons, 1968: 189, with correction to 10-cm path):

$$C_a = 11.64\,E_{663} - 2.16\,E_{645} + 0.10\,E_{630}$$
$$C_b = 20.97\,E_{645} - 3.94\,E_{663} - 3.66\,E_{630}$$
$$C_c = 54.22\,E_{630} - 14.81\,E_{645} - 5.53\,E_{663}$$

Then:

$$\text{mg chl[a,b, or c]}/\text{m}^3 = \text{C[a,b, or c]} \times \frac{v}{V} \times \frac{10}{p} \times \frac{1}{10} \qquad (1)$$

If phaeophytins are sought (cf. 19 and 20, above), also calculate chl. a and phaeophytins, as follows:

1. Subtract E_{750} from corresponding E_{665} readings.
2. chl a $(\text{mg/m}^3) = 26.7(E_{665} - E_{665'}) \times$

$$\frac{v}{V \times p} \qquad (2)$$

3. Phaeo-pigments (mg/m^3) =

$$26.7(1.7\,[E_{665}] - E_{665'}) \times \frac{v}{V \times p} \qquad (3)$$

where E_{665} = optical density at 665 mμ before acidification; $E_{665'}$ = optical density after acidification; v = volume of acetone extract (ml); V = volume of water filtered (liters); and p = light path (cm) (Ref.: Strickland and Parsons, 1968: 194). (*Note:* The "1/10" correction to 10-cm path in formula 1 is canceled out in the other three formulas.)

With Klett readings (using 4-cm light path and 10-ml extract volume):

$$\mu\text{g chl/liter} = 0.65 \times K \times \frac{1}{V} \times \frac{4}{p} \qquad (4)$$

where chl = total chlorophyll (μg); K = Klett units; V = volume filtered (liters); and p = light path (cm) (Ref.: Johnson, et al., 1970: 24).

Macrophytes

Chemicals and Reagents As above.

Procedure

1. Obtain somewhat more than 100 g of fresh material of aquatic angiosperms, bryophytes, and macroscopic algae (red algae requires special treatment, see step 2).
2. Obtain fresh weight, to 0.1 g. (If *Rhodophyta* are used, let samples stand overnight in dist. water in refrigerator to remove phycobilins, and rinse them before drying.)
3. Dry at 85°C in forced-air oven.
4. Reweigh to constant weight to obtain dry weight.
5. Grind in plant mill, mix, and take a carefully weighed sample (ca. 0.2 g is often sufficient).
6. Transfer to mortar; add a little chemically clean sand and 5 ml of 90% acetone[1], and grind with pestle (if extraction is poor, repeat using different solvent[1]).
7. Decant into 15-ml graduated centrifuge tube.
8. Add 5 ml of 90% acetone, and grind again; decant into centrifuge tube, rinsing with a little 90% acetone if necessary.
9. Make up to 15 ml with 90% acetone. Let stand overnight in dark.
10. Centrifuge 5 min at 2,500 rpm, but if turbid allow to stand overnight in refrigerator before centrifuging.
11. If color is too dense, dilute quantitatively to a convenient density; if too thin, use cuvet with longer light path.
12. Cautiously pour or draw off fluid and transfer to a spectrophotometer (or Klett) cuvet and read with spectrophotometer at 630, 645, and 663 mμ; and, if phaeophytins are desired, also read at 665 and 750 mμ (or use Klett with K66 filter).

12a. If phaeophytins are sought, add 2 drops of 50% hydrochloric acid (sol. 3) to cuvet; mix, let stand 5 min, and reread at 665 and 750 mμ.

Calculation Use the modified Richards and Thompson's formulas given above (for phytoplankton) to obtain pigment value (P);

[1] Acetone is ineffective in some algae. A solvent of 2 parts methanol and 1 part petroleum ether (bp ca. 50°C) may be necessary. (Ref.: Bogorad, L., p. 391, *in* R. Lewin, 1962, Physiology and Biochemistry of Algae. Academic Press, New York. 929 p.)

then, to express results as mg chl/g wet weight and mg chl/g dry weight of plant material, use the following formula:

$$C_u = P \times \frac{1}{A} \qquad (5)$$

where C_u = mg chl/g of plant; P = pigment, as "mg/m^3" calculated from the "phytoplankton" equations above; and A = weight of the aquatic (g).

Relationship of Pigment Content to Productivity

Where productivity rate measurements (e.g., ^{14}C uptake) are run on the same material used for the pigment analysis, then:

$$C/P_{chl} = \frac{\mu g \text{ C fixed/liter/hr}}{\mu g \text{ chl/liter}}$$

where C = carbon fixed; P_{chl} = chlorophyll pigments, and chl = chlorophyll.

Productivity per unit chlorophyll (C/P_{chl}) values from 0.1 to 2.4 have been plotted (Ref.: Yentsch *in* Goldman, 1965: 337) for open oceanic water, up to 6.2 (Ref.: Yentsch, l.c., p. 340) for coastal waters (Woods Hole, Mass.). Thus, these estimates, or a commonly used value of 0.5, can be obtained from such a relationship, as:

$$C/P_{chl} = \frac{\mu g \text{ C/liter/hr}}{\mu g \text{ chl/liter}} = 0.5$$

then:

$$\mu g \text{ C fixed/liter/hr} = 0.5 \times \mu g \text{ chl/liter}$$

For another relationship, productivity to fresh weight, one can use:

$$\text{Activity coefficient} = \frac{\mu g \text{ C/m}^3\text{/day}}{\mu g \text{ fresh weight/m}^3} \text{ or } \frac{\text{g C/m}^3\text{/day}}{\text{g/m}^3}$$

(Ref.: Nauwerk, 1963, cited by Findenegg *in* Goldman, 1965: 277).

Activity coefficient values have been obtained by Findenegg (l.c., p. 280) of 0.04–0.10. If 0.07 were taken as an empirical constant, the biomass could be estimated from productivity values obtained from Yentsch's formula above, as follows:

$$\text{Biomass } (\mu g \text{ fresh wt/m}^3) = \frac{\mu g \text{ C fixed/m}^3\text{/day}}{\text{activity coefficient}} \text{ or } \frac{\mu g \text{ C/m}^3\text{/day}}{0.07}$$

Spectrophotometry (See Also "Klett Colorimeter," Project 5a)

The spectrophotometer is an instrument for determining concentration of a color-producing solute (chromogen) by measuring the light it absorbs. This is done by comparing its absorption with that of a solution of known concentration of the solute (or with a blank, of solvent). This works because concentration is (generally) proportional to the log of the light absorbed (optical density). This relationship is defined by Beer's law.

In more complicated cases where two or more colored solutes are involved, only one of which is to be measured, the actual concentration is approximated by using just the color of light best absorbed by that solute. This is done by setting the wavelength dial, which moves a slot (door) along a spectrum thrown by a prism or grating, so as to select light of just one color (the narrower the door, e.g., 5 μ vs 40 μ, the purer the light quality). The wavelength is expressed in mμ (= nm, nanometers), and occasionally in Ångstroms (10 Å = 1 mμ).

Since different solutions vary in density, at times a longer or shorter (or fatter or thinner) or smaller diameter (tubular) cuvet is used, giving a longer or shorter light path, to make it possible to read the transmitted light with the spectrophotometer. If for a dense solution a cuvet of half the normal width is used, then the resulting concentration value must be doubled. This relationship is defined by Lambert's law.

Calculations for spectrophotometry combine these applications in Beer-Lambert laws:

$$\frac{C_s}{C_u} = \frac{E_s}{E_u} \times \frac{P_a}{P_o} \times \frac{V_o}{V_a} \text{ or } C_u = \frac{E_u}{E_s} \times C_s \times \frac{P_o}{P_a} \times \frac{V_a}{V_o}$$

where C_s = concentration of standard (mg/liter); C_u = concentration of unknown (mg/liter); E_s = extinction (optical density) of standard; E_u = extinction of unknown; P_o = light path length of original directions (cm); P_a = light path length actually used (cm); V_o = final volume of extract in original directions (ml); and V_a = volume actually used (ml).

Procedure (for Beckman Spectronic 20, and Coleman Model 14 Universal, Spectrophotometers)

1. Turn on unit in advance and allow to warm up 5 min (20 min is better) for the Spectronic 20, and 30 min for the Universal. (Use lower front left knob in the former, and main left center dial in the latter, turning from "off" to "spectro.")
2. Adjust meter line or needle to zero using lower left knob in Spectronic 20 and with coarse, then fine, adjustment dials (lower left on face) of the Universal.
3. Using carefully cleaned and wiped (with soft tissue) cuvet, fill 3/4 full with solvent (often dist. water), and insert into well. In Universal, put in lefthand hole. Line up cuvet marks.
4. Select wavelength (λ) indicated in analytical procedure.
5. Raise meter line to 100% transmittance with lower right dial of Spectronic 20, and with coarse, then fine, adjustment dials (lower left on face) of the Universal.
6. Put unknown in a second clean cuvet, and insert in place of the blank (in right cuvet hole of the Universal).
7. Cover cuvet, then read % T (and possibly the optical density).
8. To turn off, turn both control dials left to zero.
9. *Note:* In case other readings are to be made on the same solution but at other wavelengths, after completing one reading, lower the meter line, reinsert blank, select new wavelength, raise meter line to 100% T, then insert unknown cuvet and read unknown.

Calculation

$$C_u = \frac{E_u}{E_s} \times C_s$$

With solutions of unusual density, use the following:

$$C_u = \frac{E_u}{E_s} \times C_s \times \frac{P_o}{P_a} \times \frac{V_a}{V_o}$$

where C_s = concentration of standard (mg/liter); C_u = concentration of unknown (mg/liter); E_s = extinction (optical density) of standard; E_u = extinction of unknown; P_o = light path length of original directions (cm); P_a = light path length actually used (cm); V_o = final volume of extract in original directions (ml); and V_a = volume actually used (ml).

Equations in Light Penetration In the spectrophotometer or Klett colorimeter (project 5a), as with the submarine photometer measurements of light penetration of pond or sea water (project 5a), the penetration rate can be fitted by a commonly seen mathematical equation:

$$I = I_o \cdot e^{-kh}$$

The basis for this formula can be visualized in Figure 1, in which light penetration is plotted against the length of the light path, and in which a descending logarithmic curve is obtained. The curve approaches an asymptote at which the light is attentuated (stretched out) into deep water. Notice also in the figure that the original light (I_o) at zero depth becomes reduced at a decreasingly rapid rate such that the light intensity at each depth can be found by multiplying the original light intensity by e (= 2.718) raised to a negative (to indicate descending value) exponent of the light path (h) and figure (k), called the extinction coefficient, which depends upon the density of the solution. This relationship is expressed as:

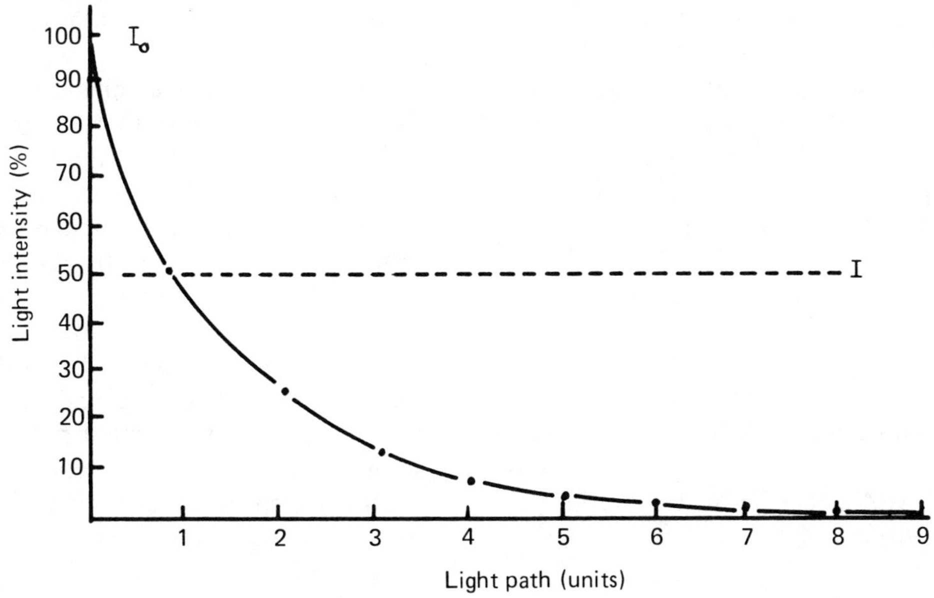

Figure 1. The equation, $I = I_o e^{-kh}$, fits normal light penetration curve. Graph is tipped on side to conform to usual mathematical treatment. View from right to see it as a penetration curve into open water. The original intensity, I_o, is reduced by ½ at each successive unit of depth. For base e, k = ca. 0.69, while for base 10, k = ca. 0.33, while the units progress 1, 2, 3, etc. (h = depth).

$$I = I_o \cdot e^{-kh} \quad \text{or} \quad \frac{I}{I_o} = e^{-kh}$$

(Ref.: Ruttner, 1963: 13; Reid, 1961: 105, where I is given as I_z and a factor, c (for concentration), is added to permit consideration of the combined Beer-Lambert laws.)

Manipulation of the Absorption Equation

$$I = I_o \cdot e^{-kh} \tag{1}$$

$$\frac{I}{I_o} = e^{-kh} \tag{2}$$

$$-kh = \log_e \frac{I}{I_o} \tag{3}$$

By changing the sign:

$$kh = \log_e \frac{I_o}{I} \tag{4}$$

$$k = \frac{1}{h} \cdot \log_e \frac{I_o}{I} \tag{5}$$

and if h = 1:

$$k = \log_e \frac{I_o}{I} \tag{6}$$

Using base 10 and equation (1), we get:

$$I = I_o \cdot 10^{-kh} \tag{7}$$

As in Equation (6):

$$k = \log_{10} I_o - \log_{10} I \tag{8}$$

And if I_o is 100% T, log 100 is 2, and h is 1, then:

$$k = 2 - \log_{10} I \tag{9}$$

Terms and Concepts in Spectrophotometry

Absorbance (absorbence, extinction): degree to which solution absorbs light (usually expressed as optical density, or Klett units).

Beer's law: concentration of chromogen is proportional to the optical density. In spectrophotometry, this is applied by making measurements on a log basis, with optical density (see equation 9), where optical density = $2 - \log_{10}$ I, and I is expressed in % T.

Dilution correction: if solution is too dense

to permit practical readings in a spectrophotometer (i.e., between 20 and 80% T), then the solution is diluted quantitatively with its solvent, and the diluted solution is read and calculations are made as follows:

$$C_u = \frac{E_u}{E_s} \times C_s \times \frac{V_a}{V_o}$$

where V_o = volume of solution prescribed in procedure and V_a = volume actually used.

Extinction: same as absorbance, and expressed in optical density (or Klett units).

Extinction coefficient: is k (equation 6, above), used under defined conditions to characterize a compound:

$$2 - \log_{10} T = \kappa \times P \times C \text{ and } \kappa = \frac{(2 - \log_{10} T)}{P \times C}$$

where $2 - \log_{10} T$ = optical density; P = light path (cm); and C = molar concentration (moles per liter $\frac{\text{g/liter}}{\text{GMW}}$). Ref.: Albert, L. S. [pers. comm.]. Sheets issued for plant physiology, Dept. Botany, Univ. R.I.)

Lambert's Law: concentration of chromogen is inversely proportional to length (depth) of solution. This is applied as:

$$C_u = \frac{E_u}{E_s} \times C_s \times \frac{P_o}{P_a}$$

Light path length correction: if the solution is so thin that a longer light path is needed in order to get a reasonable reading, or if it is so dense that a shorter light path is used, this correction can be made as follows (in accordance with Lambert's law):

$$C_u = \frac{E_u}{E_s} \times C_s \times \frac{P_o}{P_a}$$

where P_o = the light path length prescribed in the procedure and P_a = the light path actually used.

Combined light path and dilution corrections are:

$$C_u = \frac{E_u}{E_s} \times C_s \times \frac{P_o}{P_a} \times \frac{V_a}{V_o}$$

(Compare also "Klett colorimeter," project 5a.)

Limitations: there are inherent errors and limitations in spectrophotometry. An inherent error of 5% or greater is accepted in such procedures. Limitations involve both the sensitivity of the unit and properties of different solutions. Spectrophotometer accuracy drops off at both ends of the scale, and thus one aims to arrange the procedure (dilution, light path) so that readings will fall between 20 and 80% T. Concerning solutions, some do not exhibit proportional optical densities and concentration except in a very limited range. With such materials, limits are set (e.g., use 0–400 Klett units for chlorophyll) or a calibration curve is made for which known standards are analyzed throughout the range (e.g., NO_3–N and SiO_2–Si).

Transmittance, transmittancy: degree of light passed by solution (see "Transparency").

Transparency: degree to which fluid passes light, usually expressed in % T, $100 \times I/I_o$, but most spectrophotometers read in % T directly.

Centrifuge Force and Velocities

Centrifuge speeds are expressed in revolutions per minute, but the force ($F = \pi^2 S^2 RM/900$) actually applied to the material being centrifuged is expressed in multiples of gravitational force (divide through by 980 because 1 g of force = 980 dynes). The force in g's may be estimated as follows:

$$g\text{'s} = \frac{\pi^2}{882{,}000} \times S^2 RM$$

where g's = force times gravity (force-producing acceleration of 980 cm/sec/sec); S = revolutions per min; R = radius of arm (cm); and M = weight of object (g).

For example, for a 1-g water sample, spun on 20-cm radius arm, at 2,500 rpm:

$$g\text{'s} = \frac{3.14 \times 3.14}{8.82 \times 10^5} \times (2.5 \times 10^3 \times 2.5 \times 10^3) \times (2.0 \times 10) = 1{,}400 \text{ g's}$$

Table 1. Pigment occurrence in plankton and macrophytes[a]

	Red algae, blue-green algae, *Xanthophyceae, Chrysophyceae*	Brown algae, diatoms, dinoflagellates	Green algae, euglenophytes, green plants
chl a	+	+	+
chl b	0	0	+
chl c	0	+	?

[a]Reference: Smith, G. M. (1950: 3).

(Ref.: Encyclopaedia Britannica, 1965 (5:190). See "Centrifuge.")

Pigment Occurrence

For pigment occurrence in plankton and macrophytes, see Table 1.

PROJECT 15 Primary Productivity: ^{14}C Uptake

OBJECTIVE

To measure the rate of gross primary productivity by CO^2 uptake using radioactive carbon (^{14}C).

METHOD

Using a two-bottle, light-dark bottle system (project 14), fill two bottles with plankton-containing water. Inoculate each with a known activity of radioactive sodium carbonate; stopper, cover one (aluminum foil or black bag) to keep totally dark, and incubate both in growth chamber at a suitable temperature (e.g., 15°C) and light (e.g., 400 ft-c, ca. 4,300 lux) for 4–6 hrs. Filter contents of each onto Millipore filter; remove filter and dry; then count for beta radiation with ultra-thin gas flow beta counter. Also, standardize the radioisotope solution by similarly inoculating a volumetric flask, adding sufficient $BaCl_2$ to precipitate the carbonates; filter onto Millipore filter, dry, and count. Using counts from light and dark bottles, and taking account of corrections for the standard, background, instrument consistency and efficiency, etc., calculate productivity as mg C fixed/m^3/hr or μg/liter/hr.

For macrophytes, run much in the same manner except that small-leaved (e.g., *Elodea*) plants are most convenient because they can be handled in the counter, whereas other plants must be ground and filtered onto a Millipore filter. Also, the bottles should be filled with filter-sterilized raw water. If unfiltered raw water is used, blanks are necessary and will involve a 4- to 5-bottle arrangement. The wet plant material recorded after incubation should be exposed to HCl fumes to remove external carbonate deposits. Dry, obtain dry weights, make the counts of beta activity, and calculate mg C fixed/g dry wt/hr.

A convenient table for handling field data on shipboard, and satisfactory for laboratory use as well, is shown in Table 1.

Productivity of plant parts or aquatic vegetation can be studied in nature by enclosing parts in plastic bags or by covering vegetation with a thin plastic hemisphere forced into the sediment. The ^{14}C solution is inoculated through the plastic wall with a syringe. When incubation time is completed, divers bring up the bags; and, in the case of a hemisphere, push the edges down into the sediment under the plants and bring up the entire unit of water, plants, and bottom material.

For rapid estimation of growth rate of plankton in the field, Goldman (1960, and

Table 1. Sample table for field data and processing results to obtain primary productivity rate by ^{14}C uptake method (modified from Doty and Oguri, 1959: 75): sample data included with notes on handling certain steps

^{14}C ampoule batch, stock no. 4 Cruise: *Hugh M. Smith* no. 37

A	B[a]	C	D	E	F	G[b]	H	I[c]	J[d]	J′	K	L	M[f]	N[g]
Conditions, date, position or station	Bottle no.	Time in	Time out	Planchet no.	Raw counts (cpm)	Standard count (cpm)	Raw counts normalized (cpm)	C/M	Back-ground (cpm)	C/M less back-ground (I–J)	Average C/M	Time of run (D–C)	Light less dark	mg C/m^3/hr
11/21/56						123,480/5								
Sta. 4	L 137	0806	1406	910	1,275/5		1,291/5	258	25/min	233	233	6.0	190	0.1418
0800	L126			911	1,075/3		1,070/3	357		332	332	6.0	289	0.2189
						125,626/5								
	D 51			912	417/6		409/6	68		43	43	6.0		

[a]B: L = light bottle, D = dark bottle.

[b]G: Correction raw counts (F) for machine variation, the original standard source (not included in data) divided by the current reading (G) provides the correction factor; i.e.:

$$\text{from } R = r(C_O/C_C), \text{ normalized raw count (see H)} = \frac{1{,}275}{5} \text{ (see F)} \times \frac{\text{original count}}{123{,}480/5 \text{ (see G)}}$$

Original count is the first made on the standard during the run.

[c]I: Obtain count/min by dividing by minutes (e.g., I = H/5).

[d]J: C/M (see J′) = C/M (see I) – background count (see J).

[e]L: Time of incubation = time out (see D) – time in (see C).

[f]M: Subtract dark bottle count (last entry in K) from light bottle (see also K) count.

[g]N: Make corrections (on M) for self-absorption and resolving time, then determine productivity:

$$\text{Productivity (mg C/m}^3\text{/hr)} = \frac{\text{net count/min (see M)}}{\text{total ampoule count}} \times \frac{1}{\text{hours (see L)}} \times \frac{\text{mg C}}{\text{liter}} \times \frac{100}{100-\text{I}} \times 1{,}000$$

Total ampoule count is obtained by precipitating contents onto filter, counting, and correcting for self-absorption; mg C/liter is calculated from alkalinity; I = isotope effect (ca. 6.79%); 1,000 converts mg/liter/hr to m^3/hr.

summarized 1965: 125) introduced a method which involves incubating samples in the field with ^{14}C for up to an hour, then forcing filtration through small membrane filters with a syringe. The filters, stored in a coin collection case, are returned to the laboratory for later counting.

The entire procedure involves five phases, and the details of each are included under "Notes." These five phases are: 1) advanced preparations, 2) analytical procedures, 3) cleanup and monitoring area, 4) counting, and 5) calculations.

In addition, there are a number of radiological techniques or regulations outlined below which are necessary for this work. For details, see "Notes."

Basic radiological methodology:

1. Radioisotopes manipulation
2. Loss prevention
3. Detection and measurement of radiation
4. Permissible legal amounts
5. Disposal of wastes

Special procedures:

1. Establishing plateau and voltage setting of Geiger tube
2. Determining resolving time, and correcting for instrument sensitivity
3. Correcting for background
4. Correcting for self-absorption
5. Available carbon in water (as CO_2, HCO_3^-, and CO_3^{--})
6. Instrument efficiency (actually = consistency), "normalize" by use of standard
7. Isotope effect, i.e., physiologically different action with ^{12}C or ^{14}C (ca. 6.79% less for ^{14}C according to some workers)

DATA

A. Summarize and tabulate data, conversions, and corrections.

B. Present final calculated results of productivity as mg C fixed/m^3/hr or μg C fixed/liter/hr; and, for macrophytes, as mg C fixed/g dry wt/hr or μg C fixed/g dry wt/hr.

REFERENCES

APHA. 1965. (See "References" in project 5).

Buch, K. 1945. Kolsyrejämvikten i Baltiska Havet. Fennica 68: 123 (fide Steemann-Nielsen 1952).

Chase, G. D., and J. L. Rabinowitz. 1967. Principles of Radioisotope Methodology. 3rd Ed. Burgess, Minneapolis. 633 p. (Also, see 2nd Ed. 1962. 371 p.)

Doty, M. S., and M. Oguri. 1959. The carbon-fourteen technique for determining primary plankton productivity. Pubbl. Staz. Zool. Napoli 31(suppl.): 70–94.

Goldman, C. R. 1960. (See "References" in project 12).

Goldman, C. R. 1965. (See "References" in project 4).

Harvey, H. W. 1945. (See "References" in project 8).

Harvey, H. W. 1957. The Chemistry and Fertility of Sea Water. Cambridge Univ. Press, Cambridge. (1966 printing, 240 p.)

IACD. (Instruction sheets for measurement of primary production in the sea, issued with C-14 ampoules by the Agency.) International Agency for ^{14}C Determination, Charlottenlund Slot, Charlottenlund, Denmark.

JI/GTFE. 1969. (See "References" in project 12).

Saunders, G. W., F. B. Trama, and R. W. Bachman. 1962. (See "References" in project 5a).

Steemann-Nielsen, E. 1952. The use of radioactive carbon (^{14}C) for measuring organic production in the sea. J. Cons. Int. Expl. Mer. 18: 117–140.

Strickland, J. D. H., and T. R. Parsons. 1965. (See "References" in project 5).

Strickland, J. D. H., and T. R. Parsons. 1968. (See "References" in project 5).

Sverdrup, H. U., M. W. Johnson, and R. H. Fleming. 1942. (See "References" in project 5).

NOTES

^{14}C Uptake Method

Advanced Preparations

1. Assemble radiological materials in special work area equipped with facilities for radiological work, including suction, gas flow beta counter, Geiger gas, survey meter, monitoring equipment, dosimeters, isotopes (e.g., ampoules[1] with 1 μCi for coastal waters, 5 μCi for estuaries, 25 μCi for open oceans, or the 4 μCi provided by IACD laboratories for general marine use), growth chamber (usually at 15°C and ca. 3,200 lux = ca. 300 ft-c), and glassware including long-pointed medicine droppers (or 2-ml syringe with long [6-in.] needle), Millipore filtering equipment, Millipore filters (0.8-μ pore, 25-mm diam), aluminum foil, waterproof-backed absorbent paper, pipets, planchets, desiccator with soda-lime and silica gel, $BaCl_2$ powder, and neutral formalin (add borax until neutral to phenolphthalein or litmus).
2. Obtain or determine new corrections for: a) proper voltage level for counting, b) resolving time correction factor, c) self-absorption correction, and d) total carbon and carbonates in the water sample.
3. Obtain ca. 1,000 ml or more of raw water in nontoxic container, handle in reduced light, and acclimatize to temperature before beginning experiment by placing in growth chamber in dark. Filter (membrane) enough (50 ml) water for rinse purposes (see 18, below).

Analytical Procedures

1. Recharge and reset or read dosimeter. Don protective clothing.
2. Obtain the acclimatized water sample (see 3, above) from growth chamber, and work in reduced light.
3. Nearly fill two 250-ml gs bottles and a 250-ml volumetric flask with thoroughly uniformly mixed water sample.
4. After flicking top to drive all fluid into base of ampoule, file or scratch ampoule across neck, and snap off top.
5. Using sterile pipet with rubber bulb (or syringe with 6-in. long needle), draw out isotope and quantitatively deliver it to bottom of sample bottles; raise tip of pipet to near surface of fluid, suck up some water, and discharge the rinse back into water at bottom of bottle.
6. Wash neck and body of ampoule with small amount of water, and transfer residue by pipet into the bottle.
7. Repeat with other bottle and with the 250-ml flask.
8. Complete the filling of the bottles with raw water of sample, and the flask, to 250 ml; then stopper carefully and mix thoroughly by repeated inverting.
9. Cover one bottle with aluminum foil or black bag to make totally dark.
10. Put the two bottles into illuminated growth chamber, recording "time in."

To make standard and check self-absorption:

11. Prepare Millipore apparatus and filter.
12. To prepare isotope standard, mix isotope solution (or use entire contents of ampoule). With 1-ml volumetric pipet transfer 1 ml (or contents of ampoule) into test tube, alkalize with a drop of dil. NaOH, dilute by filling tube to ca. 1/4 full with dist. water, and add a little powdered $BaCl_2$, mixing carefully with glass rod until dissolved and precipitate forms. Treat as in 14, below.
13. To check self-absorption, prepare a series of several samples as in 12, but make graded series of amount of isotope added

[1] For method to make up ampoules from powdered isotope, see Doty and Oguri (1959).

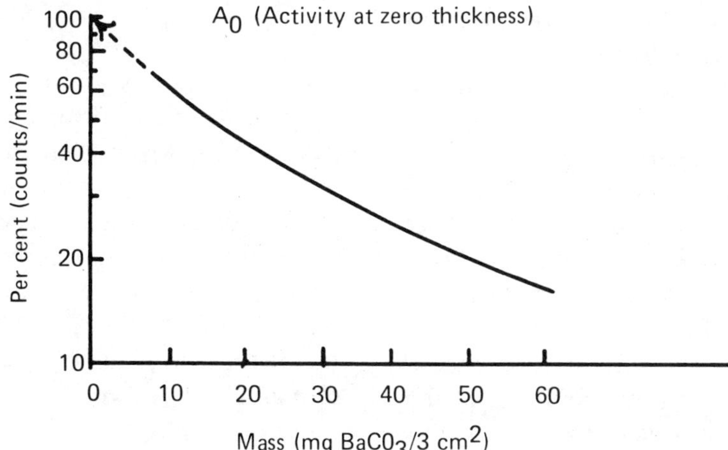

Figure 1. Self-absorption curve from counts of filters with varying amounts of precipitate but constant activity. By extending the curve to the left, one can obtain the counts/min at zero precipitate thickness.

(e.g., 0.01, 0.1, 1, 2, etc.). Treat as in 14, below, saving all filters for counting.

14. Filter onto preweighed Millipore filter, rinsing with several portions of water; expose to HCl fumes for 1 min, then rinse again.

15. Remove filter and dry in desiccator; reweigh and determine mg of carbonate precipitated. Compare with previously prepared calibration curve (or see Figure 1), and determine correction factor by which raw counts must be multiplied to obtain true counts.

16. At end of incubation time (4–6 hrs), remove the bottles from growth chamber, and record "time out."

17. Open bottles, and squirt in 1 ml of neutral formalin; mix.

18. Filter each onto Millipore filter (not exceeding 1.5 atm suction), rinsing bottle twice with 10-ml portions of filtered raw water, and scrubbing sides and bottom with rubber policeman.

19. Suck to dryness.

20. Expose filter to HCl fumes for 1 min (or rinse with 20 ml of 0.001 N HCl), followed by filtered-water rinse.

21. With uncontaminated forceps, transfer filter onto paper toweling to dry.

22. Clamp in special holder, or weight down edges with a ring; dry in desiccator over silica gel and soda-lime.

23. Spread thin layer of rubber cement onto planchet, and force filter (plankton side up) onto cement, centering carefully, and allow to dry.

24. As a blank, similarly cement a clean filter onto a planchet.

25. Label and store for later counting.

Cleanup

1. Work in hood with vacuum draft; rinse glassware with concd. HCl, then twice with running water (making sure to overflow bottles).
2. Store upside down to drain, and air dry.
3. Immerse metal filter holders in ca. 1% HCl, quickly followed by freshwater rinse.
4. Flush pipets and glass filter support in concd. HCl, and rinse several times with dist. water.
5. Collect all rinsings in jar or jug; alkalize (e.g., add pellet of NaOH), and save in plastic carbuoy for disposal through proper agencies.
6. Reread dosimeter, and record value. If much change has occurred, notify instructor.
7. Monitor self and area with good Geiger counter.

Counting with Ultrathin Window Gas Flow Beta Counter, Using Geiger Gas

1. Connect beta counting instruments to wall sockets.
2. Turn on unit, and allow to warm up for the prescribed time.
3. Run test by setting dial to "test;" set timer for 1 min and its switch to "on" (should give 3,600 counts), and then turn back from "test," if ok.
4. Slowly raise high voltage to predetermined operating value (commonly ca. 1,300, or as marked on the Geiger tube).
5. Gradually turn on valve of Geiger gas, and slowly raise pressure to ca. 5 lb/in^2.
6. Insert standard thallium source disk into carrier, carefully sliding carrier into detector (using upper position carrier).
7. Take several 1-min counts until they become consistent, and then take a series of counts and record as "standard count" (to correct for instrument inconsistency).
8. Insert planchet with clean, unused filter, and take and record 5–30 min of background reading, and record as "background."
9. Count planchet and filter for the standard isotope solution, to calculate activity of ampoule.
10. Count ^{14}C samples for the equivalent of at least 1,800 counts, recording as "raw count."
11. Repeat standard count occasionally, and record as "standard count."
12. When finished, gradually close valve on Geiger gas tank, lowering pressure to zero.
13. Leave instrument at "stand by" (i.e., lowest voltage), if it is to be used during the week, or
14. Turn off, first the high voltage, then the main switch.

Calculations Note the sequence of steps in making corrections in the data in Table 1, but also note that the activity values, A_L and A_D (= activities in light and dark, in column M), are to be corrected for resolving time and self-absorption at step N.

For phytoplankton:

$$P = \frac{A_L - A_D}{A_t} \times \frac{1}{T} \times C_t \times \frac{100}{100 - I} \times 1{,}000$$

where P = primary productivity (mg C fixed/m^3/hr); A_L = the corrected activity (cpm) in light bottle; A_D = corrected activity (cpm) in dark bottle; A_t = total original activity, as marked on ampoule or as determined experimentally; C_t = total carbon available (mg C/liter); T = time of incubation (hrs); I = isotope effect, about 6.79%; and 1,000 = factor for conversion of results from mg/liter to mg/m^3.

For macrophytes:

$$P = \frac{A_L - A_D}{A_t} \times \frac{1}{T} \times C_t \times \frac{100}{100 - I} \times \frac{1}{g}$$

where the symbols are the same as for phytoplankton, but g = fresh or dry weight of plant material, in g. When calculating on weight basis, omit the 1,000 factor used in the phytoplankton formula.

Correcting A_L and A_D for resolving time and self-absorption can be done as follows. For resolving time:

$$A_C = (A_R - A_B)\,\frac{1}{1 - (A_R - A_B)\,T_R} \times \frac{V}{V - V_n}$$

where A_C = corrected activity (cpm); A_R = raw activity (cpm); A_B = background; T_R = resolving time (min); V = volume of sample in bottle; and V_n = volume not filtered in case filter is plugged.

For self-absorption, often negligible in soft waters, correction can be made by using the factor obtained through a calibration curve (see item 4 under "Special procedures in radioisotope methodology," below). Once the factor is known, the self-absorption correction can be predicted for the amount of precipitate obtained by filtering the sample (step 15 of "Analytical procedures," above), and it can be applied to the A_L and A_D values once they have been adjusted for resolving time.

Basic Radiological Methodology

Standard techniques have been worked out for: 1) handling radioactive materials in biological and chemical manipulations, 2) preventing loss of or contamination by radioisotopes, 3) detecting presence of and measuring activity of radioactive materials, 4) limiting amounts available in any one place, and 5) catching of wastes and disposing of radioisotopes. All are governed by strictly regimented technique, and are guided by AEC regulations and checking.

Radioisotope Manipulation Wear proper protection with laboratory coat and gloves. Wear dosimeter to check dose received, and accumulate dose record to check on long-term exposure. Very hot isotopes can be moved about by remote control units or from behind lead barriers, watching manipulation by mirror. In aquatic work, prevent loss of isotope into habitat. To take care of gloves, scrub, dry, powder, and monitor, and, if clean, remove and invert (always leave used gloves inside out); then wash and monitor hands. Monitor self and shoes, and survey work area, with a good Geiger counter.

Loss Prevention Keep radioisotope bottles or vials in closed containers, propped up and standing in a container such as a beaker. Work in areas prepared to prevent escape of activity such as fume hood, and on waterproof-backed absorbent paper. With possibility of radioactive gas (e.g., $^{14}CO_2$), maintain a slight suction in hood to draw air out of room. To prevent $^{14}CO_2$ from leaving solution, alkalize liquid with pellet of NaOH to ensure alkaline condition (to litmus or phenolphthalein).

Isotope Detection Wear a dosimeter, charged and read before entering hot areas and reread on leaving. Total dose information is accumulated over the weeks or months of work with isotopes so as not to exceed safe limits set by AEC. Maximum permissible dose is:

$$(MPD) = 5(N - 18) \text{ rems}$$

where N = age in years; rem (roentgen equivalent man) = dose in rads times RBE (relative biological effectiveness), where a rad is nearly equal to a roentgen. One MPD figure is a maximal rate of 0.5 roentgen exposure during the work day, and how close you are approaching this limit can be estimated by making readings in the area with a good survey meter and by checking your dosimeter.

Monitoring devices include survey meters and special monitoring units. For ^{14}C detection, a very thin window (1.4 mg/cm^2) detector is required; in lieu of such a unit, extremely careful monitoring must be done.

The entire area should be monitored when work is finished, contaminated areas being marked for disposal or scrubbed and flushed until clean. Marked portions of absorbent paper are cut out and specially disposed of, while the rest can be discarded through normal wastepaper channels.

Permissible Legal Amounts AEC regulations vary at times, and are becoming more strict. Basically, without a license, individuals can obtain lots of 10 μCi activity, and a laboratory is to have no more than five lots (or total of 50 μCi). However, note that long half-life materials in small amounts are especially dangerous because of their continued activity. On the other hand, small amounts of short-lived but highly penetrating and destructive isotopes are damaging. For the most part, permissible unlicensed quantities are unlikely to result in lethal conditions when used with normal radiological precautions.

Disposal of Wastes AEC rules guide the method of disposal of all radioactive wastes. Clearly mark work areas or containers with radioactive materials or wastes with special radiation stickers or placards. Special waste units must be available for hot wastes, clearly marked as radioactive.

Assemble all solid radioactive material, and either hold in protected enclosure (e.g., lead pig) for 10 half-lives before spreading at random, or accumulate for disposal by authorized agencies (barrels are ordered for this purpose).

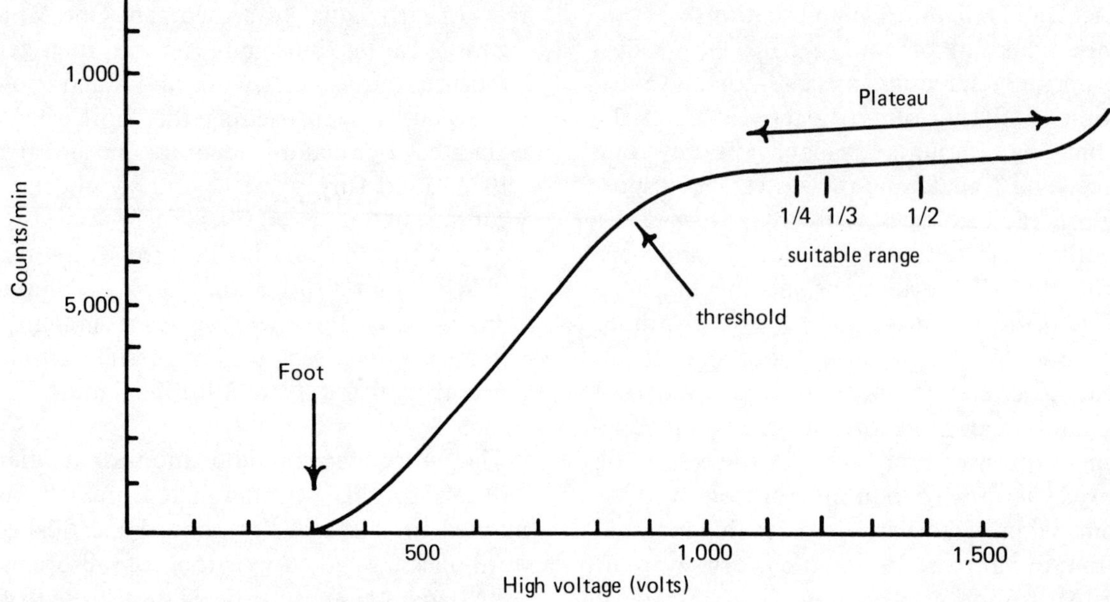

Figure 2. Diagram of high voltage-counts/min curve for Geiger tube of beta counter, showing foot, threshold, and plateau and voltage region of satisfactory operation.

Accumulate all fluid wastes; treat as necessary to prevent loss of gases (e.g., alkalize ^{14}C solutions), evaporate down, and dispose of containers as done for solid wastes.

Vent gaseous fumes in trace amounts from fume hood through a tall stack, but absorb larger amounts in fluid and precipitate chemically for disposal or conversion as solids.

For information on disposal, consult the local radiation officer and the AEC regulations.

Special Procedures in Radioisotope Methodology

Plateau and Voltage Setting of Geiger Counters Most Geiger tubes are marked with optimal operating high voltage value (see Figure 2). To check for operating voltage, proceed with a thoroughly warmed-up unit with high voltage at lowest setting. Insert radiation source in detector; raise high voltage slowly until counts are obtained. Start by taking 1-min counts, starting at 0, in steps of 25 volts each, plotting values of counts per minute (cpm) on ordinate against voltage on abscissa. Continue past "starting point" (where first counts are obtained) to "threshold" (where count rate starts to level off) to the plateau (where change in cpm per increment in voltage is nearly constant, but *stop* just as soon as the change increases again! Avoid continuous flood of counting [continuous discharge]). Lower voltage immediately in case of continuous discharge so as not to damage tube. Counting should be done at a point 1/4 (or possibly 1/3 or 1/2) of the way from lower to upper end of plateau (Ref.: Chase and Rabinowitz, 1962 or 1967).

Resolving Time*[2]*, and the Correction for Instrument Sensitivity Procedure: using paired half sources and blanks, insert one of the half sources with half blank and make

[2] *Resolving time* (recommended by Nuclear-Chicago, for use with Model 180020 solid source set):

$$T = \frac{R_1 + R_2 - R_t - R_b}{R_t^2 - R_1^2 - R_2^2} = \frac{R_1 + R_2 - (R_t + R_b)}{R_t^2 - (R_1^2 + R_2^2)}$$

where R_t = R total (i.e., R_1 and R_2), and R_b = cpm from background.

count. Insert other half source and blank and make count. Insert the two half sources and make count of combined activity. Then, take background. If the machine were 100% efficient, the sum of the two half sources would equal the combined sources; but, because the machine cannot resolve all counts, the count for the combined halves is always less than the sum of the two halves. This reduction is determined by the resolving time, if background is negligible.

$$T = \frac{R_1 + R_2 - (R_1 \text{ and } R_2)}{2(R_1 \times R_2)}$$

where T = resolving time (min); and the rates R_1 = counts per minute (cpm) of the 1st half source, R_2 = cpm of the 2nd half source, (R_1 and R_2) = cpm of the two half sources together.

The shorter the resolving time (the shortest time between two incidences detectable by a given unit), the more efficient is the unit. Therefore, by knowing the relationship between resolving time and counting efficiency, the observed counts obtained can be corrected to true count. To correct observed counts to true count:

$$R = r \times \frac{1}{(1 - rT)}$$

where R = true count (cpm); r = observed count (cpm); and T = resolving time (min).

Background Check natural radiation of area using identical conditions and geometry (i.e., same planchet, cement, filter, etc.) as normal for an extended counting time. For ^{14}C, 30 min is commonly used, recalculated to cpm.

Self-Absorption A thick layer with radioactivity absorbs a portion of its own activity (self-absorption) and gives a lower-than-true reading. Because of this complication, one strives to use thin layers or uniformly thick layers for counting.

Where self-absorption cannot be avoided or held constant, prepare a self-absorption curve by setting up a series of filters onto which identical amounts of activities are suspended in different amounts of precipitant (e.g., $BaCl_2$ to precipitate $CaCO_3$ from Na_2CO_3). Prepare stepwise gradient of progressively smaller amounts of precipitate, and filter each sample; then dry, mount, and count each one. Plot curve with mg of precipitant along abscissa, and activity on ordinate. For activity at zero thickness, extend curve to left margin and read activity at zero thickness value.

Once a self-absorption curve is prepared for given material, a correction for each observed concentration and activity can be made from the curve by noting the ratio which would occur between measured activities and the true activity at zero thickness (see curve, Figure 1) (Ref.: Chase and Rabinowitz, 1962 or 1967).

Available Carbon in Water This value is the sum of the carbon which exists as carbonates, bicarbonates, and carbon dioxide, and which through dynamic equilibrium is presumed to be available to photosynthetic organisms. It is often but not universally true that autophytes can utilize carbon in these forms. This value, although difficult to obtain with accuracy and assurance, is the heart of the ^{14}C productivity measurement and, if incorrectly assessed, can produce surprisingly large errors. A direct gasometric analysis (Van Slyke) is described by Strickland and Parsons (1968: 35), but it is far too rarely done; the simpler total alkalinity methods are employed.

The titrimetric method, if carefully done, is satisfactory; and calculations done using Saunders, Trama, and Bachman (1962) conversion factors produce comparable values for both open fresh and marine waters. Strickland and Parsons' (1968) tables are considerably more awkward, and the increased precision, if any, seems likely to fall within the limits of inherent error of the titrimetric method. For the field ecologist, the procedure outlined here doubtless will be satisfactory when used in open water areas; but if used in shallow or inshore regions, and if the objective is high precision, it leaves much to be desired. In such cases, the best suggestion is the Van Slyke; however, a new approach to the involvement of available carbon in natural waters is needed.

Procedure

1. Obtain total alkalinity, pH, and temperature (as outlined in project 5a).

2. Using temperature and pH, select correction factor from Table 2.

3. Multiply total alkalinity by the correction factor, and express results directly as mg C/liter.

Ranges Inland waters: probably 12–65 mg C/liter in normal waters with alkalinities of 10–200 and pH 5.2–8; marine: 24.7–28.5 mg C/liter (Sverdrup, Johnson, and Fleming, 1942: 198) or 2.05–2.38 mg-at C/liter.

Conversions

$$\text{mg-at C/liter} = \frac{1}{12} \times \text{mg C/liter}$$

References Saunders, Trama, and Bachman (1962); Strickland and Parsons (1968); and Sverdrup, Johnson, and Fleming, (1942).

Machine "Efficiency" (= Consistency) by Repeated Counts of Standard Many factors affect the consistency of machines. To detect shifts, a fixed activity standard, e.g., thallium, is read occasionally throughout the counting procedure. All counts are referred back to original standard count; i.e., if a change in standard count is found, the unknown count values are multiplied by the fraction of the old standard over the new:

$$R = r\left(\frac{C_o}{C_n}\right)$$

where R = corrected (normalized) count; r = observed count of unknown sample; C_o = count of original standard; and C_n = new count of current standard.

Isotope Effect The physiological use of different isotopes is not always the same as the normal element, and ^{14}C is utilized at a somewhat slower rate than is ^{12}C. This correction has been measured, and agreement centers around a value of 6.79% (see Strickland and Parsons, 1968; and Steemann-

Table 2. Factors for converting total alkalinity of open natural waters to mg C/liter[a]

pH	Temperature (°C) 0	5	10	15	20	25
5.0	9.36	8.19	7.16	6.55	6.00	5.61
5.1	7.49	6.55	5.74	5.25	4.81	4.51
5.2	6.00	5.25	4.61	4.22	3.87	3.63
5.3	4.78	4.22	3.71	3.40	3.12	2.93
5.4	3.87	3.40	3.00	2.75	2.53	2.38
5.5	3.12	2.75	2.43	2.24	2.06	1.94
5.6	2.53	2.24	1.98	1.83	1.69	1.59
5.7	2.06	1.83	1.62	1.50	1.39	1.31
5.8	1.69	1.50	1.34	1.24	1.15	1.09
5.9	1.39	1.24	1.11	1.03	0.96	0.92
6.0	1.15	1.03	0.93	0.87	0.82	0.78
6.1	0.96	0.87	0.77	0.73	0.70	0.67
6.2	0.82	0.74	0.68	0.64	0.60	0.58
6.3	0.69	0.64	0.59	0.56	0.53	0.51
6.4	0.60	0.56	0.52	0.49	0.47	0.45
6.5	0.53	0.49	0.46	0.44	0.42	0.41
6.6	0.47	0.44	0.41	0.40	0.38	0.37
6.7	0.42	0.40	0.38	0.37	0.35	0.35
6.8	0.38	0.37	0.35	0.34	0.33	0.32
6.9	0.35	0.34	0.33	0.32	0.31	0.31
7.0	0.33	0.32	0.31	0.30	0.30	0.29
7.1	0.31	0.30	0.29	0.29	0.29	0.28
7.2	0.30	0.29	0.28	0.28	0.28	0.27
7.3	0.29	0.28	0.27	0.27	0.27	0.27
7.4	0.28	0.27	0.27	0.26	0.26	0.26
7.5	0.27	0.26	0.26	0.26	0.26	0.26
7.6	0.27	0.26	0.26	0.25	0.25	0.25
7.7	0.26	0.26	0.25	0.25	0.25	0.25
7.8	0.25	0.25	0.25	0.25	0.25	0.25
7.9	0.25	0.25	0.25	0.25	0.25	0.25
8.0	0.25	0.25	0.25	0.25	0.24	0.24
8.1	0.25	0.25	0.24	0.24	0.24	0.24
8.2	0.24	0.24	0.24	0.24	0.24	0.24
8.3	0.24	0.24	0.24	0.24	0.24	0.24
8.4	0.24	0.24	0.24	0.24	0.24	0.24
8.5	0.24	0.24	0.24	0.24	0.24	0.24
8.6	0.24	0.24	0.24	0.24	0.24	0.24
8.7	0.24	0.24	0.24	0.24	0.24	0.24
8.8	0.24	0.24	0.24	0.24	0.23	0.23
8.9	0.24	0.24	0.23	0.23	0.23	0.23
9.0	0.24	0.23	0.23	0.23	0.23	0.23
9.1	0.23	0.23	0.23	0.23	0.23	0.23
9.2	0.23	0.23	0.23	0.23	0.23	0.23
9.3	0.23	0.23	0.23	0.22	0.22	0.22
9.4	0.23	0.23	0.22	0.22	0.22	0.22

[a]Directions: On the basis of the pH and temperature at time of sampling, select value and multiply total alkalinity (in ppm) by this value (after Saunders, Trama, and Bachman, 1962).

Nielsen, 1952) for ^{14}C. The correction can be made by multiplying counts by 1.05, or as done below,

$$R = r\left(\frac{100}{100-I}\right)$$

where R = actual count; r = observed count; and I = per cent reduction attributable to isotope effect (i.e., 6.79 for ^{14}C).

PROJECT 16 Mineral Cycling: Radioisotope Uptake, ^{32}P and ^{65}Zn

OBJECTIVE

To measure rates of uptake of radioisotopes (e.g., ^{32}P and ^{65}Zn) by the various plant compartments of an ecosystem.

METHOD

Using a biologically well stabilized aquarium[1], introduce sufficient isotope to produce approximately 10^{-4} μCi/ml each of a beta emitter (^{32}P) and a gamma emitter (^{65}Zn)[2]. At the start and at 24 hrs thereafter (though a geometric time pattern of 1, 2, 4, 8, 16, 32, . . ., etc., hrs would be desirable) harvest two samples of the plant material from each compartment—neuston (floating), plankton (suspended), periphyton (attached to support), benthon (bottom attached), epibenthon (lying on bottom), sediment, and water—and prepare for beta and gamma counting.

Process the samples in order to get dry weight of plant material. Beta counts on dry material attached to planchets are read with gas flow beta counter, and gamma counts of fresh material in water are read with scintillation counter and then dried. Correct data counts for machine consistency, self-absorption, machine sensitivity or resolving time, decay rate, original isotope activity, and background, as well as for weight of material used. Determine relative rate of uptake (or

---

[1] Comparable projects can be run in the field, but careful supervision and rigorous planning must be done to avoid any chance of involving health hazards or contaminating of the ecosystem. (1) In standing water, divers install hemisphere of clear plastic over community and tuck edges into mud, then introduce isotope by syringe through rubber diaphragm previously cemented to plastic at convenient point. When terminated, the plastic is forced down under community; the entire unit, water and all tightly sealed inside, is brought to surface and eased into submerged pail or tub. The unit is removed for radiological work in laboratory. (2) In flowing streams, use short half-life isotope, mix with sufficient water so that when fed into stream the downstream biota will be exposed to a sufficient concentration for a sufficient time to take up radiation. Time work carefully, based on velocity and discharge of stream, and have cooperators take scheduled samples of ecosystem compartments at stations downstream. Such projects must, in the planning stage, be cleared with the radiation officer, local residents and authorities, and possibly with the AEC.

[2] ^{65}Zn emits both betas and gammas.

Table 1. Sample table for shipboard data and processing of results for comparative uptake rates of radioisotopes: data given for sampling after 24 hrs of betas and gammas in two compartments of an aquarium

Isotopes: ^{32}P: original activity ________, date ________; ^{65}Zn: original activity ________, date ________

A	B	C[a]	D[b]	E[c]	F[d]	G	H[e]	I[f]	J[g]	K	L[h]	M[i]
						Corrections					Activity	
Compartment	Time elapsed	Activity (cpm)	Back-ground (cpm)	Standard solutions (cpm)	Standard isotope (cpm/ 2 ml)	Back-ground C–D (cpm)	Consistency (cpm)	Decay (cpm)	Counting yield (dpm)	Dry weight (g)	dpm/g	μCi/g
Benthon (betas)	24 hr	1,480/10	360/30	8,700 8,760	18,900 17,800	136	135	143.4	2,021.3	0.012	168,442	0.0759
Plankton (gammas)	24 hr	1,069	0/30	17,900 17,800	29,580 29,400	1,069	1,075	1,081.6	9,740.7	0.006	1,623,450	0.7313

Notes on calculations of betas: original activity as marked on ampoule container: 6μCi/100 ml.

[a]C: Raw data.

[b]D: Usually 30-min run.

[c]E: On standard disc or cylinder.

[d]F: Count on "standard" solution of isotope material.

[e]H: $\frac{E_o}{E_c} \times G$ (where E_o is original reading; E_c is current):

$$\frac{8{,}700}{8{,}760} \times 136 = 135.06, \text{ the normalized count}$$

[f]I: $\frac{F_o}{F_c} \times H$ (where F_o is original reading; F_c is current):

$$\frac{18{,}900}{17{,}800} \times 135.06 = 143.4$$

[g]J: $\frac{a_o}{F_o} \times I$ (where a_o is original activity; F_o is count obtained):

$$\frac{266{,}400 \text{ (from 6 } \mu\text{Ci)}}{18{,}900 \text{ (from F)}} \times 143.4 = 2{,}021.3 \text{ dpm}$$

266,400 dpm is calculated for 2 ml of 1:100 solution of 6 μCi (original activity).

[h]L: $\frac{J}{K} = \frac{2{,}021.3}{0.012} = 168{,}441.6$ dpm/g or 1.684×10^5

[i]M: $\frac{L}{(\text{cpm}/\mu\text{Ci})} = \frac{1.684 \times 10^5}{2.22 \times 10^6} = 7.59 \times 10^{-2}\ \mu\text{Ci}$

2.22×10^6 cpm/μCi for the ^{32}P (since 1 Ci = 3.7×10^{10} dps, 1 μCi = 3.7×10^4 dps or 2.22×10^6 dpm or cpm/μCi).

total activity accumulated) by each compartment, expressed in cpm/g dry weight and μCi/g. (*Note:* 1-ml samples of original isotope solution are dried on planchet [for betas] or held in a stoppered test tube [for gammas] against which to compare later readings, a step which circumvents calculating decay rates.) Table 1 provides a table for handling and processing data.

The entire project involves six basic procedures (for details, see under "Notes") as well as the knowledge of special radioisotope concepts and techniques, sampling methods, and element of danger involved.

Basic procedures:

1. Advanced preparations
2. Experimental procedures
3. Clean up and monitoring area
4. Counting
   a. Betas (see project 14)
   b. Gammas
5. Decontamination (if necessary)
6. Calculations
   a. Betas
   b. Decay rates
   c. Mixed betas and gammas
   d. Gammas

Special information for radioisotope methodology:

1. Gain
2. Window
3. Limit
4. Pulse height
5. Pulse height analyzer
6. Scintillation
7. Scintillation counter
8. Half-life

Sampling procedures for aquarium ecosystem

Range of danger from unlicensed isotopes

DATA

A. Summarize data, conversions, and corrections in tabular form.

B. Present final calculated results of activity (cpm/g dry weight), and μCi/g of each compartment after intervals of or at end of time.

C. Prepare a graph indicating these changes as per cent activity over time (Figure 1).

D. Compare graph with published results of previous workers (e.g., Whittaker, 1961).

E. Compare results with reports in literature (e.g., Odum and Odum, 1959: 470, 471).

REFERENCES

Auerbach, S. I. (See ORINS, 1963).

Chase, G. D., and J. L. Rabinowitz. 1967. (See "References" in project 15).

Odum, E. P., and H. T. Odum. 1959. (See "References" in project 13).

ORINS. 1963. (Directions for experiment in movement of radioisotopes in aquarium system.) Oak Ridge Inst. Nuclear Science, Oak Ridge, Tenn. (Assembled by S. I. Auerbach for 1963 radioecology class; mimeographed.)

USDHE&W. 1960. Radiological health handbook. U.S. Dept. Health, Education, and Welfare, Washington, D.C. 468 p. (Available from Supt. of Doc., Washington, D.C.) (Out of print.)

Whittaker, R. H. 1953. Removal of radiophosphorus contaminant from the water in an aquarium community. AEC Document HW-28636, (Fig. reprinted by Odum and Odum, 1959: 471).

Whittaker, R. H. 1961. Experiments with radiophosphorus tracer in aquarium microcosm. Ecol. Monogr. 31(2): 157–188.

NOTES

Basic Procedures for Tracer Work

Advanced Preparations

1. Prepare aquarium ca. 3 months in advance with natural water and ca. 2 cm of sediment with root parts of plants; keep it

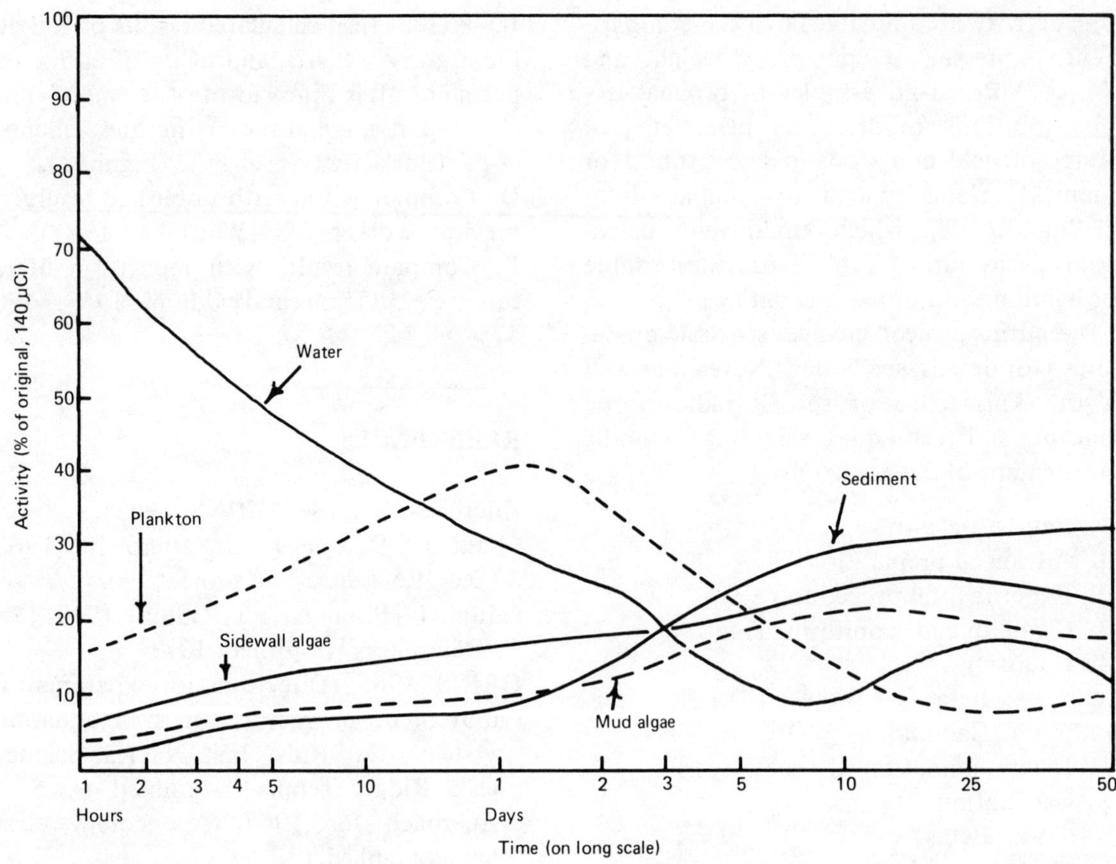

Figure 1. Radioisotope uptake, ^{32}P, in aquarium ecosystem after intervals of hours and days. (Modified from Whittaker, 1953, *in* Odum and Odum, 1959: 471.)

cool and partly shaded, adjusting conditions for maximal growth of wall scum and macrophytes. Add *Lemna* and *Elodea* prior to use if needed.

2. Order isotopes weeks in advance for delivery and calibrated for the specified day. Obtain 10 μCi of each of a beta and a gamma emitter (e.g., ^{32}P and ^{65}Zn).

3. Assemble needs in a special work area provided with facilities for radiological work, e.g., suction, gas flow beta counter, scintillation gamma counter, Geiger gas, survey meter, monitoring equipment, dosimeters, isotopes in lead brick enclosure, glassware, aquarium, contamination labels, planchets, test tubes, Millipore filters (25-mm diam., 0.4-μ pore size), sampling equipment (e.g., baster), analytical balance, scraper (e.g., razor blade held by tongs), forceps.

4. Prepare laboratory area around the aquarium. Cover table and floor with absorbent paper with waterproof backing, and have special paper-lined tray on which to do all radioisotope work. Hold isotopes in a lead container or enclosure. Put up radiation warning signs on door of room and in area of work. Keep counting equipment remote from isotope area.

5. Preweigh several 25-mm Millipore filters to 0.1 mg, and clip in fold of paper and label. If necessary, trim to fit filtering unit. It may prove necessary to pretreat these filters by drawing dist. water through them, then drying them thoroughly in desiccator. Otherwise, they sometimes lose weight, giving negative results.

6. Measure water-filled part of aquarium, and calculate volume.

7. Calculate amount of each isotope

needed to give approximately 10^{-4} μCi/ml.

8. Read activity on container label; and, if necessary, consult decay curve (e.g., USDHE&W, 1960: 115, 118, 119) and half-life data (ibid., p. 91 or 220–453) and estimate current activity.

9. Make up 100 ml of each isotope solution, using strict radiochemical techniques, pipeting the volume of isotope needed for the aquarium into the 100-ml volumetric flask containing a little water. Mix, dilute to volume with filtered aquarium water, and mix again.

10. To make final check of activity of isotope solutions, take two 1-ml samples from each flask, dry one on planchet (after mixing with drop of detergent to help spread evenly), put other in suitable test tube, and count the planchet for betas and the fluid for gammas. Keep these as standards against which to compare later readings.

11. Plan schedule for sampling, and assign one ecological compartment to each person to analyze.

12. Have gamma counter standardized and operating.

Experimental Procedures Take precautions! Cover entire area! Spill nothing! Be ready to decontaminate!

1. Don protective clothing.
2. Read dosimeter, or recharge to zero.
3. To inoculate aquarium, slowly pour isotope from flask into open water and mix gently to avoid disturbing benthos and substrate.
4. Immediately begin zero-hour sampling by taking two 1-ml water samples for beta standards and two 2-ml samples for gamma standards, and count as soon as possible. Then take samples from each compartment, as outlined below (for further sampling details, see "Sampling procedures," at the end of this chapter).

Floating

a. 1–3 leaves in planchet–dry; weigh; BETA COUNT later.

b. 1–3 leaves in 2 ml water in test tube; GAMMA COUNT; dry; weigh.

Plankton

a. 50 ml water–filter (save filtrate for later work); dry; weigh; BETA COUNT later.

b. 2 ml of water in test tube–GAMMA COUNT; filter; dry; weigh; (subtract water gamma count).

Water

a. 1 ml of plankton beta filtrate–dry; BETA COUNT later.

b. 2 ml of plankton beta filtrate in test tube–GAMMA COUNT.

Wall scrapings

a. catch on filter–dry; weigh; BETA COUNT later.

b. in test tube in 2 ml water volume–GAMMA COUNT; filter; dry; weigh.

Elodea leaf

a. 1–more leaf on planchet–dry; weigh; BETA COUNT later.

b. 1–more leaf in 2 ml of dist. water–GAMMA COUNT; dry; weigh.

Epibenthos

a. catch on filter–dry; weigh; BETA COUNT later.

b. into test tube in 2 ml water volume–GAMMA COUNT; catch on filter; dry; weigh; (subtract water gamma count).

Sediment

a. catch on filter–dry; weigh; BETA COUNT later.

b. into test tube in 2 ml water volume–GAMMA COUNT; catch on filter; dry; weigh; (subtract water gamma count).

5. Count gammas immediately, but process betas after drying.
6. Periodically, repeat counts on isotope standard made up at zero time (step 10).
7. Read dosimeter and record value, and compare with original reading.

Note Avoid spilling; but, if any occurs, immediately mark suspected area for later decontamination or disposal, or decontaminate immediately if serious.

Cleanup

1. Assemble contaminated items in one place.
2. Monitor the absorbent paper, especially where marked as spills, cut out "hot" areas, and dispose in hot waste container. Discard rest of paper with normal trash.
3. Evaporate waste water to dryness and hold for proper disposition (or until 10 half-lives have elapsed).
4. Scrub glassware and equipment with brush and moist detergent, then rinse, catching "hot" rinse water in jar. Drain and air dry glassware on absorbent paper, monitor for any trace of activity, rescrubbing if necessary.
5. Monitor entire work area, table, floor, walls, etc., and rescrub any active areas.
6. Dry down aquarium, then remove "hot" soil, pack in plastic bags, properly identify and dispose of through proper channels (or hold 10 half-lives and then, if nonradioactive, broadcast in nature).
7. Scrub gloves in "hot" sink, dry with paper towel, and monitor, rescrubbing active areas; then remove and invert, and powder down.
8. Scrub hands (at clean sink, using clean soap); monitor carefully after drying, and rescrub any active areas.
9. For final disposition of contaminated items: a) with short half-life isotopes (e.g., ^{32}P), hold for 10 half-lives, monitor, and, if no activity is noted, discard by broadcasting in nature; b) for long half-life isotopes, check for activity, discard clean portions, and handle contaminated portions as specified by AEC regulations or your local health officer.
10. Scrub and clean sink, monitor, and reclean as needed.

Counting

Betas: For use of gas flow beta counter, see "Counting with ultrathin window gas flow beta counter, using Geiger gas," in project 15.

Gammas: Count in scintillation well counter of gamma-ray spectrometer (Figure 2) (e.g., Baird-Atomic, [Bedford, Mass.]: Scaler-Timer BA-135, Amplifier-Analyzer BA-230, Detector BA-810C).

1. Turn on amplifier.
2. Turn on scaler; allow to warm up.
3. Set on "test" for "1 minute" by use of the indicated knobs; verify a count of ca. 3,600/min. Then turn to ∞, or desired K reading.
4. Raise high voltage slowly to usual level (ca. 850 volts) used with unit.
5. Calibrate with ^{137}Cs rod standard by inserting it plug-down into well, closing cover carefully, and proceeding as follows: a) set "window" (0–20V) at 2; b) set "lower limit" at 1 volt below peak (e.g., 65) for the isotope (peak of 66 for ^{137}Cs) and leave "upper limit" (5–100V) at 100; c) press "stop," "reset," and "start" buttons to clear and begin counting; d) adjust the coupled "coarse" and "fine" gain knobs by turning first the coarse gain to point of fastest counting, and then record or note that reading and select a combination of coarse and fine gain values such that their product will give the same value, and such that the coarse gain can be halved conveniently (e.g., have coarse gain at 4 to facilitate halving by turning dial to 2); e) set "coarse" gain, and adjust "fine" gain to position nearest the estimated setting which gives maximum counting rate; f) if isotope (e.g., ^{65}Zn) has a peak mev which exceeds the limit of "lower limit" dial, then halve the value (by turning "coarse" gain to half its setting), thus doubling the value of the "lower limit" setting (e.g., to obtain setting of 111.9 as needed for ^{65}Zn, halve the "coarse" gain, 111.9/2, and read "lower limit" as half its dial number [i.e., 1/2 of 111.9 = 55.9]).
6. Mix samples, insert their test tube into well of detector, and close lid *carefully* so as not to break tube.

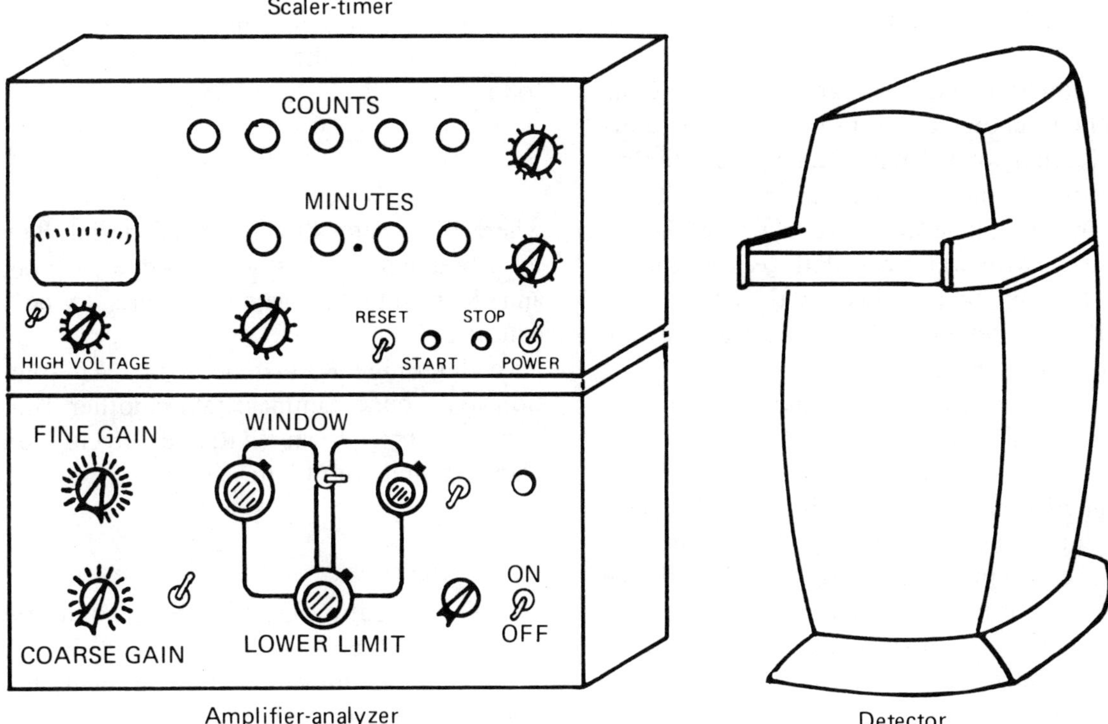

Figure 2. Units of and operation of gamma-ray spectrometer.

Detector includes the lead housing, crystal, and photomultiplier. (High voltage: 0–2,500 volts obtained from power supply in the scaler-timer unit.) Crystal is a phosphor, NaI, and path of each gamma particle glows. Light is proportional to gamma radiation. Photomultiplier senses the glowing, creating impulses proportional to it in intensity, and magnifies the impulses.

Amplifier-analyzer includes preamplifier, linear amplifier, and discriminator. Preamplifier further magnifies the impulses initiated by the photomultiplier. Linear amplifier (activated by the fine and coarse gain) permits magnifying (elongating, attenuating) the impulses. Discriminator sorts out impulses by eliminating all those below a certain amplitude (like a fence cuts out the view below its top), and this is done by the "lower level" dial (or "lower limit").

Scaler-timer contains the high voltage supply, the scaler, and the timer. High voltage supply activates the photomultiplier of the detector unit. It also provides steady current for operation of units. Scaler counts impulses received from the amplifier. A limit can be set on top right dial. Timer records the time since starting scaler, and permits stopping and clearing (reset) the decades.

7. Count at least 100 counts for each sample (depending on uniformity), recording time and number of counts.

8. Occasionally recount the cesium standard (e.g., every 5th or 10th count).

9. Finally, make background count by using clean test tube in well, and count for 5 min or 100 counts.

10. Count "standards" from isotope solutions.

11. To leave instrument running, lower the "high voltage" to "standby."

11a. To reinitiate counting, raise again to normal voltage, recount standards and background.

12. To turn off, lower "high voltage" to zero, and turn off "high voltage," turn off main switch of "scaler," then turn off main switch of "amplifier."

Decontamination In case of spillage in unprotected areas, proceed as follows.

1. See USDHE&W (1960: 18) for information.

2. Painted surfaces: a) flush with water, but be careful to avoid contaminating with waste water by catching it in container; b) moisten, sprinkle with detergent and scrub vigorously (usually the best system); c) repaint when stripped.

3. Glassware: wash or scrub with detergent, taking precautions with waste water.

4. Metal: use water and detergent, as above.

5. Concrete and brick: abrasion or vacuum blasting, taking precaution against air contamination; or vacuum cleaning, and taking care of contaminated sack and parts.

6. Wood: plane away contaminated layer, or scrub with water and detergent as above.

7. Human body: flush with water, and scrub with detergent, taking care to prevent contamination by waste water.

8. Monitor area, and continue decontamination until free of radiation.

Calculations General principle: the relative difference in radioactivity can be expressed as cpm/g dry weight of plant material, or cpm/ml of water in case of water, or in per cent of original activity. If desired, activity values can be reduced to μCi/g.

1. Beta counting is done, as in the case of project 15, on ^{14}C uptake, with the additional concern of decay rate and number of elapsed half-lives. In addition, since both ^{65}Zn and ^{32}P emit betas, it is desirable to determine the amount emitted only by ^{32}P.

2. For decay rate or elapsed half-life corrections, see USDHE&W (1960: 107–117) for tables or (l.c., p. 118, 119) for graphs, or calculate from:

$$A = A_o e^{-\lambda t}$$

where A = present activity; A_o = original activity; e = base of log (nat.) (= 2.718); λ = decay constant (= 0.69315/half-life)[3]; and t = time elapsed.[3]

> *Note* In the experimental procedure, this calculation can be avoided by taking readings on a solution of the isotopes at the start and at each interval thereafter. Thus, data are already corrected for decay.

3. For mixed beta correction, such as ^{65}Zn and ^{32}P where both betas and gammas are present but only those of ^{32}P are of interest, deduct the betas due to ^{65}Zn as follows:

$$B_p = B_t - \frac{G_z}{K}$$

where B_p = betas due to ^{32}P alone/ml; B_t = total beta count; G_z = gammas due to ^{65}Zn; and K = ratio of gamma counts to beta counts in ^{65}Zn.

To determine K, take 1 ml of ^{65}Zn solution and count gammas; take another 1-ml sample, dry down with detergent on planchet, and count betas. Then:

$$K = \frac{G_z}{B_z}$$

where K = ratio; G_z = gamma count on ^{65}Zn/ml; and B_z = beta count on ^{65}Zn/ml.

4. Gamma counting follows much the same general procedure as for betas, and similarly must be based upon apparent counts on known activity. Once this is known, then other corrections similarly involve correcting for background, machine consistency (use stock standard), machine efficiency (resolving time, if known), geometry (especially radiation absorption by water), mass of plant material, original activity, elapsed time, and decay correction for half-life. These may be assembled in a formula as follows:

$$A = (A_s - A_b) \times \frac{C_o}{C_c} \times \frac{I_o}{I_c} \times \frac{I_k}{I_t} \times \frac{I}{M} \times \frac{1}{\text{cpm}/\mu\text{Ci}}$$

where A = activity for isotope taken up, corrected back to start of experiment; A_s = count of sample (cpm); A_b = count of background (cpm); C_o = first count (less background) made on calibrated standard source (cpm); C_c = current count (less background) made on calibrated standard source (cpm); I_o = count (less background) of "standard" isotope solution at start of experiment (cpm); I_c = current count (less background) made on "standard" isotope solution (cpm);

[3] Keep these in same time units, i.e., half-lives, days, or hours.

I_k = calculated count (less background) for the "standard" isotope solution based on known activity as marked on container of isotope; I_t = count (less background) made on "standard" isotope solution at time the container calibration is valid, and it may = I_o; and M = mass of plant material (g dry weight).

The individual factor groups provide: $(A_s - A_b)$ = raw count corrected for background; C_o/C_c = correction for machine hour-to-hour performance, and results in normalizing the count; I_o/I_c = correction for decay rate, eliminating the need to make a special calculation; I_k/I_t = correction for factors that affect the proportion of the actual disintegrations that the machine records; it is called the counting yield and is expressed as counts per disintegration; I/M = expresses results in activity/g dry weight; and $1/(\text{cpm}/\mu\text{Ci}) = 1/(2.22 \times 10^6)$ = causes results to be expressed in μCi.

This calculation, valid for both betas and gammas, has certain inherent difficulties. The activity of the isotope marked on the container is not often accurate unless special, calibrated isotopes were purchased. Also, ^{65}Zn degeneration involves a complex of actions which create a slight excessive gamma count (position annihilation, x-ray release in electron capture) and slight excessive beta reading (positron release).

Special Information for Radioisotope Methodology

Gain is an amplifying procedure by which impulses are enlarged in size. The impulse obtained from a radioisotope at 0.559 mev can be doubled to 1.119 by doubling the gain. But, where the range of the machine is only 0–1, 1.119 (the mev of ^{65}Zn) cannot be read. In order to handle 1.119, halve the gain and 1.119 will be equal to 0.559. In the Baird-Atomic pulse height analyzer, the coarse and fine gain are coupled so that the actual gain is the product of the two dial settings (e.g., coarse gain of 4 and fine gain of 30 gives 120, the same as a coarse gain of 6 and fine gain of 20).

Window is the facet of the instrument which allows the operator to include a smaller or larger proportion of the impulses. In the Baird-Atomic unit, a wide open window would count all impulses up to 1.000, while a nearly closed one would count only those of a certain limited portion of that range.

Voltage from 1 to 100 on the main dial corresponds directly to 0–1 mev of isotope energy.

Pulse height is the feature of isotope radiation to make a certain charge in the instrument. If the "window" is wide open, and all pulses are counted, the total count is obtained. But, if the "window" is narrowed, then moved up and down over the array of different impulses arising from an isotope, the counts can be obtained for each class of impulses. A plotting of counts of each class of impulses is a type of action spectrum, and is characteristic of each isotope. In the present experiment, the "window" and "limit" are selected so that most of the counts are received; but extraneous ones, which are mixed with pulses arising from other sources, are excluded.

Pulse height analyzer is the unit capable of counting impulses for each selected range of impulse size.

Scintillation is the property of certain crystals (e.g., NaI) to glow when radiation, especially gamma rays, pass through them. Such a crystal is called a phosphor.

Scintillation counter is an instrument which counts nuclear activity by the impulses of light caused by the radiation penetrating it. The unit is highly sensitive to gamma radiation, but not efficient for the betas or alphas.

Half-life is the time in which half of the original activity is lost. The rate is constant for a given isotope, although the rate may be erratic over short periods. A convenient way to figure half-life and decay rate effects is found in USDHE&W (1960: 118, 119), in which the proportion (can be considered per cent, and multiplied by 100) of original activity remaining after indicated number of half-lives is given. Thus, if the half-life of ^{32}P is 14.22 days, then after 120 days (120/14.22 = 8.44 half-lives), 0.00286 of the original will remain (l.c., p. 119), or 0.286% of original amount. If the original were 10 μCi, then 0.286% remains, or = 0.0286 μCi (l.c., p. 119).

Sampling Procedures for Aquarium Ecosystem

Neuston (floating plants, e.g., *Lemna;* although skimmed surface of water may be similarly examined): record time of start

betas: 1–3 leaves–dry between blotting paper in desiccator; weigh; cement to planchet with a little rubber cement; dry cement; save to count for betas.

gammas: 1–3 leaves, in 2 ml of water in suitable test tube (to fit crystal well)–count for gammas; dry between blotters in desiccator; weigh.

Plankton: record time of start

betas: collect 50-ml sample in graduate; filter through preweighed Millipore filter; dry in desiccator; reweigh; cement to planchet with a little rubber cement; count; divide by 50 to obtain activity per ml (save filtrate for gamma work).

gammas: transfer 2 ml of plankton filtrate from beta work into test tube; count in well counter (subtract from gamma count of water, below, to get count for plankton).

Water: record time of start

betas: transfer 1 ml of sample water onto planchet; add 1 drop of detergent solution; mix; air dry; count (subtract plankton count or use filtered water from "Plankton" above).

gammas: transfer 2 ml of sample water into test tube, count in well counter (see note for "betas").

Periphyton (or wall aufwuchs): record time of start

betas: scrape wall with razor held with tongs; catch scrapings with baster; transfer to filtering unit and filter onto preweighed Millipore filter, rinsing with dist. water; dry in desiccator; reweigh; cement filter to planchet; count.

gammas: transfer scrapings to test tube; make up to 2-ml volume; count in well counter; filter onto preweighed Millipore filter; dry; reweigh.

Benthon (attached plants, e.g., *Elodea*): record time of start

betas: follow directions for "Neuston," above.

gammas: follow directions for "Neuston," above.

Epibenthon (or thin layer of algae lying on bottom): record time of start

betas: draw up cautiously with baster or propipet-equipped pipet; then follow directions for "Periphyton," above.

gammas: draw up cautiously; then follow directions for "Periphyton," above.

Sediment (thin layer of sediment particles): record time of start

betas: draw up sediment particles with baster; then follow directions for "Periphyton," above.

gammas: draw up sediment particles with baster; then follow directions for "Periphyton," above (use only a small amount of sediment, a layer 1–2 grains thick).

Range of Danger from Unlicensed Isotopes

Some idea of the relative danger from unlicensed isotopes can be obtained from data in USDHE&W (1960: 139, 183) where:

1. One Ci of ^{65}Zn yields gamma radiation at 1 m of 0.26 R/hr.
2. No large-scale drop in life span is found after many months of exposure to 0.5 R/day (0.02 R/hr).
3. AEC unlicensed amounts, e.g., 10 μCi (1/100,000 Ci), would give a dose at 1 m of ca. 0.0000026 R/hr—far less than that which would affect life span, even if continuous.

Thus, at 1 m, unlicensed isotopes are safe enough; but, if absorbed on or in the body, or kept at close proximity to the body, the radiation can be dangerous. A note of caution, however; although radiation may have no evident lethal effects, one wisely avoids excess exposure and possible unseen long-term damage, especially to genetic patterns.

RAWSON'S NOMOGRAM

A Nomogram for Determining Oxygen Saturation Values at Various Temperatures and Altutudes

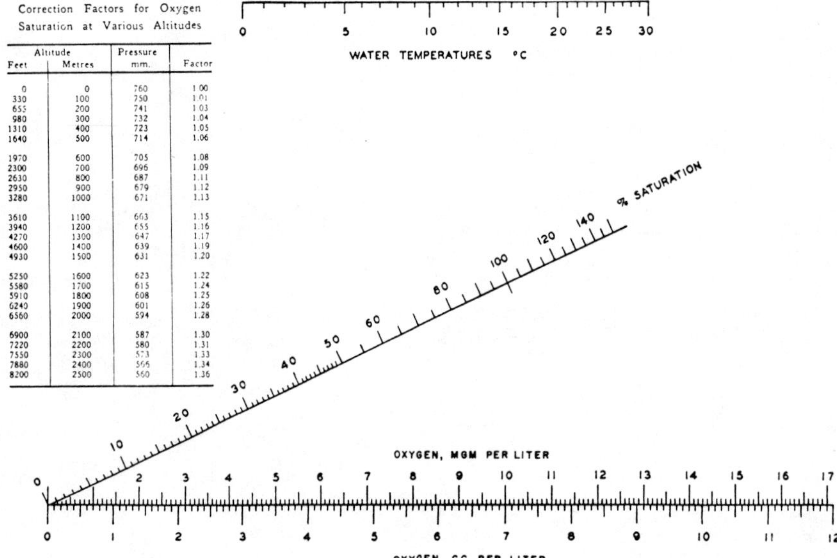

Correction Factors for Oxygen Saturation at Various Altitudes

Altitude Feet	Altitude Metres	Pressure mm.	Factor
0	0	760	1.00
330	100	750	1.01
655	200	741	1.03
980	300	732	1.04
1310	400	723	1.05
1640	500	714	1.06
1970	600	705	1.08
2300	700	696	1.09
2630	800	687	1.11
2950	900	679	1.12
3280	1000	671	1.13
3610	1100	663	1.15
3940	1200	655	1.16
4270	1300	647	1.17
4600	1400	639	1.19
4930	1500	631	1.20
5250	1600	623	1.22
5580	1700	615	1.24
5910	1800	608	1.25
6240	1900	601	1.26
6560	2000	594	1.28
6900	2100	587	1.30
7220	2200	580	1.31
7550	2300	573	1.33
7880	2400	566	1.34
8200	2500	560	1.36

In practice, a straightedge is used to connect observed temperature and dissolved oxygen concentration. The point of intercept on the inclined scale gives the per cent of saturation. Correction for altitude is made by applying the factors given in the table in the upper left. (From Rawson, D. S. 1944. The Calculation of Oxygen Saturation Values and Their Correction for Altitude. Limnology and Oceanography publ. no. 15. Courtesy, American Society of Limnology and Oceanography, Inc., Milwaukee, Wisc.)

Abbreviations

Abbreviations common in hydrobotanical literature for the most part as recommended in *CBE Style Manual,* published by the American Institute of Biological Sciences, Washington, D.C. (3rd Ed., 1972).

′: minute
″: second
%: per cent
^{0}/oo: parts per thousand

A: acre, ampere
A: absorbance, activity, area
Å: Ångstrom
A_0: activity at start
abs: absolute
A-ft: acre foot
alk, ALK: alkalinity
alt: altitude
A.M.,a.m.: before noon
amp: ampere
amt: amount
at: atoms (as in μg-at)
atm: atmosphere(s)
at.wt.: atomic weight
av, avdp: advoirdupois system of weights

b: breadth
b̄: mean breadth
BeV(Bev): billion electron volts
BOD: biochemical oxygen demand
bp: boiling point
Btu(BTU): British thermal units (convert to joules)
β^+: positron, + electron
β^-: betatron, − electron

(c)Ci: curie
c: centi-, prefix for 10^{-2}
C: Celsius (centigrade), °C
ca.: about
cal: calorie
Cal(kcal): kilocalorie
cc(cm^3): cubic centimeter
centi-: prefix for 10^{-2}
cf: see, compare (use discouraged)
cfs(ft^3/sec): cubic feet per second (convert to metric)
cg: centigram
cgs: centimeter-gram-second system
chl: chlorophyll
Ci(c): curie
Cl: chlorinity, chlorosity
cm: centimeter
C/N, C:N: carbon-nitrogen ratio
C:N:P: carbon-nitrogen-phosphorus ratio
coef: coefficient
concd: concentrated
concn: concentration
cp: chemically pure
cpm(counts/min): counts per minute
cps(counts/sec): counts per second
C.V.: coefficient of variation

d: depth; deci-, prefix for 10^{-1}
d: density, depth
d̄: mean depth
d_{13}: density at 13°C
d_{max} : maximum depth
d_{max} : maximum density
DC: direct current
deci-: prefix for 10^{-1}
deka-: prefix for 10^1
det.: determined by
df: degrees of freedom
dg: decigram
diam.: diameter
dil: dilute(d)
diss.: dissolved
dist.: distilled
dm: decimeter
dN/dt: growth rate
DO: dissolved oxygen
dpm: disintegrations per minute
dps: disintegrations per second
dry wt: dry weight
Δ: increment; freezing point depression

e: base of $\log_e$(2.718)
E: east
E: extinction (optical density)
E_0: electrode potential at standard
E_7: redox at pH 7
EC: electron capture
EDT: eastern daylight saving time
EDTA: ethylenediaminetetra-acetic acid
e.g.: for example
E_h: redox compared to H electrode
emf: electromotive force
eq: equivalent
EST: eastern standard time
eV(ev): electron volt
η: viscosity

F: Fahrenheit
F: focal length (optics)
Fig., Figs.: figure(s)
fl.: fluid (as in fluid ounces)
fm: fathom
fp: freezing point
fps(ft/sec): feet per second
FR: far red light
ft: foot
ft-c: foot-candle
ft/sec(fps): feet per second
ft^3/sec(cfs): cubic feet per second, discharge of

g: gram; unit of gravitational force
G: gravitational constant (see also g's)
gal: gallon
gal/min: discharge at gallons per minute
g-at(g-atom): gram-atom (gram atomic weight of material)

g-at/liter: gram-atom per liter
GAW: gram atomic weight
g-cal,gcal: gram calorie (also cal)
g-cal/sec: gram calorie per second
g-eq/liter: gram equivalent per liter
GEW: gram equivalent weight
g-mol: gram molecule
GMW: gram molecular weight
grad.: graduated
gs: glass-stoppered
g's: gravitational force, times gravity
γ: gamma ray quantum

h: hecto-, prefix for 10^2; Planck's constant; hour
(H^+): hydrogen ion concentration
ha: hectare
HHW: higher high water (tide)
hp: horsepower (convert to watts)
hr(h): hour
Hz: Hertz (cycles of electromagnetic waves)

I: intensity
I: current
i.e.: that is
in(in.): inch (use metric)
indet.: unidentified (taxonomy) (see det.)
ips: incidences per second (radiology)
IR: infrared radiation

J: joule
JTU: Jackson turbidity units

k: kilo-, prefix for 10^3
K: coefficient; constant; specific conductance; temperature, Kelvin or absolute
kc(KHz): kilohertz (kilocycle)
kcal: kilocalorie
KeV(kev): 1,000 electron volts
kg: kilogram
km: kilometer
kn(kt): knot
κ: specific conductance
$\kappa_{18} \times 10^6$: specific conductance in reciprocal megohms (or in micromhos)

L: Lambert
(L,1): liter (spell out)

lat.(lat): latitude
lb: pound
lb/in^2(psi): atmospheric pressure, pounds per square inch
LD: lethal dose
LD_{50}: lethal dose at 50% survival; mean lethal dose
LLW: lower low water (tide)
lm: lumen
ln: $\log_e$(natural logarithm)
log: logarithm; $\log_{10}$ = logarithm to base 10; $\log_e$ = natural logarithm, to base e (2.718)
long.(long): longitude
ly: Langley
λ: wavelength; microliter; decay constant

M: molar; mass; mega-,prefix for 10^6; molecular weight
m: meter; milli-,prefix for 10^{-3}
max: maximum
mb: millibar
mCi(mc): millicurie
mega: prefix for 10^6
meq: milliequivalent
MeV(mev): million electron volts
mg: milligram
mho: reciprocal ohm (proposed: siemens)
MHz: megahertz; megacycles per second
(mi): mile (spell out)
milli-: prefix for 10^{-3}
min: minimum; minute
ml: milliliter
MLD: minimum lethal dose
MLW: mean low water (tide)
MLWN: mean low water neap (tide)
MLWS: mean low water spring (tide)
mm: millimeter
mo: month
MO: methyl orange alkalinity (total alkalinity)
mol, mole(M): molecule, molecular weight
mp: melting point
MPD: maximum permissible dose (radiology)
mph(mile/hr): velocity, miles per hour
msl(MSL): mean sea level
MT, m.t.: metric ton, megaton
mv: millivolt
(myria-): prefix for 10^4 (use discouraged)
$m\mu$(nm): millimicron (use discouraged)

μ: micro-, prefix for 10^{-6}; mean
μCi(c): microcurie
μg: microgram
μg-at: microgram-atoms
μm(μ): micrometer
μmg: micromilligram (use ng)
μmho: micromho
μv: microvolt
$\mu\mu$g: micromicrogram (use pg)

n: nano-, prefix for 10^{-9}
$n_D^{20}(N_D^{20})$: refractive index at 20°C for sodium light
N: north; normal; nitrogen; neap tide
NA: numerical aperture (microscopy)
nCi(nc): nanocurie, 10^{-9} curie
NE: northeast
ng: nanogram
nl: nanoliter
nm: nanometer = 10^{-9} m or millimicron
n.mi(nmi): nautical mile
no.: number
N/P, N:P: nitrogen-phosphorus ratio
NTP: normal temperature and pressure
ν: frequency

OD: optical density
opt: optimum; optical
oz: ounce (both fluid and dry)
Ω: ohm

p: photosynthesis; pico-, prefix for 10^{-12}; page
p: probability
P(Pr): productivity
PAAP: provisional algal assay procedure
pCi(pc): picocurie (10^{-12} curie)
pg: picogram
pH: log $1/(H^+)$
Ph-th: phenolphthalein alkalinity
pico-: prefix for 10^{-12}
pK: log 1/dissociation constant
P.M., p.m.: after noon
ppb: parts per billion = ng/liter
ppm: parts per million = mg/liter
ppt: parts per thousand, or ‰; precipitate
Pr(P): productivity
psi(lb/in^2): pounds per square inch
pt: pint
π: pi = 3.1416

Q: discharge (fl.); charge (electricity); quantity
Q_{10}: temperature coefficient (van't Hoff's law)
qt: quart
qual: qualitative
quant: quantitative

r: correlation coefficient
R: roentgen; rate, count
R: resistance
rad: unit of radiation doses of 100 ergs/g or 10^{-2} J/kg
RBE: relative biological effectiveness (radiology)
rem: roentgen equivalent, man
rev/min(rpm): revolutions per minute
RH: relative humidity
rpm: revolutions per minute
RQ: respiratory quotient
ρ: density

(s)sec: second
S: south, salinity, entropy
sc: screw-capped
SD(σ): standard deviation
SE: standard error
sec: second
sin: sine
sp.: species (taxonomy)
sp act: specific activity
sp gr: specific gravity
spp: species (plural) (taxonomy)
ssp: subspecies (taxonomy)
STP: standard temperature and pressure
(σ) SD: standard deviation

t: t-values (statistics)
t: ton
T: time; transmittance
T: temperature
$t_{1/2}$: half-life
Tab.: table
tan: tangent
temp: temperature
TL_{50}: tolerance limit at 50% survival
TLC: thin-layer chromatography
tr: trace
TRIS: tris(hydroxymethyl)-aminomethane

USP units: carotenoid units
UV: ultraviolet light

V,v: volt
V,v: velocity
vac, Vac: vacuum
(vel): velocity (use *V* or *v*)
vol: volume; volumetric
vol/vol(v/v): solution concentration (see v/v)
vs: as against
v/v: solution concentration, volume fluid to total volume

W: west
W(w): watt
W: work
wet wt: wet weight
wk: weak; week (spell out)
wt: weight
wt/vol: solution concentration, weight of solute to volume of solvent
w/v: solute concentration, solute weight diluted to volume

$\bar{x}$: "x-bar" for mean, average
χ^2: chi square

Y/G: yellow-green pigment ratio
yd: yard (use metric)
yr: year (spell out)

Glossary: Constants, Terms, and Units

absolute (abs) *assimilation:* C fixed/m^2/unit time (cf. relative)

biomass: g/m^2

humidity: partial pressure of atmospheric gases consisting of water vapor

temperature: Kelvin (273 K = 0°C)

absorbance (*absorbency, extinction*): $\log_e I_o/I$ or $2 - \log_{10} T$

abyssal: of deep regions of the oceans

acceleration due to gravity(*g*): ca. 980 cm/sec/sec, but varies with location and altitude

acre: 40.47 ares = 43,560 ft^2 = 0.4047 ha = 4,047 m^2 = 1.562×10^{-5} mi = 4,840 yd^2

acre-foot(*acre-ft*): 43,460 ft^3 = 1,231.6 m^3

activity(*a*, A)

coefficient (*Nauwerk's*): ratio of productivity to fresh weight

degree of radioactivity (radiology)

aerenchyma: air-holding tissue common in aquatic vascular plants

afternoon(P.M.)

air embolism: dangerous rupturing of lung tissue on ascent with SCUBA on failure to breath regularly

air pressure: 760 mm Hg at STP (sea level)

alkalinity(ALK): milliequivalents of hydrogen ions neutralized by 1 kg of water (see also phenolphthalein alkalinity)

allochthonous: arising from outside the habitat (esp. turbidity)

altitude (alt) and pressure: changes 1.07 in. Hg/100 ft

amount(amt)

Ångstrom(Å,A): = 0.1 mμ or nm

are: 0.0247 acres = 100 m^2 = 119.6 yd^2

area: see acre, are, hectare, square centimeter, decimeter, meter, millimeter, micron

ASA unit: unit of illumination (photography, = Weston Units). For value, see Weston unit

assimilation: photosynthesis

association: basic phytosociological unit of vegetation

atmosphere(atm): 1.013 bar = 29.92 inches of Hg = 1.0335 kg/cm^2 = 1,013 mb = 14.7 lb/in^2 all at STP (sea level); 33.9 ft H_2O

atomic number(*z*)

atomic weight(at. wt.)

attenuation: gradual decrease in intensity of radiation on penetrating water, etc.

aufwuchs: organisms attached to, or associated with those attached to, submerged structures

austral: southern

autecology: ecology of the individual

autochthonous: indigenous, native, arising from within the habitat (esp. of turbidity)

autotrophic: producing food from raw materials (esp. photosynthetic)

Avogadro's number: 6.0225×10^{23} molecules/liter of gas

backwash: action of wave washing back down over beach (see swash)

bar: unit of atmospheric pressure, = 1 megadyne/cm^2 = 750.06 mm or 29.53 inches of Hg (at STP, sea level), and 0.987 atm

barometric pressure: 760 mm or 29.92 in. Hg = 1013.2 mb at STP, sea level

benthon: organisms living on the bottom; (the word form, although not well established, parallels that of plankton, neuston, etc.)

biochemical oxygen demand(*BOD*): ml diss. oxygen/liter used in 5 days

biomass: g dry wt/m^2 (see absolute, relative)

biotope: a habitat

black zone: uppermost algal intertidal zone

boiling point(bp)

boreal: northern

brackish: of intermediate salinity

British termal unit(BTU): 0.252 kcal = 252 gcal

buffer: action-reducing change (e.g., of acidity due to weakly ionized acids and their salts)

calomel electrode: reference electrode for pH meter, generates 0.243 volts
calorie(cal, g-cal, gcal): heat required to raise 1 g of water 1°C
candle power(cp): light produced by standard candle (at 1 ft = 1 ft-c = 12.577 lm and 10.76 lux, convert to candela(cd)
carbon fixed to chlorophyll ratio(C/P_{chl})
carbon-nitrogen ratio(C/N;C:N)
carbon-nitrogen-phosphorus ratio(C:N:P): in seawater is 41:7.2:1
carrier: stable atoms mixed with radioisotope of the same element
carrier-free: radioisotope without stable atoms of the element
Celsius(°C): temperature, centrigrade = $\frac{5}{9}(F - 32)$
centigram(cg): 0.01 g = 0.000527 oz
centimeter(cm): = 0.394 in = 0.01 m
chemical concentration: see equivalent, gram-atom, gram atomic weight, gram equivalent weight, microgram atom, milligram atom, milliequivalent, millimole
chi square(χ^2): index of degree to which observed data approach expected data,

$$\chi^2 = \frac{\Sigma(f - F)^2}{df}$$

where f = sample count, F = expected count, df = degrees of freedom (see Snedecor, 1956: 29, for probability tables)
chlorinity(Cl): g halides/kg water, as ⁰/oo (see chlorosity)
chlorosity(Cl): g halides/liter at 20°C; chlorosity = chlorinity × density at 20°C
chop: short, sharp waves
chromogen: colored solute which colors a liquid
clone: genetically uniform population derived by vegetative propagation
coefficient(coef): a factor or constant, for a formula
coefficient of variation(C.V.): = $\frac{s}{\bar{X}}$ (100) where s = standard deviation, X = the mean
coincidence: occurrence of two or more simultaneous events (radiology)
colligative properties: properties of fluid dependent on number, not nature, of molecules present, e.g., freezing point, osmotic pressure
community coefficient (of associations): see similarity index
compare(cf)
compensation point: intensity at which photosynthesis equals respiration (usually referring to light) (cf. critical light intensity)
concentrated(concd.)
concentration(concn.): see chemical concentration equation for: VN = vn
conductance(κ in Europe): see conductivity; specific conductance, e.g., $\kappa_{18} \times 10^6$ reciprocal megohms
conductivity(cond): degree to which a solution conducts electrical current
correlation: degree of similarity of occurrence patterns of two variables
correlation coefficient(r): =

$$\Sigma x_1 x_2 / \sqrt{\Sigma (x_1)^2 (x_2)^2}$$

where x_1 and x_2 are variables
cosmic rays: radiation from beyond the atmosphere having high energies, mostly protons and nuclei
counts per minute(cpm)
counts per second(cps)
critical light intensity: intensity just sufficient to support a photosynthetic species (or system) from day to day; it is higher than compensation point
critical tide levels: levels at which organism distribution limits occur
cubic
centimeter(cm^3, cc): = 0.06102 in^3 = 10^{-3} liters = 1 ml = 0.0338 oz (fl)
decimeter(dm^3): = 100 cc = 61.023 in^3
foot(ft^3): = 28.317 dm^3 = 2.83×10^7 ml = 7.481 gal
inch(in^3): = 16.387 cc = 0.554 fl. oz
kilometer(km^3): = 3.5313×10^{12} ft^3
meter(m^3): = 35.315 ft^3 = 264.17 gal = 1,000 liters = 1,056.7 qt = 1.3079 yd^3
microns(μ^3): = 10^{-9} mm = 6.0694×10^{-14} in^3
millimeter(mm^3): = 10^{-3} cm^3 = 0.061 in^3 = 3.38×10^{-5} oz (fl)
mile(mi^3): = 1.4719×10^{11} ft^3 = 4.16 km^3 = 4.16×10^9 mm^3
nautical mile($n.mi^3$): = 2.2478×10^{11} ft^3 = 6.4 km^3 = 6.4×10^9 m^3
curie(c,Ci): unit of radiation = 3.7×10^{10} disintegrations per second

datum: accepted base level for mapping
decay constant(λ): factor: $e^{-\lambda t}$ where $N = N_o e^{-\lambda t}$
decay rate: dN/dt
decimeter(dm): 0.1 m = 10 cm = 3.937 in = 0.328 ft
deep scattering layer: zone of relatively concentrated animal life (esp. euphausiids) detectable by depth sounders
degree: arc(°)
freedom(df): N – 1
temperature(°C or °F)
density(d): mass/ml, e.g., seawater (d_{13} = 1.029), d_{max} = –4°C
depth gauge: diver's depth gauge (see also fathometer, inclinometer)
determinavit(det.): determined by
detritus: organic particulate nonliving matter
diel: 24-hour cycle, or study
discharge(Q): quantity of water moving per unit time
discontinuity layer: thermocline, chemocline
disintegrations: atomic transformations which release radiation
dissociation: separation of molecules into ions
dissociation constant(pK):

$$\frac{[Ca]\ [Anion]}{molecules} = pK$$

dissolved oxygen (DO)
diversity: range of variation; number of species/m^2 or unit
dry weight(dry wt)

ecosystem: an interacting environmental complex
electromagnetic spectrum: continuum of radiations, cosmic, gamma, x-rays, ultraviolet, visible light, infrared, radio waves, electric current
electromotive force(emf): voltage
electron volt(ev,eV): potential gained by 1 electron traversing potential of 1 volt (see mev, bev) (radiology)
embolism: see air embolism
entropy(S): a measure of disorder of a closed thermodynamic system, S increasing with disorder
equivalent(eq): grams of substance required to replace 1 g of hydrogen
equivalent weight(GEW): gram molecular weight/valence
erg: unit of energy or work of 1 dyne/cm
error: see per cent error
eu-: prefix for true
euphotic: water stratum with light, and photosynthetic organisms
euplanktonic: true plankton
eury-: prefix for wide range
euryhaline: tolerant to wide range of salinity
eurythermal: tolerant to wide range of temperature
extinction(E): absorbency, optical density: = $\log_e I_o/I$ or $2-\log_{10}T$

Fahrenheit(°F): temperature, $F = \frac{9}{5}C + 32$
far red(FR): radiant energy beyond red light (ca. 700–900 mμ)
fathom(fm): = 6 ft = 1.829 m = 2 yd
fathometer: electronic unit for measuring depth
fetch: distance upwind over which waves can build
flushing time: time for a given mass of water in estuary to be replaced

$$t_f = \frac{S_s - S_f}{S_s} \times V_f \times \frac{1}{V_d}$$

where t_f = flushing time, S_s = salinity at mouth, S_f = salinity of estuary, V_f = volume, V_d = volume daily moving in and out (e.g., Great South Bay, N.Y., t_f = 48 days)
foot(ft): = 12 in = 30.48 cm = 0.3048 m = 0.333 yd
foot-candle(ft-c): total light at 1 ft from a standard candle (= 10.76 lux)
freezing point(fp): of seawater (S = 35 ‰, fp = ca. −2°C)
freezing point depression(Δ): a colligative property, the lowering of freezing point caused by solutes (for seawater at S = 35 ‰, Δ = ca. 1.88°C)

gallon(gal): US gal = 4 qt = 8 pt = 231 in^3 = 0.13368 ft^3 = 3.785 liters = 128 fl. oz
glass electrode: of pH meter
glass-fiber filter: comparable to membrane filters, especially useful in pigment extraction (e.g., Whatman GF/C)
glass-stoppered(gs)
gram(g): = 0.03527 oz = 0.001 kg = 2.2046 × 10^{-3} lb
gram-atom(g-at): mass of element equal to the atomic weight
gram-atom per liter(g-at/liter): to find, use

$$\text{g-at/liter} = \frac{\text{GAW}}{\text{GMW}}\ \text{g/liter}$$

gram atomic weight(GAW)
gram equivalent weight(GEW): = GMW/valence
gram equivalent weight per liter(g eq/liter): to find, use

$$\text{g eq/liter} = \frac{\text{valence}}{\text{GMW}} \times \text{g/liter or } \frac{1}{\text{GEW}} \times \text{g/liter}$$

gram molecular weight(GMW)
grapnel or *grapple:* hook or anchor with several recurved prongs
gravitational acceleration: 980 cm/sec^2, but varies with location
gravitational forces(F): often expressed as g's, = ca. 980 dynes/g
gravity, centrifugal force(g's): number of times centrifugal force on a material or body exceeds gravity (see preceding)
gross productivity: P + R (photosynthesis plus respiration)
ground swell: long low waves
growth rate: dN/dt
heat of fusion(Hf): heat required to vaporize with no temperature change (H_f of H_2O = 500–600 cal/g)
heat of vaporization: for dist water = 500–600 cal
hectare(ha): area of 10,000 m^2 = 2.471 acres = 1.07 × 10^5 ft^2 = 10^{-3} km^2 = 0.0038597 mi^2
hecto-: prefix for 10^2
holo-: prefix for completely
holoplankton: plankton which are always planktonic
horsepower(hp): unit of power required to drive machinery, = 746 watts = 33,000 ft-lb of work per min
hydrogen electrode: electrode for pH meters which generates a voltage taken as the basic reference, as 0 (see calomel electrode, 0.243 v)
hydrogen ion concentration(H^+): moles of hydrogen ions per liter, = 10^{-7} for cp dist. water; usually converted to pH
hypsographic curve: graph showing per cent of area at each depth relative to that of the surface

inch(in, in.): 2.54 cm = 0.083 ft = 0.0254 m
inclinometer: unit for measuring angle of towing line to aid in calculating depth of towing

infrared(IR): radiation beyond 900–10^7 mμ range
integrated productivity, Talling's: planimetric measurement of photosynthesis under the curve obtained from a series of DO measurements expressed as mg $O_2/m^2/hr$
intertidal: seashore area between highest and lowest nonstorm tides (HHHW–LLLW)
ionization constant(K): see dissociation constant
iso-: prefix for same, equal
isobar: line connecting points of equal atm pressure
isobath: line connecting points of equal depth
isopleth: line connecting points of equal value of some parameter
isotope effect: differing effectiveness of isotopes of an element

Jackson turbidity unit(JTU): measure of turbidity, reduction in light transmittance by 1 mg/liter of Fuller's earth; being replaced by more permanent standards
joule(J): unit of work, J = 10^7 ergs

kilo-(k): prefix for 10^3
kilocalorie(kcal): 10^3 calories
kilogram(kg): 10^3 g = 2.2046 lb = 35.274 oz
kilogram/hectare(kg/ha): equal to g/m^2
kilometer(km): 10^3 m = 3,280.8 ft = 0.6214 mi (statute) = 0.5394 n.mi = 1,093.6 yd
knot(kn): velocity, 1 n.mi/hr = 1.15 mi/hr = 0.54 km/hr
Koehler illumination: in microscopy, a system for getting maximum resolution by control of lens focus and diaphragm adjustments

Lambert(L): 1 lumen/cm^2
Langley(ly): unit of total radiation, in gcal/cm^2
latitude(lat.)
length: see centimeter, decimeter, fathom, foot, inch, kilometer, millimeter, micron, mile, nautical mile
lentic: very slowly flowing water habitats (see lotic)
lethal dose(LD): at 50% survival = LD_{50}
light energy: solar constant (at surface of atmosphere) 1.92 gcal/cm^2/min; average at surface of sea, 0.159 gcal/cm^2/min
light units: see candle power, foot-candle, lumen, lux; also see electromagnetic spectrum
liter(do not abbreviate): volume of 10^3 ml = 61.025 in^3 = 33.85 oz(fl) = 1.0567 qt; 1 liter of dist. water weigh 1,000 g
load: suspended sediments carried by stream (often expressed as MT/day, i.e., metric tons/day)
longitude(long.)
lotic: rapidly flowing water habitats (see lentic)
lumen(lm): unit of luminous flux, 1 lm/ft^2 = 0.796 candle power; 1 lm/m^2 = 1 lux = 0.93 ft-c; 1 lm/cm^2 = 1 Lambert(L)
lux(lx): unit of illumination, 1 lux = 0.093 ft-c

macrophyte: large plants, sometimes restricted to tracheophytes
marl: soil or sediment gritty with rock particles, primarily $CaCO_3$
mass(m): weight
maximum(max)
mean(μ): letter covered with bar, e.g. $\bar{x}$; average, $\Sigma x_i/N = \bar{x}$ where Σ xi = sum of values (x_i), N = number of values, $\bar{x}$ = mean
mega-(M): prefix for 10^6
megahertz(MHz): 10^6 Hertz (cycles/sec)
megohm: 10° ohms (see reciprocal ohm)
melting point(mp): seawater (35 ^{o}/oo S), ca. -2°C; dist. water, 0°C
mero-: prefix for partly
meromictic: lake only partly mixed, i.e., with permanent bottom higher density portion (often saline)
meroplankton: forms which are planktonic for only a portion of the life cycle
meso-: prefix for middle
mesohaline: intermediate salinity (5–20 ^{o}/oo S)
meter(m): unit of length, = 100 cm = 39.37 in = 3.28 ft = 1.0936 yd = 6.214 × 10^{-4} mi
meter wheel: pulley block with dials recording length of line run out
methyl orange alkalinity(MO): total alkalinity
metric ton(MT,M.T.,m.t.): 10^3 kg = 1.1023 tons (US) = 2,204.62 lb
mho: reciprocal ohm (conductivity)
micro-: prefix for 10^{-6}
microcurie(μc,μCi): 10^{-6} curies, 3.7 × 10^4 dps
microgram(μg): 10^{-6} g
microgram atom(μg-at): mass of element equal to GAW × 10^{-6}
microgram atom per liter(μg-at/liter): find by

$$\mu\text{g-at/liter} = \frac{\text{GAW}}{\text{GMW}}\ \mu\text{g/liter}$$

microliter(μl): 10^{-6} liter = 10^{-3} ml
micromole(μ-mol): GMW × 10^{-6}
micromole/liter(μ-mol/liter): find by

$$\mu\text{-mol/liter} = \frac{10^6}{\text{GMW}}\ \text{g/liter}$$

micron(μ,μm): 10^{-6} m or 10^{-3} mm = 3.93 × 10^{-5} in
mile(mi): 5,280 ft = 1.609 km = 1609 m = 0.869 n.mi = 1,760 yd
milli-: prefix for 10^{-3}
millibar(mb): 10^{-3} bar = 0.75007 mm or 0.02853 in. Hg (at STP, sea level, air pressure = 1,013.2 mb)
millicurie(mc,mCi): 10^{-3} curies, 3.7 × 10^{-7} dps
milliequivalent(meq):

$$\frac{\text{GMW}}{\text{valence}}\ \frac{1}{10^3}$$

milliequivalent/liter(meq/liter): find by

$$\text{meq/liter} = \frac{\text{valence}}{\text{GMW}}\ 10^3\ \text{g/liter}$$

milligram(mg): 10^{-3} g = 3.527 X 10^{-5} oz
milligram atom(mg-at): GAW X 10^{-3}
milligram atom per liter(mg-at/liter): find by

$$\text{mg-at/liter} = \frac{\text{GAW}}{\text{GMW}} \text{ mg/liter}$$

milliliter(ml): 10^{-3} liter = ca. 1 cc = 6.103 X 10^{-2} in^3
millimeter(mm): 10^{-3} m = 0.1 cm = 0.00328 ft = 0.03937 in
millimicron(mμ,nm): 10^{-6} mm = 10^{-9} m = 10 angstroms = 1 nm
millimole(m-mol): 10^{-3} GMW
millival(meq/liter): see milliequivalent per liter
millivolt(mv): 10^{-3} volt
minimum(min): d_{min} for seawater (35 °/oo S) = ca. −4°C, for dist. water = +4°C
minimum lethal dose(MLD)
minute(min,′): time (min); or arc (′): 1′ lat = ca. 1 n.mi = 6,080.2 ft
mixis, mixing: as suffix -mictic, especially of lakes (e.g., amictic, dimictic, holomictic, meromictic, polymictic)
molal(M): solution of 1 GMW + 1 liter of water, useful by having ideal osmotic activity
molar(M): 1 GMW/liter
mole(mol): gram molecule (GMW)
molecular extinction coefficient: the constant relating extinction and gram molecular concentration
molecular weight(mol wt, GMW)
mud: soil or sediment slimy and sticky in nature due to high content of clay or silt

nannoplankton: small plankton, passing 25-mesh plankton net (ca. 5–60 μ), obtained by centrifugation
nano-(n): prefix for 10^{-9}
nanometer(nm): 10^{-9} m = 1 mμ
nautical mile(n.mi): 6,080.2 ft = 1.854 km = 1.15 mi (statute) = 2,026 yd; = ca. 1′ lat. (recently → 6,076.12 ft)
neap tide(N): biweekly period of minimum tides, e.g., HLWN = higher low water neap tide
nekton: swimming organisms
neritic: water mass over continental shelf
net coefficient: factor relating number of plankton collected to number actually present per unit volume
net productivity: photosynthesis less the respiration; the photosynthesis figure obtained until corrected for respiration
neuston: life of water surface film, includes epineuston, hyponeuston, and pleuston
normal conditions(NTP): normal temperature and pressure
normal solution(N): 1 GEW/liter
nuclide: any of some 1,000 different atoms with characteristic amounts of protons (z) and neutrons (N) and mass (A), such that A = N + z; many are radionuclides

number(no.)
numerical aperture(NA): lens characteristic, engraved on lens mount, expressing resolving power and brightness of image

ohm: unit of resistance, amp = volt/ohm (see mho)
Ohm's law: $I = E/R$, amp = volts/ohms
oligo-: prefix for low
oligotrophic: low in nutrients; clear lakes with little plankton
optical density(OD,*E*): degree of absorption of light from clear solution as $\log_e I_o/I$, also $\log_{10} I_o/I$ or $2 - \log_{10} T$
organic matter: ca. dry weight − ash weight
osmotic pressure(OP): potential pressure a solution could develop in an osmometer; a measure of solute concentration
ounce(oz)
  dry: = 28.349 g = 0.0624 lb
  fluid: = 1/16 pt = 1/32 or 0.03125 qt = 1.8045 in^3 = 0.02957 liters = 29.57 ml
oxidation reduction potential(E_7,E_h): electrical potential developed between a platinum electrode and a hydrogen electrode, indicating balance between tendency to gain (reduction) and lose (oxidation) electrons in the system
oxygen, dissolved(DO): *per cent saturation:* oxygen held in solution compared with what it would hold when water is in gaseous equilibrium with air

parameters: values which define an environment
partial pressure: that portion of the total gaseous pressure exerted by one gas, e.g., for oxygen, 20/100 of 760 mm Hg = 152 mm Hg
parts per million(ppm): = mg/liter
parts per thousand(°/oo,ppt)
peat: partly carbonized (under water) soil or sediment largely or partly decomposed
pelagic: of open water
per cent(%)
per cent error:

$$\frac{\text{larger} - \text{smaller}}{\text{larger}} \cdot 100$$

per cent saturation(% sat): see oxygen
pH: unit of measure of acidity,

$$\text{pH} = \log_{10} \frac{1}{(\text{H}^+)}$$

phaeophytins: breakdown products of chlorophyll pigments
phenolphthalein alkalinity: alkalinity based on acid required to lower pH to phenolphthalein endpoint
phi scale: measure of soil/sediment particle size; $\log_2$ of diameter in mm where coarse sand = 0
phosphor: crystal which glows when penetrated by radiation
phyco-: prefix for algal

phycobilins: blue and red vascular pigments of red and blue-green algae
phyto-: prefix for plant
phytoplankton: microscopic or near microscopic planktonic plants, suspended in water
pico-(p): prefix for 10^{-12}
picocurie(pc,pCi): = 10^{-12} curies, 3.7 X 10^{-2} dps
pigment ratio(Y/G): ratio of carotenoid to chlorophyll by optical densities (extinctions) at indicated wavelengths, E_{430}/E_{665}
pint(pt): fl, = 1.671 X 10^{-2} ft³ = 0.4732 liters = 473.2 ml = 16 oz = 0.5 qt
Planck's constant(h): universal constant relating energy of quantum (photon) and its frequency, E = h, h = 6.626 X 10^{-27} erg-sec
plankton: organisms suspended in open water
pleuston: life in surface film of water (cf. neustron)
poly-: prefix for large
polysaprobic: very polluted
positron(β^+): positively charged electron
potamoplankton: river plankton
pound(lb): = 453.59 g = 0.4536 kg = 16oz (dry)
primary productivity: organic matter synthesized by autophytic organisms (see gross and net productivity), usually as g dry wt/m²/day
productivity(Pr): see primary productivity
profundal: of deep regions with insufficient light for photosynthesis (of inland waters)
proton: positively charged nuclear particle with mass of 1
psammon: organisms inhabiting sand

quart(qt): = 0.25 gal = 0.946 liter = 946.3 ml = 32 oz (fl) = 2 pt
quenching: reducing by absorption, of light, electronic noise, etc.

radionuclide: nuclide which emits radiation
reciprocal ohm:

$$\text{unit of conductance} = \frac{1}{\text{ohm}};\ \frac{1}{\text{megohm}} = \mu\ \text{mho} = K_{18} \times 10^6$$

redox(E_7,E_h): see oxidation reduction potential
refractive index($n\frac{20}{D}$): ratio of angle of incidence (i) to refracted (r) light, as $\frac{\sin i}{\sin r}$, at 20°C for sodium light
relative assimilation: carbon fixed per volume or weight (see absolute)
relative biomass: g per various factors or measures other than earth's surface or sea volume, e.g., g dry wt/g chl or area of host
relative humidity: per cent of vapor in air to that which it could hold at saturation
resolving time (*dead time, coincidence*): length of time between two incidences that can be resolved by the detector (radiology)
respiratory quotient(RQ): ratio of volume of gas released to that absorbed, especially ml CO_2/ml O_2
revolutions per minute(rpm)
roentgen(R,r): unit of exposure dose of x- or gamma rays

salinity(S): equivalent NaCl which would give the same osmotic pressure; S = 0.03 + (1.805 X Cl) where Cl is °/oo chlorinity
saprobe: organism typical of polluted conditions
saprobic: polluted
scaler: unit for counting impulses (radiology)
scintillation: light produced in phosphor when penetrated by radiation
sea level(MSL,msl): mean sea level, established by recordings over years
Secchi disk transparency: depth of visibility of disk, = ca. depth at 5% transmitted light. *E* = ca 1.7/ D,D(m)
second(sec, ″): arc (″); latitude (1″ = ca. 101 ft or 30.9 m); time (sec)
seiche: periodic oscillations in limited bodies oı water, t = 2L/gh where t = oscillation time (sec), L = length of basin (cm), g = gravitational acceleration (980 cm/sec/sec), h = height (cm)
seston: particulate organic matter in water, both living and nonliving
settling rate: Stoke's law:

$$V = \frac{2}{9}\frac{(d_1 - d_2)}{\eta}\ gr^2$$

where V = rate (cm/sec), g = gravitational acceleration (980 cm/sec/sec), d_1 and d_2 are densities of body and liquid, η = dynamic viscosity of the liquid, r = radius of body
similarity index, coefficient(S): Søensen's index, a measure of relative similarity of two stands or associations,

$$S = \frac{2c}{a + b} \times 100,$$

where c = number of species in common, a and b = numbers of species in the two separate stands
sine(sin): sin a = opposite/hypotenuse
solar constant: energy received at outer surface of atmosphere, 1.92 gcal/cm²/min; average energy at ocean surface = 0.159 gcal/cm²/min
Sørensen's index: see similarity index
species(sp.)
specific activity (sp act): activity per unit mass, e.g. μCi/μ-mol
conductance(κ in Europe): conductance of cm² section of fluid at 18°C (of 0.1 N KCl = 0.0001413 mhos or 1413 μmhos) (see conductivity)
heat: heat required to raise 1 cc water 1°C (for dist. water = 1 gcal)

spectrophotometry:

$$\frac{\text{optical density}_1}{\text{optical density}_2} = \frac{\text{concentration}_1}{\text{concentration}_2}$$

Square
centimeter(cm^2): = 0.001076 ft^2 = 0.155 in^2 *square* = 100 mm^2
decimeter(dm^2): = 100 cm^2 = 1,076 ft^2 = 15.5 in^2
foot(ft^2): = 144 in^2 = 929.03 cm^2 = 0.0929 m^2 = 0.111 yd^2
inch(in^2): 6.4516 cm^2 = 0.00694 ft^2 = 6.45 16 $\times 10^{-4}$ m^2 = 645.16 mm^2
kilometer(km^2): = 247.1 acres = 1.0764 $\times 10^7$ ft^2 = 100 ha = 0.386 mi^2
meter(m^2): = 0.01 ares = 2.47 $\times 10^{-4}$ acres = 10^4 cm^2 = 1,550 in^2 = 10.764 ft^2 = 1.1959 yd^2
micron(μ^2): = 10^{-8} cm^2 = 10^{-12} m^2 = 1.55 $\times 10^{-9}$ in^2
mile(mi^2): = 640 acres = 2.7878 $\times 10^7 ft^2$ = 258.99 ha = 2.589 km^2
millimeter(mm^2): = 10^{-2} cm^2 = 1.55 $\times 10^{-2}$ in^2
nautical mile($n.mi^2$): = 3.697 $\times 10^7$ ft^2 = 4.1047 $\times 10^6$ yd^2
yard(yd^2): = 2.066 $\times 10^{-4}$ acres = 8,361.27 cm^2 = 0.83613 m^2 = 1,296 in^2 = 8.361 $\times 10^{-5}$ ha

standard deviation(s,SD): unit of deviation from the average (mean) which includes over 66% of the values within ± 1 s and over 95% within ± 2 s,

$$s = \sqrt{\frac{\Sigma(X - \bar{x})^2}{n - 1}}$$

where X = each value, $\bar{x}$ = average, $X - \bar{x}$ = one of the deviations, n = number of values, n − 1 = degrees of freedom (df)
steno-: prefix for narrow
stenohaline: restricted to narrow salinity range
stoichiometric: pertaining to weight relations in chemical reactions
Stoke's law: law defining factors involved in rate of settling (see settling rate) as densities of body and fluid, gravity, viscosity of fluid, and radius of the body
strand line: line of debris left by high water or tide
sublittoral: marine shore zone below lowest tidal level (LLLW)
surface tension(T): in dynes/cm^2
swash: flood of water from broken wave onto beach (see backwash)
swash line: line of debris left on beach at upper limit of swash

tangent(tan): tan a = opposite/adjacent
temperature (t, T, temp.)
terrigenous: sediment derived from land
thallophytes: nonvascular plants (see tracheophyte)
thermodynamic laws: I. conservation of energy—energy may be transformed but not created or destroyed; II. in energy transformations, there is always a degradation from concentrated to dispersed form (i.e., heat cannot be transferred from colder to hotter body); the degree of increasing dispersion (disorder) is measured as entropy (S)
time conversion: EST → EDT (+ 1 hr in April); EST ← EDT (− 1 hr in October)
tolerance limit at 50% survival (LD_{50})
ton
US ton(T): = 2,000 lb = 907.185 kg
metric ton(MT): = 2,204.6 lb = 1,000 kg = 1.1023 US tons
total alkalinity(ALK,MO): same as methyl orange alkalinity (see alkalinity)
tracer: radionuclide incorporated into a compound providing tag to enable compound or element to be followed through reaction or experiment
tracheophytes: vascular plants (see thallophytes)
transceiver: portable unit for two-way telecommunication (CB walkie-talkie)
transducer: sensitive probe of fathometer (depth sounder)
tripton: nonliving suspended matter in water
tsunamis: earthquake waves
turbidity: degree of reduction in transmittance of light due to suspended matter, compared to a standard suspension of 1 mg/liter Fuller's earth, expressed in JTU
turnover rate: rate at which material changes from one environmental phase to another
tychoplankton: plankton not regularly present; derived from bottom shallows, etc.

ultraplankton: microscopic plankton below 5-μ size range
ultraviolet light(UV): radiation of shorter wavelength than visible light (390–10 mμ range)
upwelling: surfacing of deep-water currents against shore or coastline
USP unit: unit of concentration of carotenoid phytoplankton pigments; 1 USP = ca. 1 mg β-carotene

van't Hoff's law(Q_{10}): chemical reactions double at each 10°C rise in temperature
variation, coefficient of(C.V.): see coefficient of variation
velocity(v): distance per unit time, expressed as ft/sec, cm or m/sec or min, knots, mph, etc.
versus(vs.): as against, contrasted with
vertical exaggeration: times by which vertical scale is increased over the horizontal scale to give acceptable pictorial effect
viscosity(η): descriptively, an internal friction of fluid, expressed in dyne-sec/cm^2 or poise
volt(v): unit of electrical potential; I = E/R (amp = volt/ohm)
volume: see acre-foot, cubic centimeter, gallon, liter, cubic mile, microliter, fluid ounce, pint, quart
voucher: specimen preserved to support a record (taxonomy)

watt(w): unit of power, = 1/746 hp; note that P = w/t = joules/time
wavelength (λ)
wave velocity(v): in shallow water,

$$v = \sqrt{gh};$$

in deep water,

$$v = \sqrt{\frac{g\lambda}{2\pi}},$$

in both where v = velocity (cm/sec), h = depth of water (cm), λ = wavelength (cm), g = 980 cm/sec^2
weight(wt): see gram, kilogram, microgram, metric ton, milligram, ounce, pound, ton

Weston unit: unit of illumination (I) used in photography in which 16 units = 6,400 ft-c, 15 = 3,200 ft-c, etc., conforming to $I = 6{,}400/2^{16-W}$, where I = ft-c, W = Weston unit; = ASA unit

x-rays: radiation originating by shift of electrons between orbital rings, and comprise those of the 1–100 angstrom, 10 ev to 1 kev

yard(yd): = 91.44 cm = 36 in = 3 ft = 0.9144 m = 5.68×10^{-4} mi
yellow-green pigment ratio(Y/G): see pigment ratio
yellow substances: apparently carotinoid breakdown products in the sea
yield: e.g., MT/mi^2, lb/acre, MT/ha

Annotated Author Guide to Literature Cited

Complete reference occurs on boldface page. The major topic covered is enclosed in parentheses.

Albert, L. S. (pers. comm.). (spectrophotometry) 117, 124

APHA. 1965. (standard methods) **24**, 28, 30, 31, 32, 33, 41, 42, 43, 44, 45, 46, 48, 49, 51, 52, 55, 56, 62, 64, 74, 75, 76, 96, 97, 99, 129

Armstrong, F. A. J. 1951. (silicates) 28, **62**

Atkins, W. R. G. 1923. (phosphates) 28, **52**

Auerbach, S. I. 1963. (aquarium ecosystem) 141

Baldwin, M., C. E. Kellogg, and J. Thorp. 1938. (soil classification) **19**

Bogorad, L. 1962. *In* R. Lewin. (pigment extraction) **120**

Braun-Blanquet, J. 1932. (phytosociology text) **80**, 82, 83

Brunel, J., G. W. Prescott, and L. H. Tiffany. 1950. (algal culture) **108**

Buch, K. 1945. (^{14}C-uptake) **129**

Carney, E. J. (pers. comm.). (multifactor analysis program) **102**

Chapman, C. F. 1968. (seamanship) **24**, 28, 31, 32, 58, 97

Chapman, V. J. 1960. (salt marshes) **80**

Chapman, V. J. 1964. (coastal vegetation) **89**

Chapman, V. J., and C. B. Trevarthen. 1953. (intertidal zones) **89**

Chase, G. D., and J. L. Rabinowitz. 1962, 1967. (radioisotope technique) **129**, 134, 135, 141

Chemical Rubber Publ. Co. (current issues). (chemical-physical data) **24**

C&GS. 1968. (salinity curves) **80**, 81

C&GS. 1969. (tide tables) **89**, 92

C&GS. (current issues). (hydrographic charts) **1**, **80**

CNCA. 1959. (skin and SCUBA diving) **24**, 57

Coker, R. E. 1954. (streams, lakes, and ponds) **1**

Conard, H. S. 1959. *In* W. T. Edmondson. (mosses) **7**

Dahl, E. 1960. (mathematical phytosociology) **80**, 83

Dansereau, P. 1959. (vascular plant communities) **13**, 15, 24, 28, 31

Dansereau, P. 1959a. (aquatic phytosociology) **80**

Davis, R. E., and J. W. Kelly. 1942. (surveying) **68**

Deevey, E. S. 1940. (data on ponds) **28**

Denigès, G. 1920. (phosphates) 28, **52**

Doty, M. S. 1946. (critical tide factors, intertidal zonation) 88, **89**

Doty, M. S. 1957. *In* J. W. Hedgpeth. (intertidal zonation) **89**, 95

Doty, M. S., and M. Oguri, 1957. (photosynthetic periodicity) **113**

Doty, M. S., and M. Oguri. 1959. (^{14}C-uptake method) 128, **129**

Eastman Kodak Co. 1946. (photography) 28, **55**

Edmonds, S. J., and H. B. S. Womersley. 1958. (algal ecology) **90**

Edmondson, W. T. 1959. (pollution testing) **74**

Elster, H. J. 1965. *In* C. R. Goldman. (productivity, absolute and relative) **113**, 114, 115, 116

Eppley Co. (pers. comm.). (radiation units) **105**

Encyclopaedia Britannica. 1965. (gravitation) **125**

EPA. 1971. **108**

Fassett, N. C. 1940, 1957. (aquatic plants) **7**, 9, 10, 11

Fenneman, N. M. 1938. (physiography) **1**

Fernald, M. L. 1950. (higher aquatic plants) **7**, 9, 11

Findenegg, I. 1965. *In* C. R. Goldman. (productivity) **118**, 121

Fjerdingstad, E. 1962. *In* C. M. Tarzwell. (saprobic system) 73, **74**

Fjerdingstad, E. 1964. (pollution zones) 73, **74**

Fogg, G. H. 1965. (algal culturing) **109**

Fosberg, F. R., and M.-H. Sachet. 1965. (herbarium techniques) **7**, 8, 11

FWPCA. 1968. (water quality criteria; pollution) **74**

Gaufin, A. R., and C. M. Tarzwell. 1956. (pollution indicators) **74,** 75

Gehu, J. 1961. (phytosociology) **81**

Goldman, C. R. 1960. (primary productivity) **109,** 127, 129

Goldman, C. R. 1965. (productivity) **19,** 109, 113, 115, 116, 118, 121, 129

Golterman, H. L. 1969. (see IBP. 1969)

Golubic, S. 1968. (bisect illustrations) **14**

Goodall, D. W. 1952. (quantitative phytosociology) **81,** 83

Hargraves, P. E., and R. D. Wood. 1967. (periphyton) **24,** 26, 66

Hartman, R. T. (pers. comm.). (biomass values) **19**

Hartman, R. T., and D. L. Brown. 1965. *In* R. G. Wetzel *In* C. R. Goldman. (productivity rates) **115**

den Hartog, C. 1959. (algal phytosociology) 88, **89**

Harvey, H. W. 1945. (seawater analysis) **81,** 84, 96, 129

Harvey, H. W. 1957. (seawater and carbon analysis) **129**

Hedgpeth, J. W. 1957. (marine ecology) **89**

Hodgman, C. D. 1943. (chemical, physical, mathematical data) **24**

Hubbs, C. L., and C. Hubbs. 1953. (graphing method) **14,** 16

Hunt, C. B. 1967. (physiography) **1**

Hutchinson, G. E. 1957. (limnology text; salinity) **84**

IACD. (current issue). (^{14}C-uptake technique) **129**

IBM. 1966. (computer programs) **102**

IBP. 1969. (fresh-water chemistry) **28,** 30, 74

Industrial Instruments Inc. (pers. comm.). **34**

JI/GTFE. 1969. (algal assay procedure) **109,** 129

Johnson, D. W. 1919. (seashore structure) **1**

Johnson, J. M., T. O. Odlaug, T. A. Olson, and O. R. Ruschmeyer. 1970. (algal assay procedures) **118,** 120

Knudsen, M. 1901. (hydrographical tables) **81**

Lewin, R. 1962. (pigment extraction) **120**

Lewis, J. R. 1957. (intertidal communities) 88, **89**

Lewis, J. R., and H. T. Powell. 1960. (intertidal communities) 88, **89**

Little, T. M. 1966. (correlation) **104**

Lobeck, A. K. 1957. (interpreting topographic maps) **1**

Lohmann, H. 1908. (plankton volume measurement) **96**

Mackenthun, K. M. 1969. **74,** 75

Mackereth, F. J. H. 1963. (limnological methods) **24,** 28, 31, 33, 43, 102

Margalef, R. 1963. *In* E. P. Odum. (succession in cultures) **109,** 110

McLean, R. C., and W. R. Ivimey-Cook. 1946. (ecological methods) **19**

Miller, W. R., and F. E. Egler. 1950. (salt marsh) **81**

Millipore Corp. 1968. (coliform counting) **74**

Muenscher, W. C. 1944. (aquatic plants) **7**

Muenscher, W. C. 1959. *In* W. T. Edmondson. (aquatic plants) **7**

Mullin, J. B., and J. P. Riley. 1955. (nitrates) 28, **42**

Nauwerck, A. 1963. (plankton volume and biomass) **96,** 118, 121

Needham, J. G., and P. R. Needham. 1962. (pollution detection) **74**

Neushul, M. 1967. (divers' transects) **14**

Northcraft, R. D. 1948. (intertidal algal succession) **89**

Odum, E. P. 1963. (succession in cultures) **109,** 110

Odum, E. P., and H. T. Odum. 1955. (trophic structure of reef) **118**

Odum, E. P., and H. T. Odum. 1959. (ecology text; radioisotopes, primary productivity methods) **113,** 141, 142

Olsen, F. C. W. 1960. (morphometry method) **68**

Oosting, H. J. 1948. (aquatic communities) **14**

ORINS. 1963. (aquarium ecosystem experiment) **141**

Palmer, C. M. 1959. (algae of water supplies) **74**

Patrick, R. 1949. (teamwork stream study) **28**

Phillips, E. A. 1959. (ecological methods) **19**

Poole and Atkins. 1929. 57

Pratt, D. M. (pers. comm.). (chemical procedures) 28, 42, 51, 52

Pratt, D. M. 1959. (seasonal marine phytoplankton) **96**

Prescott, G. W. 1954, 1962, 1969. (fresh-water algae) **7,** 11

Pringsheim, E. G. 1951. *In* G. M. Smith. (algal culturing) **109**

Randall, B. (pers. comm.). (computer programs) **87,** 102

Reid, G. K. 1961. (limnology-estuary text) 21, **24,** 31, 32, 44, 48, 57, 68, 102, 113, 123

Subject Index

Boldface pages indicate a definition, formula, or special discussion.